TEXTS AND STUDIES

CONTRIBUTIONS TO

BIBLICAL AND PATRISTIC LITERATURE

EDITED BY

J. ARMITAGE ROBINSON B.D.

HON. PH.D. GÖTTINGEN HON. D.D. HALLE

NORRISIAN PROFESSOR OF DIVINITY

VOL. III.

No. 1. THE RULES OF TYCONIUS

THE BOOK OF RULES

OF

TYCONIUS

NEWLY EDITED FROM THE MSS WITH AN INTRODUCTION
AND AN EXAMINATION INTO THE TEXT OF THE
BIBLICAL QUOTATIONS

BY

F. C. BURKITT M.A.

Wipf & Stock
PUBLISHERS
Eugene, Oregon

Wipf and Stock Publishers
199 W 8th Ave, Suite 3
Eugene, OR 97401

The Book of Rules of Tyconius
By Burkitt, F.C.
ISBN: 1-59244-892-5
Publication date 9/29/2004
Previously published by Cambridge, 1894

TO

E. E. BOWEN Esq. M.A.

HEAD MASTER OF THE MODERN SIDE
IN HARROW SCHOOL
FROM WHOM I LEARNT THE ELEMENTS
OF THE CRITICISM OF ANCIENT DOCUMENTS
I MOST GRATEFULLY
DEDICATE
MY FIRST BOOK

PREFACE.

IN trying to find a pre-Augustinian African writer, who from his date and locality might be presumed to quote from a Version similar to that used by S. Cyprian, I came across Tyconius, the author of the *Liber Regularum*. A very slight study was enough to shew that it was impossible to ground any satisfactory work upon the printed texts of that book. All the editions hitherto printed are derived from a single late and faulty MS, so that the language appears almost wholly incomprehensible. Indeed it is not too much to say that the *Liber Regularum* is here printed for the first time in something of the form in which Tyconius wrote it.

It is, I believe, mainly this corrupt state of the text which has prevented the recognition of the very important place which Tyconius holds in the history of Biblical Interpretation in western Europe. I have approached the subject almost entirely from the point of view of the textual criticism of the Old Latin Versions, and have tried to vindicate for the quotations of Tyconius their true position as the only considerable body of evidence for the Latin text of the Prophets current in Africa between the epochs of S. Cyprian and S. Augustine. But there is another side to the *Liber Regularum*. It is the first book in western Christendom which attempts to treat of the meaning and Inspiration of the Bible as a whole, and which tries to find a method of interpretation more thorough and scientific than the almost hap-hazard selection of proof texts. The work of Tyconius seems to be entirely original; there are hardly any traces of the influence of previous writers in it. But it profoundly influenced succeeding Latin writers from the time of S. Augustine onward.

I hope that the improved text contained in this volume may induce some scholar to investigate Tyconius' methods and ideas, which are well worthy of a more careful study than I feel myself competent to give to them. A system of interpretation which frankly recognises the historical meaning of prophecy without thereby detracting from its spiritual essence should have some interest in the present day.

The present work has grown out of the Kaye Prize Essay for 1891, upon the Old Latin Versions of the Prophets. I attempted to shew that an improved text of Tyconius was essential towards a clearer understanding of this subject, and the adjudicators of the Prize have kindly allowed me thus to modify both the title and the contents of the Essay.

It remains now to thank the many friends who have helped me at various stages in the preparation of this book, among whom I wish especially to name Father Bollig, of the Vatican Library, M. Henri Jadart, of Reims, and Dr Ceriani, of Milan, through whose good offices I was able to procure a transcript of the Monza Epitome. The Editor of this Series has been unwearied in his help both in the Text and the Introduction; it is chiefly due to him that the work is not disfigured by many crudities of style and expression. To the never-failing kindness of the late Prof. W. Robertson Smith I owe several suggestions and references, besides a brilliant emendation in the text of Rule I.

F. C. B.

July, 1894.

CONTENTS.

ERRATA.

Introd. p xlix, line 8 *for* canta V* *read* canta V

Text 10[24] *omit comma after* mansionem

30[15] *for* insequabantur *read* insequebantur *and let the note read* insequebatur V

60[9] *for* difinitur *read* definitur *and insert in the notes* difinitur RV

70[24] *for* domu *read* domo *and let the note read* domu R

77[12] *for* nouissimis *read* nouissimus

INTRODUCTION.

I. *The writings of Tyconius.*

TYCONIUS the African lived in the latter half of the fourth century and was a member of the Donatist community. This schismatic Church came into existence after the great Diocletian Persecution, having separated itself from the main body on the question of the Lapsed. In Africa the Donatists formed a strong party and kept up their organisation for a couple of centuries, holding Catholic doctrine, but refusing communion both with the lapsed and those who had received the lapsed. They were thus an isolated body of Latin-speaking Christians. There were no Greek Donatists, so that the Donatist Church had less temptation than the rest of Western Christendom to revise its Bible from Greek Codices. So far as I know, the 'Italic,' *i.e.* Augustinian, type of text is never found in their works, and at a much later date than Tyconius they seem still to have used the Old Version when S. Jerome's translation had become the Catholic text. Thus in the curious Dialogue *Contra Fulgentium Donatistam*, printed in the appendix to S. Augustine[1], where a Catholic and a Donatist are made to dispute together, the Donatist uses an Old Latin text, while the Catholic quotes from the Vulgate. These considerations explain the absence of Greek influence in the works of Tyconius whether in regard to his ideas or to the text of his Biblical quotations. He was an African by nationality and an African by religion.

[1] Migne xliii 763.

Tyconius seems to have occupied a prominent and independent position in the internal disputes of his Church[1]. His book on the Donatist controversy called *Bellum Intestinum* has unfortunately perished, and the little that is known about his life comes chiefly from references scattered up and down in the works of S. Augustine. Tyconius appears to have recognised the existence of the true Church outside the Donatist community elsewhere than in Africa, and on this ground he seems to have quarrelled with his party, yet without joining himself to the Catholics. "Contra Donatistas," says S. Augustine[2], "inuictissime scripsit, cum fuerit Donatista; et illic inuenitur absurdissimi cordis, ubi eos non omni ex parte relinquere uoluit." His greatest influence, however, both on his contemporaries and on succeeding generations, was due to his two exegetical works: the Book of Rules edited in this volume, and the Commentary on the Apocalypse.

The Commentary of Tyconius on the Apocalypse is believed to be lost. No MS is known to exist at the present time, though the Monastery of S. Gall possessed one in the 9th century. A great portion of the work has however been incorporated by various authors, as has been lately shewn by Dr Haussleiter in the *Zeitschrift für Kirchl. Wissenschaft*, 1886, pp. 239—257, where the whole question of the extant sources has been fully worked out. The chief writers who used Tyconius as their main authority in explaining the Apocalypse were Primasius, Bede, the author of the Pseudo-Augustinian Homilies[3], and above all Beatus, a Spanish priest contemporary with Charlemagne, whose book on the Apocalypse is little more than a series of extracts from our author. This last work is very scarce; the only edition (by Florez, Madrid, 1770) was not reprinted for Migne. There is a copy in the Bodleian, but none in the British Museum or in the Cambridge University Library. According to Dr Haussleiter, the influence of the Commentary of Tyconius is further visible even

[1] See Tillemont, vi 145—150, and the article *Tichonius* in the Dict. of Christian Biography, for further information on the relations of Tyconius with his party. From the point of view of the textual critic the one important factor of the Donatist position is their isolation in Latin-speaking Africa. For the spelling of the name Tyconius see Appendix II on Orthography.

[2] Aug *de Doct Christ* iii 30.

[3] Migne xxxv 2417; see Tillemont, vi 150, and Haussleiter, pp 240, 242.

in the ordinary recension of the Commentary of Victorinus of Pettau, although this author lived a little before Tyconius, and his genuine interpretations were quite different from those of the African Donatist.

The Book of Rules has met with a better fate than the Commentary on the Apocalypse. Two independent MSS survive, besides an extensive Epitome and some interesting quotations in subsequent writers.

In this work Tyconius attempts to deal with a real problem. The Church had inherited the Old Testament and held fast to the belief that the ancient scriptures wholly testified to the New Covenant. Many Jewish prophecies are appealed to by the N. T. writers, by the early apologists, and in such works as S. Cyprian's *Testimonia*. But there still remained an enormous residuum which was not obviously edifying, so that many verses from the Prophets have been quoted by no ancient writer. It was this unsurveyed region, the "prophetiae inmensa silua," which Tyconius set himself to explore and map out. Consequently his longer quotations are often from passages which no one else has touched. His aim was to find general rules of interpretation which would cover every case, and which therefore might be applied to the most unpromising subjects and images. Whatever we may think of his results, they certainly seemed to meet the wants of the men of his own time. It is a most extraordinary fact that the Catholic world should have accepted the work of a schismatic as a text-book of exegesis; that it was so accepted is the best testimony to the success of the Book of Rules.

Tyconius divides all prophecies into two classes: those which refer to Christ and His Church, and those which refer to the Devil and his followers. It is acknowledged that many passages in the prophetical books refer to Christ. But Christ is One with His Church, the Body of which He is the Head. A prophecy therefore which begins with something referring to our Lord may go on to say something about the Church which is the Body of Christ. Again, the Body of Christ is made up of parts; there is the Right Hand and also the Left,—in other words true and false Christians. Thus in any given prophecy one verse may refer to our Lord Himself, and the next to the black sheep among the flock.

Tyconius is careful to explain that reason alone can decide which is meant.

A few examples will make our author's method clearer. He begins with Isaiah liii. He quotes the well-known words "Hic peccata nostra feret......ipse uulneratus est propter facinora nostra," &c., which, as he says, the mouth of the whole Church refers to our Lord. But then he goes on to quote from Is liii 10, 11: "Et Deus uult purgare illum a plaga et uult Deus a dolore auferre animam eius, ostendere illi lucem et formare illum prudentia[1]." This, he says, can refer only to the Church, and not to Christ. As the two verses in which these words occur are passed over by S. Cyprian, though he quotes the rest of the chapter in full[2], it is probable that he too felt a difficulty in applying them to Christ. Yet the verses cannot be separated arbitrarily from the rest. Tyconius saw this, and provided an explanation by saying that to the mind of the prophet the Church and Christ form one whole.

Again, in Cant v 1 the Bride says: "I am black and comely[3]." This Tyconius understands to refer to the mixture of the good and the bad in the Church, and he goes on to say: "Never can I think that the Church, *which hath neither spot nor wrinkle*, which the Lord with His own Blood cleansed for Himself, can in any part be black, except in the left, whereby *the Name of God is blasphemed among the Gentiles*." He then explains how it is that the Church can have any part black. The Bride, he says, —that is of course the Church—is black and comely "as the tent of Kedar, as the curtain of Solomon." Here we have implied in a single sentence the whole story of Hagar and Sarah, the bondwoman and the free. For Kedar is the son of Ishmael, who was rejected; while Isaac was chosen, whose heir is Solomon. Ishmael or his representative is always with the Church, and in each age is again cast out. Sometimes the bad part is called Ishmael, sometimes Esau; but it is always reappearing, and, as Tyconius tells us in another place[4], the Church now suffers from false brethren, but they will soon be cast out at the approaching end of the age.

[1] p 2.
[2] *Test* ii 13 and 15.
[3] p 10.
[4] pp 29—31.

Rules I and II are occupied in expounding the above theory. Rule III is an excursus explaining the author's idea of the antithesis of Faith and Works, of the Promises and the Law. In Rule IV he goes back to Prophecy, and tries to find a method of extracting edification out of those parts of the Old Testament which obviously refer to special towns or countries. He makes a distinction between what he calls *Genus* and what he calls *Species*. Genus includes those statements which are universally true, the general principles of God's providence; Species includes particular promises or threats which are fully appropriate only to the individual cities or nations. In the view of Tyconius Genus and Species are mixed up together in an almost inextricable confusion, —he calls it "Spiritus eloquium subtile." In successive verses Genus may give place to Species or *vice versa*, or the whole verse may be assigned to either category. "For while," he says[1], "the prophecy is still referring to the particular instance, the transition is often made to the general promise in such a way that it is not at once clearly visible. We often find words used at first which suit either interpretation, until at last some detail is introduced too wide for the Species, and we discover that the sense has become general." Thus Nahum prophesied against Nineve, and much that he says will suit the story of the destruction of the ancient city on the Tigris, but to shew that 'Nineve' is not to be confined to that special city, some words are added which are too great for a single town, such as "There was no end to the nations thereof," and "Thou hast multiplied thy merchandise above the stars of the heaven,"—that is, the Church[2].

In Rule V there comes a truly marvellous dissertation upon Times, Seasons and Numbers. Nothing less than a quotation of the original in full would do justice to the extraordinary ingenuity by which almost any number can be made to mean any other. Thus the time between the Death of Christ on the cross and His Resurrection is proved to have been three days and three nights by the following process of reasoning. The time in question appears to be the evening of Friday, the whole of Saturday, and until sunrise on Sunday. Tyconius says:—any part of Friday or Sunday may stand for the whole day, because it is written "Vespera et

[1] pp 31, 32.

[2] Nah iii 3, 16, p 42.

mane dies unus" (Ge i 5). But Saturday must be complete, for we read "A uespera in uesperam obseruari diem sabbatorum" (Lev xxiii 32). Finally, the Resurrection took place when it was yet dark (Jn xx 1) on Sunday morning, because "competit operibus Dei, ut non dies obscuraretur in noctem sed nox lucescat in diem. ipsa enim nox inluminatur et efficitur dies, quod est figura eorum quae facturus erat in Christo[1]." This is a happy thought, whatever we may think of it as exegesis.

The sixth Rule is devoted to what Tyconius called *Recapitulatio*. This is by no means identical with what we usually mean by 'recapitulation'; and the neglect of the distinction has given rise to a certain amount of misunderstanding from the time of S. Augustine onward, and has produced a confusion in the text of one of our principal manuscript authorities[2]. According to the terminology of Tyconius a 'recapitulation' is made when a Biblical writer is speaking both of the type and the antitype, the promise and the fulfilment. For just as the Church and her Head are not two but one according to the "subtle eloquence of the Spirit," and may therefore appropriately be the subject of the same prophecy, so also the type and the antitype are in a measure one in the prophet's mind. Thus we read in Mt xxiv 15: "When ye see that which was spoken by Daniel the prophet, then let them which are in Judaea flee to the mountains." What was spoken by Daniel had come to pass long ago, for the direct fulfilment had been only one of the types of the general coming of Antichrist. But the Evangelist 'recapitulates' this and joins the events together by saying 'then'; that is, when a similar state of things is seen again in the world. Tyconius seems to realise that others might feel the difficulties of this method of interpretation, in which both the class of beings to which a prophecy refers and the time for which it is appropriate are left to the intelligence of the reader. He therefore makes a digression to shew that in several texts, even in the Epistles, much is really hinted at rather than expressly stated, and that simply to take

[1] Similar reckonings of the "three days and three nights" are found in Aug *Serm* ccxxi (=*Eug* 445) and *Quaest Ev* I 7 (=*Eug* 447). In these passages S. Augustine seems to be influenced by Tyconius. See also Cassian, *contra Nest* vi 23.

[2] See pp xxxvi, xxxvii.

what the Apostle says, and no more, would lead to manifest absurdity.

The seventh Rule is occupied in shewing that prophecies about the Devil and his followers are subject to the same rules as those about Christ and His Church. As the Church is the Body of Christ, so the wicked are the Body of the Devil. There is however one difference. In the Church are false brethren. Jacob and Solomon and other types of the Church have also a wicked side; for the Church is black as well as comely. But the followers of the Devil are altogether bad. Esau, Seir, Theman are types of the bad alone. Even if the Evil One is said to be ornamented with precious stones[1], these ornaments are only the "men of excellent intelligence and powerful genius" whom he has stolen from God: "Omnia enim quae fecit Deus bona sunt; horum diabolus usum non naturam mutauit[2]."

II. *The Date of the Book of Rules.*

The date of the work is of some importance in estimating the value of the text of the Biblical quotations, as we cannot suppose that the Donatist Bible entirely escaped the tendency to eclectic revision which prevailed in the fourth century. A few years difference in the date of the publication of the Book of Rules might conceivably have produced a very considerable change in the text of the quotations.

The principal external evidence for the date is derived from the consideration that the work is decidedly earlier than 426 AD, the date of the second edition of the treatise *de Doctrina Christiana*, in which S. Augustine contrasts the time when Tyconius wrote with his own. "Non erat expertus hanc haeresem (Pelagianorum), quae nostro tempore exorta multum nos...... exercuit[3]."

A passage in Rule V (de Temporibus) supplies a further clue within the work itself. It runs as follows: "Vnus dies aliquando C anni sunt, sicut de Ecclesia scriptum est iacere *in ciuitate ubi et*

[1] Eze xxviii 13.

[2] Rule VII, p 82[8].

[3] See *de Doct Christ* iii 33.

Dominus eius *cruci fixus est tres dies et dimidium* (cf. Ap xi 8, 9), et: *Oportet filium hominis Hierusalem ire, et multa pati a senioribus et principibus sacerdotum et scribis, et occidi, et post tres dies resurgere;* ipse enim tertio surrexit[1]." The "Son of Man," by which expression Tyconius here understands the Church, not Christ[2], will come to the end of the long struggle in three days and a half—that is 350 years—after the Crucifixion. This brings us to 383 AD at the latest: therefore it would seem that Tyconius wrote before 383 AD.

III. *The Literary History of the Book of Rules.*

The Rules of Tyconius are explained and criticised by S. Augustine in his treatise *de Doctrina Christiana* III 30—37. This is no doubt the most important event in the history of the book. The great African theologian suggests a fresh title for Rules II and III, and gently complains that the treatment of Promises and Law is not quite full enough for the times of the Pelagian controversy. He also warns readers not to forget that Tyconius was not a Catholic: "Caute sane legendus est, non solum propter quaedam in quibus ut homo errauit, sed maxime propter illa quae sicut Donatista haereticus loquitur[3]." But this is S. Augustine's hardest word, and indeed throughout the whole review he treats Tyconius as an authority to be explained rather than as a theorist to be criticised.

S. Augustine is moreover a prime authority for such of Tyconius' Biblical Quotations as he himself quotes. The only passage of Tyconius' own writing which is given word for word is the preface, but wherever S. Augustine quotes a verse to shew how it is explained by Tyconius, he quotes it directly from the Book of Rules.

Two examples are given below to make this clear. The right-hand column contains quotations of the same verses from other works of S. Augustine.

[1] p 61. [2] See pp 4, 7.

[3] *de Doct Christ* iii 30.

Eze xxxvi 23

de Doct Christ iii (=Tyc. p 33)	*contr ep* 2 *Pelag* iv
et sanctificabo	et sanctificabo
nomen meum	nomen meum
sanctum illud magnum	magnum
quod *pollutum* est	quod *profanatum* est
inter nationes	*in gentibus*
quod polluistis	*et profanastis*
in medio e*a*rum,	in medio eorum,
et scient gentes	et scient gentes
quoniam ego sum	*quia* ego sum
dn̄s,	dns, *dicit Adonai dn̄s*,
dum sanctificabor	*cum sanctificatus fuero*
in uobis	in uobis
ante oculos eorum.	ante oculos eorum.

Esai xiv 12 (after "Quomodo cecidit de caelo lucifer mane oriens")

de Doct Christ iii (=Tyc. p 70)	*de Genesi ad litt* xi
contritus est	contritus est
in terr*a*	in terr*am*
qui *mittit*	qui *mittebat*
ad omnes gentes	ad omnes gentes

In the last instance, the difference of reading corresponds to a difference of interpretation; for "contritus est in terra" is explained to mean that the Devil is defeated on earth in the person of wicked men who perish, while "contritus est in terram" is referred to the fall of the Evil Angels.

It is worthy of notice in passing that the whole passage in *de Genesi ad litt* xi from which Isaiah xiv 12 is quoted above seems to shew the influence of Tyconius on S. Augustine. Tyconius is not named, but S. Augustine argues from Isaiah xiv and Ezekiel xxviii as in Rule VII, though the text of these passages as he quotes them is independent of Tyconius. Such words as these seem an echo of the Book of Rules: "*Tu autem dixisti sensu tuo, In caelum ascendam, super sidera caeli ponam thronum meum*......et cetera, quae in figura regis uelut Babylonis in diabolum dicta intelleguntur, plura in eius corpus conueniunt, quod etiam de humano genere congregat... Sicut enim qui erat diabolus homo dictus est, ut in Evangelio: *Inimicus homo hoc fecit,* ita qui homo erat diabolus dictus est... Et sicut corpus

Christi, quod est Ecclesia, dicitur Christus,...eo modo etiam corpus diaboli, cui caput est diabolus...dicitur diabolus... Itaque lucifer qui mane oriebatur et cecidit, potest intellegi apostatarum genus uel a Christo uel ab Ecclesia, quod ita conuertitur ad tenebras amissa luce, quam portabat[1], quem ad modum qui conuertuntur ad Deum a tenebris ad lucem transeunt, id est qui fuerunt tenebrae fiant lux[2]."

In Cassian *contra Nestorium* vi 23 (C.S.E.L. xvii), about 429 AD, is a short *résumé* of the first part of Reg v, but Tyconius is not mentioned by name.

The Book of Rules is next referred to in the "Liber de Promissionibus" which is usually bound up with the works of S. Prosper of Aquitaine, and which seems to have been written in Africa between 450 and 455 AD[3]. I have thought it worth while to quote the reference to Tyconius in full, as it shews how his eschatological calculations were explained away by readers in the succeeding century. The passage is *de Promissionibus* iv 13 (Migne li 848): "......septimus dies qui mane tantum, et uesperam non habebit. quam requiem sabbati omni praecepto diuinitas ipsa seruandam commendat[4], ut uacantes ab omni opere malo *mane astemus* (Ps v 5), ut contemplemur eum *qui coronat in miseratione et misericordia* (Ps cii 2), omnes iuste iudicans et inique neminem damnans. sed de his Tyconius multa conscripsit. consummationem uero perfectionemque temporum trium annorum et sex mensium —qui dicti sunt dies MCCLX, et menses faciunt XL et II—non tantum Apocalypsis Iohannis quantum et Daniel propheta commendat, quibus *ciuitatem sanctam calcari* (Ap xi 2)[5] ut aestimatur ab haereticis et maxime Arianis, qui tunc plurimum poterunt."

The next reference to the Book of Rules is found in the commentary on the Pentateuch compiled by John the Deacon. This John the Deacon certainly lived before Gregory the Great, and he may be identical with Pope John III. A MS of the commentary exists at Paris[6], from which Dom Pitra edited some portions. The work consists of extracts from earlier writers, among which is found one passage from Rule V[7]. This is pub-

[1] Cf Reg VII, p 83[22, 27].
[2] Cf Regg IV, p 48[20]; V, p 57[18 ff].
[3] See Migne li 731, 732.
[4] Cf Reg V, p 62.
[5] Cf Reg V, p 61.
[6] Cod Lat 838.
[7] See pp 55, 56.

lished in *Spicilegium Solesmense* i 294, 295. The extract is introduced as a comment on Ex xii 40, and it is most likely that John the Deacon was induced in this single instance to quote the Book of Rules, because S. Augustine had mentioned Tyconius when commenting on that verse[1]. But the reference itself is in any case independent, as John the Deacon makes an exact quotation of some length, while S. Augustine merely refers to the interpretation of Tyconius.

In the 6th century the Book of Rules is praised in general terms by Cassiodorus, and recommended to students of Scripture[2]. His contemporary Primasius on the other hand does not mention this work, though his commentary on the Apocalypse is based on that of Tyconius.

S. Isidore of Seville, about the beginning of the 7th century, describes the Rules in the "Liber Sententiarum[3]." Tyconius is not once named, but the Rules are said to be the work of "certain wise men." S. Isidore's description is mainly taken from *de Doct Christ* iii, but he must also have been familiar with the Book of Rules itself. Thus in describing Rule IV he quoted Isaiah xiii 17, adding Tyconius' explanation[4], though that passage is not mentioned by S. Augustine. The text of the quotations themselves is assimilated to the Vulgate, as in the other works of S. Isidore.

The account of the Rules which Bede prefixed to his *Explanatio Apocalypsis* is entirely taken from S. Augustine. There is however an interesting reference to them in Hincmar (Migne cxxv 297). He is speaking of the heretic Godescalc: "imitari uolens Isidorum de Ticonio et aliis sapientibus septem in sacris scripturis regulas excerpentem, satis insulse nausiauit." As S. Isidore never names Tyconius it may well be that Hincmar himself had read the Book of Rules. We shall see in the next section that the oldest and best MS of it now known was among the books which Hincmar gave to the Cathedral library at Reims.

The remaining *Testimonia Veterum* to the Rules are the Epitomes and the "Memoria Technica." The latter is a set of seven Hexameters, first published in the French Departmental Catalogue of 1849 (vol i 88) from a 13th cent. MS at Laon. I

[1] *Quaest in Hept* ii 47.
[2] Cassiod *de Inst diuin litt* x.
[3] Isid *Sent* i 19.
[4] Reg IV, p 51^{25}.

have found the lines in two MSS at Rome, of the 14th and 15th centuries respectively. From the extensive variations in these MSS it is evident that the common original must have been much earlier than the oldest of the three, but there is no proof that the verses are independent of S. Augustine's review[1].

Two Epitomes of the Rules were published by Dom Pitra in vol iii of the *Spicilegium Solesmense.* One[2] is merely a repetition of S. Augustine's remarks, and only noticeable for the statement that S. Augustine added three more Rules to the Seven. As a matter of fact, in the earlier chapters of *de Doct Christ* iii S. Augustine gives some rules for interpreting certain classes of Scripture passages, but in no sense does he attach them to the Rules of Tyconius[3].

The other Epitome, published in *Spicil. Sol.* iii 397, is more interesting, though it also has no direct connection with the work of Tyconius, being entirely based on SS. Augustine and Isidore. This comes out very clearly from an examination of the text of the Biblical quotations. S. Isidore conforms Tyconius' quotations to the Vulgate, but S. Augustine quotes them exactly. The Epitome agrees with S. Augustine as far as he goes, but where S. Isidore refers to a quotation of Tyconius not given by S. Augustine the text of the Epitome agrees with S. Isidore,—that is, with the Vulgate. For example, both S. Isidore and the Epitome quote Isaiah xiii 5 and 11 together thus: *Et disperdam omnem terram, et uisitabo super orbem mala,* which is word for word with the Vulgate, except that the latter has *ut disperdet*[4]. On the other hand the direct dependence of the Epitome on S. Augustine is unmistakeable in the description of Rule V: "Duobus autem modis ualet haec regula aut tropo synecdoche quod expositum est, aut legitimis numeris quos eminentius diuina Scriptura commendat." This is word for word from S. Augustine, except that he writes "uigere dicit hanc regulam," and that the phrase "quod expositum est" stands for S. Augustine's explanation.

[1] See p 86. [2] *Spic. Sol.* iii 445.

[3] Jacob Perez of Valencia, who also gives ten rules in his commentary on the Psalms (AD 1506) in imitation of the rules of Tyconius, is entirely dependent for them on S. Aug *de Doct Christ.*

[4] Contrast Reg IV, pp. 50^{23}, 51^{10}.

Three MSS of this Epitome are mentioned in the *Spicilegium Solesmense*, one being of the 12th cent. I have seen two others, one at Paris (Bibl. Nat. MS Lat. 14402), and one at Oxford (Canonici Patr. Eccl. 88). No doubt there are several more[1]. The Epitome generally occupies the fly-leaf at the beginning or the end of a Biblical or quasi-Biblical MS.

The discussion of the Monza Epitome belongs to the section treating of the MSS of the Book of Rules.

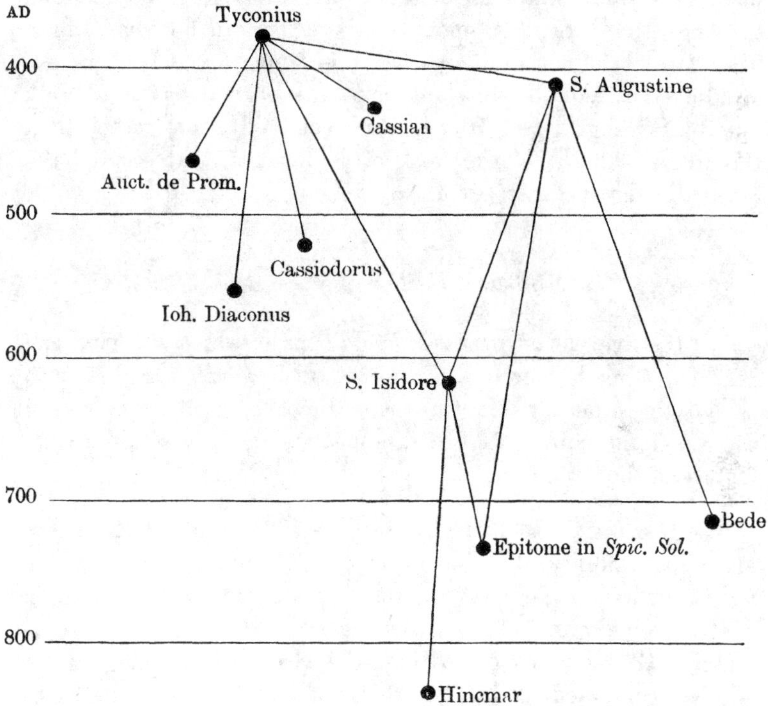

The mutual relations of the Patristic references to the Book of Rules will be seen at a glance by the diagram here annexed. Yet it hardly does justice to the preponderating influence of

[1] Such a one must be Munich, Cod. lat. 22239 (*Windberg* 39), written AD 1279: "*f* 226 de Tyconii vii regulis, id est modis loquendi diuersis in sacra scriptura; *f* 227 Arbores historiarum, etc." The lost Cluny MS may also have merely contained the Epitome, not the Book of Rules itself; see p xxviii.

S. Augustine, for the sole reference to Tyconius' book independent of the review in *de Doctrina Christiana* is that by the author of the *de Promissionibus*. He was an African, and perhaps for that reason familiar with the book which his countryman had written less than a century before[1]. But Cassian and John the Deacon quote the Book of Rules only to illustrate a passage where Tyconius' explanation had been already noticed by S. Augustine; Cassiodorus names Tyconius only in the sentence in which he recommends the study of the *de Doctrina Christiana*; S. Isidore follows S. Augustine's remarks more than the original Seven Rules. Therefore it is not unlikely that the fame of the book in the Middle Ages and its preservation to the present day is entirely due to S. Augustine. It was his recommendation, rather than the intrinsic merit of the work of a Donatist, that secured the respect of Latin Christendom.

IV. *The MSS and Editions of the Book of Rules.*

Of the five MSS of the *Liber Regularum* of which we have any knowledge one is now lost. The lost MS however, together with two of the others, was a transcript direct or mediate of one of the remaining pair, so that its disappearance only affects the later history of the text.

1. CODEX REMENSIS (R), *saec.* ix. Cod. lat. 364 of the Municipal Library at Reims (Haenel's 252 *bis*), formerly part of the Cathedral Library. A vellum quarto of 35 leaves written in neat Caroline minuscules with two columns of 28 lines on a page, making 139 columns of writing, the last column being blank. R never contained the last two-thirds of Reg VII; the text breaks off in the middle of a sentence and the colophon FINIT LIBER TYCONII is added in red. The present binding is modern, and the only signatures (*foll.* 1r, 9r, 17r, 25r and 33r) are also modern and in Arabic numerals. At the foot of *foll.* 16v, 17r an ancient hand has scrawled in capitals HINCMARVS ARCHIEPS DEDIT SCAE MARIAE REMENSI. The same words appear on the last page.

[1] See above, p xx, and *Tillemont*, xvi 28.

At the bottom of the first page also is DEDIT etc, so that the Rules may once have been bound up with some other work, on the last page of which was written *Hincmarus Archieps*; but as it appears from a scrawl on the fly-leaf at the end, written May 14, 1412, that R then as now contained only the *Liber Regularum* "sine primo folio," the loss must be ancient, if indeed what is now missing was ever more than the fly-leaf at the beginning. The same words (*Hincmarus Archieps* etc) in the same hand appear in the 9th cent. MS of Victor of Capua's Harmony, which also came from the Cathedral Library. As there is some evidence[1] that Hincmar knew of Tyconius independently of S. Isidore, there is little reason to doubt the historical accuracy of the statement that the book was given by him.

The text of R is divided into short paragraphs with capitals at the beginning of them outside the line. These paragraphs seem to be older than the MS itself, as they now and then preserve the right divisions in places where the text of R is corrupt[2]. The usual contractions are found in R; ę for ae is rare, ae being generally written in full; & is used even in such cases as d&e for *de te*; i is lengthened before n at the beginning of a word to distinguish 'in' from 'm.' Quotations generally have ; placed against them in the margin. Titles, subscriptions, etc, are in regular red capitals. The ink is still very black and the MS in excellent condition. The changes in the text seem all contemporary. There are several long erasures underneath the present writing, but the character of the text does not seem specially affected at these points[3].

Sabatier was the first to make critical use of Cod. R. In the year 1727, in the midst of the preparation of his great collection of all the pre-Hieronymian Biblical quotations then available, he was obliged to leave Paris on account of the Jansenist troubles, and retired to a sort of exile at Reims[4]. This was the occasion of his coming across our MS. He was for a time Librarian in

[1] See p xxi, and compare Berger, *Vulgate*, p 281.

[2] See Reg I, pp $5^{21,22}$, $7^{23,24}$.

[3] Thus in the long erasure pp 6^{24}—7^{6} R is the only witness for the certainly genuine '*Lucan*' for '*Lucam*,' and '*generaui*' for '*genui*.'

[4] O. Lat. Bibl. Texts I xxvii, and *Sab*. III xxviii.

the Monastery of S. Nicasius[1] and made a catalogue of the MSS there, but he also quotes from the MSS belonging to the Cathedral. In the earlier parts of the Bible Sabatier simply cites Tyconius from the *Maxima Bibliotheca Veterum Patrum*, tom. vi, pp 49—67, but from Hier xxv 35 (chap xlix *Hebr*) onwards he makes considerable use of R.

I collated R in July 1891, and saw it again in May 1892. The Editor of this series also was kind enough to re-examine several doubtful passages in September of the latter year, so that I hope a considerable degree of accuracy has been insured. I have not noticed all the interchanges of *e* and *ae*, but with that exception I have tried to include every variation.

2. CODEX VATICANUS REGINENSIS 590 (V), *saec.* x. A vellum quarto containing the Book of Rules (*ff* 91—146), preceded by the Life of S. Fulgentius and his two books *de Remissione Peccatorum*. The writing is in one column with hardly any divisions; those which are found are often badly placed and have no connection with the paragraphs in R. Rules V and VI also are divided differently. The style of writing is the ordinary minuscule. 'Ecclesia' and its oblique cases are often written 'eccł' without any termination. There are many changes in the text by a contemporary corrector (V*corr*), mostly designed to improve the orthography and grammar, but including a few conjectural readings. Besides the regular corrector there are a few changes made by a later hand, possibly none other than the scribe of the Paris MS. V is described in Reifferscheid's *Bibliotheca Patrum Latinorum Italica*, p 407, but the text has never been published. I collated the MS in March and April 1892.

3. COD. PARISIENSIS (P), *saec.* xi, now Bibl. Nat. Lat. 2359, but formerly belonging to the Monastery of S. Martin des Champs near Paris. The original contents of P were Bede on the Acts, followed by S. Fulgentius and the Book of Rules as in Cod. V. These are now preceded by a 12th cent. MS of S. 'Ildefunsus,' but in the 13th century catalogue of the library of S. Martin des Champs the two books are separate. Collated in September 1891.

[1] *Sab.* III xxix.

4. COD. OXONIENSIS (O), *saec.* xii *exeunt.*, now *Marshall* 21 in the Bodleian, but formerly at the Church of S. Peter in Ghent. O contains Hilary on S. Matthew with the Book of Rules following it. The initial letters of each work are illuminated in colours. Collated in June 1891.

5. "*Cod. Claromarisci Abbatiae iuxta Audomaropolim, quem contulit P. And. Schottus, Soc. Iesu, anno* 1618." This MS has disappeared, and it is only known by the readings inserted in the margin of the edition of 1622. What remained after the Revolution of the books of the Cistercian Abbey of Clairmarais near S. Omer were removed to the S. Omer Municipal Library, but the Tyconius is not there. As however the Abbey Library was burnt in 1638, and moreover as only 117 out of the 270 MSS which were at Clairmarais in 1789 are now to be found, it is no wonder that this book is among the lost. Its readings are quoted with the sign C.

6. A paper MS at Basle of the 16th century. It is unbound and without class-mark[1]. Quoted as B.

7. CODEX MODOETIANUS (M), *saec.* ix—x, numbered $\frac{c-2}{62}$ in the Cathedral Library at Monza near Milan, is a vellum MS of 210 leaves about 10 in. × $6\frac{3}{4}$ in., containing 'Ambrosiaster' on the Pauline epistles (including Hebrews). The last five leaves are occupied with an abridgment of the Book of Rules. The extracts embrace matter found on pages 1—39 and 50—68 of this edition, and are simply headed with the words VII · TICONII REGVLAE. At the end of the volume is the note "ego Liuthprandus scripsi hoc librum."

I first heard of M through a communication kindly made to the Editor of this series by Dom Amelli of Monte Cassino in the summer of 1893. I was unable to go to Monza myself, but Dr Ceriani of the Ambrosian Library at Milan most kindly had a complete transcript prepared for me, which is given in full in Appx. I (pp 89—98)[2].

[1] "*Ex Museo Faeschii,*" Haenel 656 *bis*.

[2] I have also to thank Dr Varisco of Monza for kindly sending me very full preliminary information concerning the MS.

M has been for a long time at Monza, possibly ever since it was written. It seems to be identical with the volume described in the catalogue of AD 1275: "Item in alio uolumine augustinus super epistolas pauli" (Frisi's *Monza* II 135). S. Augustine did not write a commentary on the Pauline epistles, but other errors occur elsewhere in the Catalogue, so that the commentary of 'Ambrosiaster' may really be meant. Our MS is described in Frisi III 30, No. LXVII.

In the 12th cent. catalogue of the Cluny Library (published by Delisle[1]) No 274 is thus described: *Volumen in quo continentur vii libri Ticonii de multiplici uarietate et passiones sanctorum Nazarii et Celsi et sermones et hymni et misse, etc.* If this was a MS of the Book of Rules it is quite lost, but the rest of the contents of the Codex suggest that it may have been only the second Epitome described on p xxii.

The text of the Book of Rules was first published by Grynæus at Basle in 1569 among the Orthodoxographa. Grynæus' text was repeated (with several misprints[2]) in the *first* edition only of de la Bigne's *Bibliotheca Patrum*, Paris 1575[3].

In 1622 the Jesuit Andreas Schott edited the Rules for the Appendix of the *Magna Bibliotheca Veterum Patrum.* In the margin he inserted several readings from the lost S. Omer MS, and he also appears to have now and then emended the text from the same source[4]. But this is of very rare occurrence, and for the most part even the misprints of the *editio princeps* are repeated. Schott's edition appears again in the *Maxima Bibliotheca,* from which Sabatier mainly quotes, and the pages of which appear in the margin of this edition. In 1772 another edition

[1] ii 237.

[2] E.g. 'esis' for 'eris' in the last line.

[3] The other editions of de la Bigne do not contain the Rules; see *Tillemont*, vi 148.

[4] Thus in Reg II, p 11[8] *nequam ille seruus* is the reading of the MSS; Grynæus left out *nequam*, but it is inserted by Schott, though it is a reading quite different from the Vulgate. On the other hand he leaves *mente* for *monte* (Reg I, p 2[22]), though that is a simple printer's blunder, and changes *sæuere*—a mistake of the editio princeps for *sed seuere* (Reg III, p 16[7])—into *sed vere*, which has remained in all subsequent editions.

of Tyconius came out in Galland, tom. viii. Some of the misprints in Schott's edition were removed, and a few conjectures made without any warning to the reader, but no MS was used. Finally, Galland's edition was reprinted in Migne, tom. xvii, with several fresh misprints.

V. *The Genealogy of the MSS.*

The object of this section is to shew that Cod. V is the sole ancestor of Codd. P O B C and the Editions. For the sake of clearness I give here what I conceive to be the relations of the MSS to one another, including the Monza Epitome (M). Greek letters represent hypothetical lost MSS.

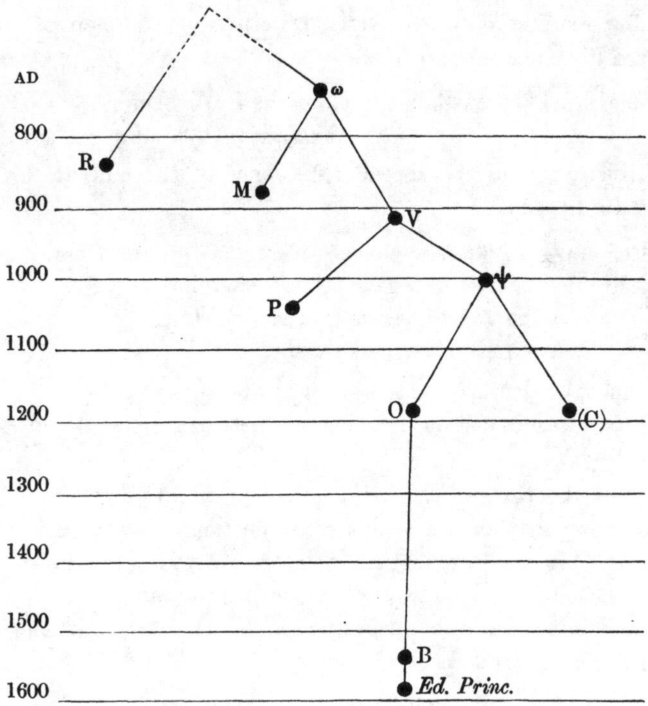

1. Derivation of B and *p* (the *editio princeps*) from O.

A large number of the extraordinary corruptions which have

hitherto defaced the printed text of Tyconius come from O, the MS now in the Bodleian.

For example:

Reg I, p 5^9 nouissimo aduentu Domini...nemo ut aliqui putant *mentietur* R V*corr* P M

metietur V*

mercietur O

mereretur p, altered by Schott into *moreretur*!

Tyconius is talking of "false Christs," and says they appear before, not at the time of the Last Advent.

Reg III, p 15^7 sed minus *liquet* quid sit...ex fide R

licet VP

lucet O *p*

The reading of O is evidently a mere correction of 'licet,' though it makes sense in itself.

Reg IV, p 33^{16} custodiatis et *faciatis* R VP Aug$^{\text{loc cit}}$

operemini O *p* (= *Vg*, Eze xxxvi 27)

An illustration of the sporadic influence of the Vulgate on late Patristic MSS.

Reg VII, p 79^{18} tres pueri, qui regem...unum Dominum asserendo *eiusdem Dei praesente uirtute* confuderunt VP

eiusdem Dei praesente (om *uirtute*) O C

eodem Dei praesente all edd.

Schott conjectures *eiusdem Dei praesentia.*

This instance shews a connection between Codd. O and C not shared by VP.

Thus the texts of the *editio princeps* and Cod. O stand very near to one another. The link of connection is the paper MS B at Basle. This MS is evidently printers' 'copy.' In the margin are red chalk marks and the numeration of the pages of *p*, the exact points where the pages begin being marked in the text, with the catchwords printed out, thus:

1353 et crescendo / terram / omnem texit......

The greater part of B is written in a large clear Italic hand, but the first page is not so professional in appearance. It seems almost as if Grynæus himself had begun it, and then ordered a copy to be made by a writer. At the top left-hand corner are the words

ex bibliotheca sti petri Gandensis,

which have been run through with a pen. The corresponding words in O are on the fly-leaf at the end: Lib' ſi petri gand.' ecclę. The opening words in B are *incipit liber Tichonij*, as in O, but this has been altered in the MS to *Tichonij liber* (without *incipit*), which is the title in *p*. As far as relates to the text, we find that, near as O and *p* stand together, B is nevertheless between the two. Three examples will be enough.

Reg I, p 2[28] accepit omnem potestatem R VP C O M

For *potestatem* B has *p'tatem*; accordingly *ed. princ.* and all other editions have *pietatem*, though since Schott's time *potestatem* has had a place in the margin.

Reg III, p 22[21] fidelis Deus R
fideles Deus VP (C) O

fidelis Deus is in the text of both B and *p*, but in the margin of B is *al' fideles*, and in the margin of all editions is *alias fideles*.

Reg VII, p 73[20] illum ab Aquilone persequar R VP O
illum persequar ab Aquilone B *p* and edd.

The Greek of Joel ii 20 is *τὸν ἀπὸ βορρᾶ ἐκδιώξω*.

Both external and internal evidence therefore prove that *p*, the *editio princeps*, was made from B, and that B is a copy of O. In what follows the readings of O alone will be quoted.

2. Proof that Codd. VP O C constitute one family.

Reg III, p 20[23] Salomon *in prece dedicationis* templi...inquit R
in praedicationis V
in predicatione P
in dedicatione O and edd.

P and O here give independent emendations of V.

Reg III, p 29[11] quod pars mala simulet se Iacob
et *sint duo sub* uno nomine R
...et *sine dubio* uno nomine VP O and edd.

Reg IV, p 48[11] minatur Deus ignem ex igni Israhel regi Assyriorum, et *dicit arsurum uelut* stipulam R

et *dicitur sýrum uel ad* stipulam V*

et *dicit ad syrum uel ad* stipulam V*corr* P O and edd.

V's ancestor seems to have written *a* in the form *cc* (as indeed we sometimes find in V itself); this is easily confused with *u*.

But some of the most striking and convincing proofs of the close connection of the family VPOC come from the text of the Biblical quotations. It must be borne in mind that for at least two hundred years before the earliest of our MSS was written the Vulgate had been the only Biblical text known in Western Europe. Nearness therefore to the exact words of the LXX is a proof of textual fidelity.

Reg IV, p 42[26] sacerdotes eius *profanant* sacra R

prophetant VPO

βεβηλοῦσιν LXX Soph iii 4

Reg IV, p 42[27] Dominus...iustus *in medio* eius R

in templo VPO

ἐν μέσῳ LXX Soph iii 5

Reg IV, p 44[4] quoniam dedit timorem suum super

terram *uitae, dormiet* R

...*uitae dormiret* V*

...*ut dormiret* V*corr* P

...*uitae ut dormiret* O

The Greek of Eze xxxii 32 is *ὅτι δέδωκα* (*ἔδωκεν* Lucian) *τὸν φόβον αὐτοῦ ἐπὶ γῆς ζωῆς καὶ κοιμηθήσεται.*

As is so often the case, the corrupt word in V*—'dormiret'—is unchanged by the correctors and copyists, while the words which were faithfully transmitted are still further corrupted by conjecture.

Reg IV, p 46[15ff] accipe *citharam, uagulare,* ciuitas fornicaria oblita; bene citharizare, *multa canta,* ut tui commemoratio fiat. R (R has the misspelling 'citharizari,' a mistake not shared by the others)

1. *cytharam angulare* V; *cytharam angularem* PO
2. *multa cantica canta* VPO

The Greek of Esai xxiii 16 is *λάβε κιθάραν ῥέμβευσον πόλις πόρνη ἐπιλελησμένη, καλῶς κιθάρισον πολλὰ ᾆσον ἵνα σου μνεία γένηται.*

The rather harsh phrase *multa canta* is a literal rendering of *πολλὰ ᾆσον,* and therefore *cantica* in VPO is not genuine. *Angularem* in PO comes from *angulare* in V, which is a corruption of R's word *uagulare.* 'Vagulari' seems to be a *ἅπ. λεγ.* to express *ῥεμβεύειν,* a word which occurs here only in the whole Greek O. Test.[1] 'Vagari' is the word used in this passage by Ambrose and Jerome.

Reg IV, p 49[17] *Confringantur* arcus in Aelam R

συντριβήτω (Cod. A etc, but *συνετρίβη* B) *τὸ τόξον Αἰλάμ,* Hier xxv 36.

confringānair VP

confringam nair O, and as '*nair*' was otherwise inexplicable it has been spelt with a capital N in all the editions, and treated as a proper name! It was this corruption which seems to have made Sabatier suspicious of the printed texts of Tyconius, and which led him to publish some readings of R.

Reg IV, p 50[1] *eritque* in nouissimis diebus *auertam* captiuitatem Aelam R

καὶ ἔσται ἐπ' ἐσχάτων τῶν ἡμερῶν [καὶ] ἀποστρέψω κ.τ.λ. Hier xxv 39

erit......aeternam captiuitatem aelam VP

erit......in aeternam captiuitatem elam C

erit......in aeternum captiuitatem elam O and editions

This instance makes it quite clear that C also belongs to the same family as VP and O.

3. Proof that V is the actual parent of P and O.

The instances given above only shew the close relationship of VPO. Something more is needed to prove actual parentage. It must not be a mere corruption in V, for that might have arisen by faithfully copying a damaged exemplar. It must be some peculiarity in the MS itself, which has been mistaken by subsequent

[1] A similar instance is found in Reg IV, p 45[28], where, to express *θρήνημα* in Eze xxvii 32 (which only occurs in the LXX at that place), we find *lamenta* in R, which is changed in V and PO to *lamentum.* For *lamenta* see Rönsch 86.

copyists. From the nature of the case such instances are rare, but I have noticed the following examples.

a. There are several cases where RV* are together, while O and P follow V*corr.* Thus

Reg I, p 1[19,20] Dominum eiusne corpus, id est Ecclesiam, Scriptura loquatur, sola ratio discernit] R

That is: "Reason alone decides whether in a Messianic passage the Scripture is speaking of the Lord Himself, or of His Body the Church."

For *eiusne* VPO have *eiusque*, which destroys the whole sense. Nevertheless *loquatur* was read by V* as in R; but as there was now no particle to govern the subjunctive, *loquatur* was changed by the corrector into *loquitur*, and *loquitur* is the reading of P and O.

Reg VII, p 76[1] Abductosque non soluit. potest istud in speciem conuenire] V*corr* P (*hiat* R)

For *abductosque* and *istud*, V*O have *abductoque* and *inquit*. The first was obviously wrong, so the amended reading *abductosque* is in the editions, but *inquit* was never changed back in them to *istud*.

b. Accidental defacements in V a cause of corruption.

Reg IV, p 47[27] ista sunt] R
ista faciant VO

faciant is in the last line of a page of V, and the letters *ac* have been injured by damp, not erased by a scribe. The reading of P is *fiant*.

Reg VII, p 74[4] quasi] RVP, *om* quasi O and edd.

By some accident—I think some ink has come over from the opposite page—'quasi' has been nearly blotted out in V.

c. Marginal corrections in V misunderstood or neglected.

Reg I, p 5[28] Dauid totam Ecclesiam Christum dicit] RM

V* omitted *Christum*, but it was added in the margin. P puts the word in the text at the right place, but in O it is inserted between *totam* and *Ecclesiam*.

Reg IV, p 49[13] ex omnibus gentibus uenientibus] R
ἐκ πάντων τῶν ἐθνῶν τῶν ἐλθόντων Zech xiv 16

V* omits *gentibus*, but it is given in the margin, apparently by the first hand, and a sign of omission is placed thus:

omnibus ^ uenientibus.

gentibus is read by PO, but both these MSS mistook the sign of omission for the mediæval contraction for *con*, and so read '^ uenientibus' as *conuenientibus.* The contraction for 'con' occurs nowhere in V.

d. Miscellaneous.

Reg IV, p 51[9, 10] et tenebrescet oriente sole lumen et non permanebit lumen eius] R (R has *tenebriscet*, as elsewhere)

This corresponds to Esai xiii 10 *καὶ σκοτισθήσεται τοῦ ἡλίου ἀνατέλλοντος, καὶ ἡ σελήνη οὐ δώσει τὸ φῶς αὐτῆς.*

V omits *oriente sole lumen,* leaving a space for about 25 letters. P and O also omit, leaving no space.

Reg III, p 24[15] stultum est et proteruum credere] R

et proteruum has been corrupted in V into *et propterea*m, which the scribe wrote

& $\overline{\text{pp}}$ eum

V*corr* expunged these words by putting dots below; they are altogether omitted in P and O.

Reg V, p 63[8] adducent fratres uestros] R (= *τοὺς ἀδελφοὺς ὑμῶν* Esai lxvi 20)

for *fratres uestros* V has $\overline{\text{f}}\overline{\text{f}}$

This is read as *omnes fratres* by P

and *filii filiorum* by O

The reading of P is influenced by the Vulgate, which has *omnes fratres uestros.*

There can, I think, be no other explanation of all these passages except that V is the direct ancestor of both P and O. With regard to C we cannot indeed take the paucity of readings preserved by Schott as satisfactory evidence for identity of text in O and C, yet even among these readings is one specially characteristic of O, viz 'diei' CO for 'Dei,' p 57[18]. This was so obviously a blunder that it did not appear even in the *editio princeps.* But if C and O be closely connected in error, then C is also descended from V through an ancestor which contained the blunders which C shared with O.

VI. *The Text of the Monza Epitome.*

i. Contents. (See pp 89—98.)

With three exceptions M consists of passages taken from the first six Rules arranged in their proper order. Many sentences are curtailed, and for the most part the Biblical quotations are omitted, or only the beginnings and endings of the passages are given. Some of those which are retained have had their text assimilated to the Vulgate. The general aims of the compiler seem to have been brevity and clearness. Difficult sentences and phrases are often passed over altogether[1], and the remarks of objectors introduced by Tyconius are left out[2].

The three passages where M deserts the order or the text of the Book of Rules will be found on pp 93, 98. The first of these is the passage "non de omnibus...unum corpus," which belongs to Rule III, p 26^{7-10}. It is the only instance of such a transposition. The remaining pair are from S. Augustine. The closing words of the Epitome (p 98) from "Omnes homines saluos fieri" to "decimatis omne olus" are taken from the *Enchiridion* § 103, and the passage "Et in genesi...nouissima hora est" comes from *de Doct Christ* iii 36 (Eugippius 873—875), part of S. Augustine's review of the Book of Rules.

This last paragraph merits special discussion, as it has a *prima facie* appearance of being a part of the original text of Rule VI, lost in Codd. RV from *homoeoteleuton.* In our MSS Rule VI, after a remark on the obscurity of 'Recapitulation,' begins with a quotation of Lk xvii 29—32, which is explained as one of the passages where all this present time in which our Lord's Advent is taking place is spoken of as a 'day' or an 'hour.' In *de Doct Christ* iii S. Augustine prefaces his description of Rule VI by explaining Recapitulation in its ordinary sense of a summary, giving several Biblical examples. He then says: "Fit ista recapitulatio etiam obscurius," and goes on to quote Lk xvii 29—32 followed by a paraphrase of the explanation of it by Tyconius. Thus the first

[1] E.g. ista...uidentur, $4^{11,12}$; sed hunc...subornauit, 5^{20-25}; et Spiritus...uideri possit, 31^{17-20}; et eo...properantes, 66^{4-9}.

[2] E.g. sicut quidam...Christus, 2^{18-25}.

part of S. Augustine's remarks does not correspond to anything in our MSS of Rule VI, and when we find the passages reappearing in M, we might suppose at first sight that there had been a lacuna at this place in the ancestor of R and V.

But a closer inspection proves that M is here directly derived from S. Augustine. In fact M altogether deserts the Book of Rules at this point and quotes Lk xvii not from Tyconius but from S. Augustine, giving afterwards S. Augustine's explanation of it. This explanation is beyond question in S. Augustine's own words, not those of Tyconius; if then we find M following S. Augustine here, there is no difficulty in believing that the previous section also was taken directly from the same source.

ii. The text of M.

The author of the Epitome treated the text of the MS before him with such freedom that singular variations of M are entitled to little weight. Nevertheless he made use of a good exemplar, so that M is often of great value in helping us to decide between the readings of R and V. The combination RM against V is more frequent than VM against R in the proportion of six to five, but this is only the result of the numerous blunders of V. M and V are in fact closely connected, and fall into common error in several places.

The most important of these errors for the genealogy of the MSS is to be found in Rule V, p 56[11,12]. I give the passage in full. (*D* is the commentary of John the Deacon. See p xx.)

R*D* sicut autem in prima parte
cuiusque temporis
tempus est,
ita et nouissima hora
totus dies est.

autem] enim *D* cuiusquam *D*
tempus est] *om* est *D*

VM sicut autem in prima parte
cuiusque temporis
totum tempus est,
ita et nouissima,
ut nouissima hora totus dies sit.

cuiusque] cui: M
cuiusque temporis totum] temporis cuiusq. temporis cuiusq. V
ita et] M; ita in V

"But just as the whole time (of any epoch) is (mystically contained) in the first part of the epoch, so the last hour (of an epoch) counts as a whole day."

Here the important reading in which VM unite against R is the addition of *ut nouissima* to *et nouissima*, with a consequent change of *est* to *sit*. Either reading by itself is grammatical, though I believe that of VM really contradicts Tyconius. But however that may be, we have at this point a fourth witness independent of RVM in the Commentary of John the Deacon (see above p xx). He quotes the passage independently of R, but like R he omits *ut nouissima* and ends with *est*, not *sit*. R then is right here against VM, and therefore VM are not textually independent, and their united witness not always conclusive against R.

Other coincidences of MV against R in wrong readings are

1. 6^{28} sed qui] R V*corr*; sed quis V*M V*corr* gets *qui* from the preceding quotation, while M makes the following sentence run easier by omitting *dicens* 7^{1}.

2. 7^{5} lucan] R; lucam MV 'Lucan' is the *old* spelling.

3. 11^{27} in omnibus] R; omnibus gentibus VM.

4. $16^{10,11}$ si enim mandaret a se prouentum postulari, et
legem destruxerat et fidem. ut quid enim legem daret,
si legem in omnibus facturum polliceretur ?] R
si legem in omnibus factorum... V
si se legem in omnibus factorum... M.

5. 32^{8} ab specie in genere aut a genere in specie
in specie] R; in speciem MV (*but not* "in genus").

6. 39^{22} achar] R; achan M; acham V*corr* (a×××× V*).

7. 51^{25} cui enim hosti non opus est auro] R
cui enim ostis non opus est auro V
quis enim hostis aurum non quaerit M

Here M had the corruption (h)ost*is*, but makes grammar by changing the construction.

8. $55^{7,8}$ et affligent] R*D*; et affligent eos MV

Here again the presence of *D* enables us to decide that R is right and MV wrong.

9. 56^{9} mensis] R*D*; mensis mensis M; mensis decimus V.

10. $60^{15,16}$ dies saluationis] R; dies salutis M; dies salutationis V.

11. 66^{10} legem] R; lege MV.

12. 66^{16} die quo] R *Aug* (*incl* M *when quoting* Aug); die qua MV.

13. 68[1] omnis] RV*corr*; omnes V*; $\overline{\text{oms}}$ M.

Of these instances I lay especial weight on 4, 8, 10, and 12.

Besides these there are several places where both M and V have been influenced independently by the Vulgate, e.g. in those quotations which have been altogether assimilated to the Vulgate in M.

The following I believe to be a complete list of apparent coincidence of R and M in wrong readings against V.

Coincidence in omission.

6[20] *uocatus apostolus*] V (= *Vg* and all MSS of Ro i 1); *om* RM

This omission may be due to Tyconius himself.

24[22] qui liberi deo seruiunt] V; *om* RM

This is undoubtedly a genuine clause. These are the only two clauses omitted by R and M together, and their agreement in these two cases proves nothing, as M omits so many clauses both in the quotations (e.g. 9[3,28], 37[13], etc) and in Tyconius' own words (e.g. 7[4], 13[21], 14[8], 19[7], 24[23], etc).

Addition of m *to ablatives.*

9[11] in gloria enim mea] V; in gloriam enim meam RM

32[15] in terra] V; in terram RM (possibly right)

Readings such as these again prove very little, since even if they be not correct they might occur independently.

·ē· *for* ē

65[22] idem] idē V; id·ē· M; id est R

This is the only occasion where RM go wrong together in this way.

Real various Readings.

23[27] quaesiuit fidelem cui id donaret] R*corr* V; quaes. fid. cui donaret R*M

May not this be accidental? R*corr* does not seem to have had a different exemplar to R*

59[25] *laudabo te*] V *Aug* [= the Verona Psalter, (Gk and Lat)]; *laudem dixit tibi* R; *laudem dixit* M

The Vulgate and the old Psalters (exc *Veron*) have *laudem dixi tibi.* M so often deserts the true text of Tyconius' quotation for the Vulgate that it is probable the scribe intended to write 'dixit.'

VII. *The Accuracy of Tyconius' Quotations.*

1. Before applying the quotations of Tyconius to the criticism of the LXX or even of the Old Latin Versions, it is most necessary to examine how far he can be trusted as a witness at all. Patristic citations are valuable for textual criticism in proportion as they simply reproduce the codex used by the author, or at least enable us to see what was the reading on which the writer is basing his remarks. A Biblical MS professes at least to reproduce its inherited text, but a writer who is merely illustrating his own words by quotations is under no such restriction. We ought not to use the quotations of Tyconius as fragments of the African Latin or any other Version, without enquiring what standard of accuracy these quotations habitually reach. The African Fathers differ greatly in this respect. S. Cyprian is very exact, and if he quotes a passage a second time he almost always does so in the same words. Tertullian on the other hand is acknowledged to be often paraphrastic, while Prof. Sanday remarks of a contemporary of Tyconius: "it may be said to be characteristic of Optatus that he is able to recast a scriptural passage almost entirely in his own words[1]." Both slavish accuracy and free adaptation are found; it is not necessary to postulate a fresh version of the Bible for every deviation from the customary word-for-word rendering.

There is a *prima facie* probability that in a single work an ancient writer used, besides his memory, a single MS only; and there is also a *prima facie* probability that in an original work on the interpretation of Scripture the text familiar to the author—the text, that is, that he means to quote from when he quotes from memory—is the text of his own MS. To prove that variations in the quoted texts have any other source than the inaccuracy of the author the variations must have some outside authority.

What, after all, are the proofs that a Latin Father is quoting the Bible accurately, that is, from a book, or from a memory as good as a book? Practically the proof is one of two: either the quotations agree verbally with some other Latin Father or a Latin MS of the Bible, or, where a knowledge of Greek is excluded,

[1] O. Lat. Bibl. Texts ii, p lxxxviii.

the quotations agree verbally with some form of the original Greek. Where neither of these is the case, only the strongest internal evidence can remove the suspicion that the writer was unable to give the exact words, or more probably did not care to do so.

2. The standard of accuracy in the shorter quotations of Tyconius is not always high. Though there are many verses quoted which shèw complete agreement either with some other Old Latin authority, or else with every particle of the Greek, yet in many passages we find renderings which are quite unsupported, passages which are in fact simply paraphrases, conscious or unconscious, and which have no real connection with the text of any Latin Version.

The two instances given below shew Tyconius at his worst. The first might be passed over as an allusion, but the second professes to be a direct quotation.

(*a*) Reg III, p $18^{26\text{ff}}$

Superabundauit (gratia) in omnem carnem reuelata in Christum, qui ueniens *restaurare quae in caelo et quae in terra euangelizauit* fidem *his qui proxime et qui longe.*

The italicised words are from Eph i 10 and ii 17, and the variants can all be paralleled by various Old Latin authorities. But 'fidem,' the point of the quotation, is unique. The Greek is *εἰρήνην*, both in Eph ii 17 and in Isaiah lvii 19, the passage in the mind of S. Paul. This is rendered by 'pacem' in *Tert Cyp Hil Hieron Aug*$^{5}/_{5}$ *Ambst* as well as in the Vulgate and the Graeco-Latin bilinguals. It is therefore highly improbable that *fidem* ever existed as a real variant to *pacem.* We need not suppose that Tyconius himself intended to suggest that 'faith' was here spoken of in the Epistle: but 'faith' is the subject of his discussion at this point, and he has used Scriptural language to clothe his own thought. But from our present point of view we have an inaccurate quotation.

(*b*) Reg III, p $26^{18\text{ff}}$

Quid de illa lege dicemus quae aperte promissioni uidetur aduersa? sicut scriptum est in Esaia: *Si me audisses Israhel, esset sicut harena maris numerus tuus.* ecce increpatur Israhel quod uitio suo non fuerit factus sicut harena.

(Cod. V omits *sicut* after *aduersa*, and R by homoeoteleuton omits from *maris* to the second *harena*. But the text as given above must be correct, as the quotation from Isaiah is repeated on p 28^7.)

If any quotation in Tyconius ought to be accurate it is this. It is quoted twice in identically the same form, and it is the subject of two pages of discussion. Yet it is a mere paraphrase.

It seems to be meant for Isaiah xlviii 18, 19. The extant Old Latin of Esai xlviii 18, 19 is given by a quotation of Lucifer *de Reg Apost* xi. It runs as follows: *Sic dicit...Sanctus Israhel, Ego sum Deus, ostendam tibi uiam in qua ambules; et si audisses mandata mea, facta fuisset ut fluuius pax tua et iustitia ut fluctus maris, et factum esset sicut arena maris semen tuum et nati uentris tui.* This is in accordance with the LXX; Tyconius is alone in reading 'me' for 'mandata mea' (τῶν ἐντολῶν μου), in introducing the vocative 'Israhel,' and in reading 'numerus tuus' for 'semen tuum.' Perhaps 'me' and 'Israhel' come from Ps lxxx 14 and 'numerus' from Esai x 22, but all that concerns us here is that the citation is inaccurate, in spite of its formal introduction.

I do not know that any other explanation of these two passages can be given, except that Tyconius had a treacherous memory and that he did not always verify his references.

3. But the occasional lapses of Tyconius only throw into relief his habitual correctness, especially in the long quotations.

A good example may be found in Eze xxvi 15—18, the only passage in his quotations from the Prophets where both our fragmentary Old Latin MSS are extant. These are the *Weingarten* fragments (*w*) and the *Würzburg* Palimpsest (*h*)[1], both assigned by their editor E. Ranke to the fifth century.

In what follows, as it is the general correctness of Tyconius rather than recensional peculiarities which is under discussion, singular readings of *h w* or *Tyc* are italicised, singular omissions marked with a caret, and singular variations in order marked with a star.

[1] The notation of *w* and *h* (Cod. Herbipolensis) is taken from Cornill.

h	*w*	Tyc
	15 *Propterea quod*	
15 Haec dicit dm̅s	haec dicit dm̅s	15 Haec dicit Dominus
ad *te* sor	ad sor.	ad Sor,
non a uoce	non a uoce	Non*ne* a uoce
ruinae tuae	ruinae tuae	ruinae tuae
in gemitu	in gemitu	in gemitu
uulneratorum	uulneratorum.	uulneratorum,
tuorum	*in euagina*tione	*dum* interfici*untur*
∧ interf*e*ctione ∧	gladi*i*.	gladi*o*
in medio tui	in medio tu*o*	in medio tui
commouebuntur	commouebuntur	commouebuntur
insulae	insulae.	insulae?
16 et descendent	16 et descenden*s*	16 et descendent
a sedibus ∧	a sedibus suis	a sedibus suis
omnes principes	omnes principes	omnes principes
maris	*de gentibus* (=LXX) maris	maris
et auferent mitras	et auferent mitras	et auferent mitras
a capitibus suis	*de* capitibus suis.	∧
et uestem	et uestem	et uestem
∧ suam	uariam suam	uariam suam
se despoliabunt	se dispoliabunt	despoliabunt* se.
in stupore mentis	in stupore mentis.	in stupore mentis
et *dementia induentur*	et stupebunt	∧ (=LXX) stupebunt
super terram	super terram	∧
sedebunt	sedebunt	∧
et timebunt	et timebunt	et timebunt
perditionem eorum	interitum eorum	*in* interit*u tuo*[1],
∧ ingemescent	et ingemescent	et ingemescent
super te	super te	super te,
17 et accipient	17 et accipient	17 et accipient
super te	super te	super te
lamentationem	lamentationem	lamentationem,
et dicent tibi	et dicent tibi.	et dicent tibi,
quomodo	quomodo	Quomodo
destructa es	destructa es	destructa es*t*
de mari	de mari	de mari
ciuitas illa	ciuitas illa	ciuitas illa
laudabilis	laudabilis	laudabilis,
quae dedit	quae dedit	quae dedit
timorem su*per*	timorem suum	timorem suum
omnibus habi-	omnibus habi-	omnibus *in*habi-
-tantibus in ea	-tantibus in ea.	-tantibus in ea!
18 *nunc* timebunt	18 et timebunt	18 et timebunt
insulae ex die	insulae ex die	insulae ex die
ruinae tuae	ruinae tuae	ruinae tuae.

[1] The reading of both R and V is *tuo*, but Sabatier by error edited *suo* for R.

In these four verses *w* has 6 points peculiar to itself, *h* has 12, and Tyconius 12. *Tyc* differs from *h* 21 times and differs from *w* 15 times, but *h* differs from *w* 17 times. In other words our text of Tyconius only differs from our fifth century MSS about as much as they differ from one another[1].

4. In books of the nature of a commentary, where discrepancies are found between the text as quoted at the head of a section and as quoted in the commentary, it is often a very delicate matter to judge between the relative authority which should be given to the two. Regarded as a question of the textual criticism of the author, there is no doubt that the short quotations in the commentary are generally less likely to suffer than the long quotations. The shorter quotations are often bound up grammatically with the author's remarks, while on the other hand the scribe is apt to weary of a long extract from the Bible. He often becomes careless and hurries over his work[2]. Sometimes scribes are worse than careless, and out of mistaken ingenuity they emend Biblical quotations from the current version, especially in places where there is some corruption already. Happily in the case of O. Test. quotations made by Latin Fathers, who used a version derived from the LXX, we can detect at once emendations made from S. Jerome's Vulgate, which was translated from the Hebrew[3].

The long Biblical quotations in Ecclesiastical writers are thus exposed to subsequent corruption by scribes, and we may often recover the Biblical text used by the writers from the shorter quotations and allusions which occur in the midst of their argument. But the case is entirely altered whenever the real text of the writer himself is ascertained. The long Biblical quotations are, it is true, exposed to subsequent corruption; but in the form in which they were originally written down by the author, they represented more nearly the text he used than the shorter allusions to the same passages in the course of his argument. It was worth

[1] In Eze xxvi 15—18 the Greek codd. *Alex.* and *Vat.* differ nine times.

[2] A conspicuous instance may be found in the long quotation from Eze xxviii 2—19, pp 77, 78, where V, our only authority, has omitted four long clauses and several single words, all of which nevertheless appear in the commentary which follows.

[3] *Cf* p xxxv for an instance in the secondary MSS of Tyconius.

while to copy out five, six, or a dozen verses, but in quoting the verses a second time a writer would not always take the trouble to look up the passage in the MS again, or even to refer to what had been copied out above[1]. When in the commentary a particular phrase is singled out and used to explain some doctrine or point in the argument, then the form the quotation assumes is of the greatest weight. It is attested by all the authority of the writer. But where the quotation is merely repeated, without particular stress being laid on the form of the words, we are simply dependent on the writer's memory and habit of mind as to whether it represents the text he used or not.

The chief variations in the repeated quotations of Tyconius are given below. They do not include minor variations of order, etc, nor the obvious superficial blunders of cod. V in the quotation of Eze xxviii 2—19 on pp 77, 78[2]. The number following the reading refers to the page of the text. Where V alone is extant the references are followed by the letter V.

1.	2 Regn vii 14	arguam eum 37^{18}	arguam...delicta eius $38^{27, 28}$ (*cf* Ps lxxxviii 33)
2.	Esai xiv 13	contritus 70^{14}	confractus 71^{9}
3.	16	concitat 70^{20}, 75^{10} V	incitat 71^{15}, $75^{17, 20}$ V, 76^{32} V
4.		mouet 70^{21}	commouet $75^{11, 17, 20}$ V
5.	18	reges gentium 70^{23}	reges terrae 76^{18} V
6.	20	quomodo uestimentum $71^{1, 2}$	[quomodo uenisti] sicut uestimentum $77^{3, 4}$ V
7.		erit 71^{2}	est 77^{4} V
8.	Hier xvii 27	consumet 62^{29}	conburet 64^{1}
9.	xxxii 26	omnia regna 53^{29}	uniuersa regna 54^{8}
10.	29	quia 54^{3}	quoniam $54^{11, 12}$
11.		super ipsam 54^{1}	in ipsa 54^{12}
12 a.	Eze xxviii 4^{a}	sapientia 77^{20} V	scientia 79^{21} V
b.	4^{b}	doctrina 77^{21} V	sapientia 79^{21} V
c.	5, 7, 17	doctrina $77^{22, 27}$, 78^{15} V	scientia 79^{23}, 80^{2}, 83^{31} V
13.	7	propter hoc 77^{25} V	propterea 79^{35} V
14.	9	dicturus es 77^{29} V	[narrans] narrabis 80^{15} V (*cf* Ps xxi 23)

[1] I am assuming throughout that Tyconius is an independent author. The whole state of things is changed in the case of a writer like Primasius, in whose work on the Apocalypse the text at the head of the sections differs from that in the commentary, because the commentary was taken for the most part from one source, the text from another.

[2] E.g. morte 78^{13}, *for* monte; inferorum 78^{14}, *for* igneorum.

15.	Eze xxviii 13	deliciis paradisi 78^{2}, 80^{31} V	paradiso 80^{29} V
16.	19	perditio factus es 78^{22} V	perditio facta es 85^{27} V
17.	xxxii 7	cooperiam 44^{13}	operiam 45^{6}
18.	10	†erit ad† ruinam 44^{22}	expectantes 45^{12} V (expugnantes R)
19.	2 Co iii 18	a claritate in claritatem 19^{11}	in gloria ex...gloria 19^{17} a gloria in gloriam $21^{9, 10}$
20.	2 The ii 7^{a}	obtinet 52^{9}	[detinens] detinet 74^{28} V* (detinens ē detineat V*corr*)
21.	7^{b}	donec 52^{9}	quoadusque 74^{28} V
22.	Ap xxii 17	sponsus 3^{28}	sps 71^{27}

Out of these twenty-two readings many may be seen at once to be merely the result of Tyconius' inaccuracy. Thus *terrae* 76 for *gentium* 70 in Esai xiv 18 (τῶν ἐθνῶν) is a mere slip, absolutely unattested elsewhere in any language; it could hardly have been found if Tyconius had been in the habit of verifying his quotations by his codex when he repeated them, or even if he had been in the habit of referring to what he had previously written. The argument in fact has a double conclusion: the general accuracy and occasional inaccuracy of Tyconius makes it improbable (i) that he could have consulted his codex for the inaccurate quotations, and (ii) that he could have done without his codex for the accurate quotations. But if we are obliged to resort to the hypothesis that Tyconius did not verify his quotations on repetition in order to explain the merely careless blunders like *terrae* for *gentium* (No. 5) and *paradiso* for *deliciis paradisi* (No. 15), the same hypothesis may be used to explain most of the substitutions of synonyms, such as *incitat* for *concitat* (No. 4). These substitutions are neither in the first nor the second series of a peculiarly 'African' or other cast. The only instance to the contrary is that of the variation between 'gloria' and 'claritas' in 2 Co iii 18, where however 'claritas' is also the word used in the Vulgate.

Seven of the passages demand special treatment. These are the complicated variations which I have grouped under No. 12, and Nos. 4, 18, 22, and 6, 14, 20, where there is reason to think that our MSS are corrupt. No. 12 mainly turns on the translation of ἐπιστήμη. In Eze xxviii 3, 4^{a}, 5 and 7 ἐπιστήμη is rendered in *w* (cod. Weing.) by *doctrina*; in verse 17, where *w* is wanting, *doctrina* is found in *m* 675. Thus 'doctrina' is well supported, and it is found as the rendering of Tyconius' version, pp 77, 78, in vv. 5, 7, and 17. But in the repeated quotation on pp 79, 80 and 83 we find 'scientia' instead. Moreover in v. 3 'sapientia' renders ἐπιστήμη both in 77^{20} and 79^{15}, while in v. 4 corresponding to the Greek ἐπιστήμῃ...φρονήσει we find *sapientia...doctrina* in $77^{20,21}$, but *scientia...sapientia* in 79^{21}. The rendering of ἐπιστήμη by *sapientia* in v. 3 is supported by Optatus. The valuable pair of Greek cursives 62-147 transpose ἐπιστήμη and φρόνησις in v. 4, and *w* has in that verse the corrupt reading "numquid doctrina eorum doctrina est tua aut sapientia tua fecisti," etc, which seems to have arisen out of a dittography of *doctrina*.

These variations are best shewn by a table:

Eze xxviii	Gk MSS	62-147	*w*	Tyc (1st quot)	Tyc (2nd quot)
3	ἐπιστήμη	ἐ.	doctrina	sap. (= *Opt*)	sap.
4ª	ἐπιστ.	φ.	doctrina *bis*	sap.	scientia
4ᵇ	φρόνησις	ἐ.	sapientia	doctr.	sap.
5	ἐπιστ.	ἐ.	doctrina	doctr.	scientia
7	ἐπιστ.	ἐ.	doctrina	doctr.	scientia
17	ἐπιστ.	ἐ.	[doctrina *m* 675, *hiat w*]	doctr.	scientia

Thus *scientia* in the repeated quotation stands for *doctrina* in the original, and if we suppose that *sapientia* and *doctrina* have got transposed in verse 4 in cod. V (our only authority) this is true without exception[1]. For the rest, it seems as if *doctrina* were the original rendering of ἐπιστήμη in all five places, but that in verse 3 *sapientia* had been substituted in the codex of Tyconius as in that of Optatus, while in the remaining four passages Tyconius himself replaced *doctrina* by a third word *scientia*.

In Nos. 4, 18, and 22 the probable explanation of the differences in quotation is simple corruption in the MSS. In Esai xiv 16ᵇ (No. 4) it is easy to see how 'com' might be lost after 'ram' in the sentence *concitat terramcommouet reges*, especially when the constant use of the simple verb 'mouere' with 'terra' for 'earthquake' is considered. Again in Ap xxii 17 (No. 22) Tyconius expressly quotes the text on p 3 for the sake of the curious

[1] *Cf* 21^{1}, 32^{24} in V.

reading "sponsus et sponsa." Yet on p 71 both our MSS have "sps et sponsa," that is "Spiritus et sponsa." This must be a clerical error in codd. RV, as Tyconius appears to have supported 'sponsus' in his Commentary on the Apocalypse, if indeed he did not invent that reading[1]. As to Eze xxxii 10 (No. 18), "erit ad ruinam suam" p 44^{22} corresponds to *προσδεχόμενοι τὴν πτῶσιν αὐτῶν*, yet on the next page Tyconius repeats the verse with the correct translation 'expectantes' for 'erit ad.' Is it possible that the corruption was already in his codex and was copied out mechanically by him?

The remaining instances (Nos. 6, 14, and 20) form a class by themselves. In each case the second quotation occurs in that part where V is our only authority, and I believe the text has in each case suffered corruption by dittography.

The readings are as follows. I have bracketed the corrupt anticipations of the following word in giving the readings of V.

6. Esai xiv 20 *ὃν τρόπον ἱμάτιον*
 quomodo uestimentum 70^{23} RV (= *Habetdeus* 315)
 [quomodo uenisti] sicut uestimentum $77^{3,4}$ V

14. Eze xxviii 9 *λέγων ἐρεῖς*
 dicturus es 77^{29} V (= *w*)
 [narrans] narrabis 80^{15} V

20. 2 The ii 7 *ὁ κατέχων*
 qui obtinet 52^{9} (R)V (quod obtinet R)
 qui[d] [detinens] detinet 74^{28} V*
 qui detinens ē detineat V*corr*

I should not have ventured to assert that these readings were corrupt and produced in the same way in all three cases, were it not that readings of this kind are extremely common in V, so common in fact, that it would be unlikely that the portion of text in which we are dependent on V alone should contain no examples. Below is a complete list of these cases of false repetition. Those marked V have been unnoticed by correctors and have passed into the later MSS and the printed editions; those marked V* have been altered. The readings of M are given wherever it is extant.

[1] *Cf* Ps-Aug[loc] (Migne xxxv 2452). 'Sponsus' found its way into the later MSS of the Vulgate, though not into the printed Editions.

5^{21} synonymis] si non nimis R	non nimis nouimus V
7^{20} unum] R	uniunum V
11^{9} non totum] RM	totum non totum V
24^{19} data] R	data data V*
25^{31} operatrix] R	operatrixrix V*
32^{13} sic Dominus] sed ds R; *om* M	sic dicit dns V*
44^{26} uirtus eius] R	uirtus eorumeius V*
46^{17} multa canta] R	multa cantica canta V*
$52^{10,11}$ ostendit omnes] R	oms ostendit oms V* oms ostendit V*corr*
56^{11} cuiusque temporis] R, cuiusquam temporis *D*, cui: temporis M	temporis cuiusq. temporis cuiusq. V
56^{12} ita et nouissima hora] R*D*	ita in nouissima ut nouissima hora V(M) (ita et...M)
$68^{19,20}$ Verbum carne(m) factum quid persequitur Verbum in carne] R	*pr* Verbum carne factum quid persequitur in carne V
71^{26} de se et] de sede & R	de se & de se & V*......

Besides these, there are the three passages under discussion pp 74^{28}, $77^{3,4}$ and 80^{15}.

Somewhat similar as shewing a tendency to amplification are the following:

56^{9} primus dies mensis est] R*D*	primus dies mensis decimus est V primus dies mensis mensis est M
$59^{24,25}$ VII spiritus Ecclesiae] RM	septem sps ecclesiae septem V
64^{30} tempus est] R	totum tempus est V
69^{6} Dominum Iesum] R	dnm ihm xpm V
73^{27} Dominus noster Iesus Christus] R	dns ds nr ihs xps V

These numerous cases of repetitions both simple and corrupt in the text of V (in which it is important to notice that the corrupt reading generally precedes the true reading[1]) are sufficient to shew the probability of the phenomenon occurring also where R is lost. It only remains to prove that in each of the three cases mentioned on p xlviii the reading of V is impossible as it stands,

[1] Some of these readings may have been due to corrections in the text of V's ancestor, misunderstood by the scribe of V. Compare p 48^{4}.

and to explain the variation which remains between the text as emended and the other form in which the quotations are found.

In Esai xiv 20 the text *quomodo uestimentum* as it appears in both codd. R and V on p 70 is in literal agreement with the text as quoted by Habetdeus the Donatist at the Council of Carthage. As we might expect, the text of the Version used by him is most closely related to that of Tyconius. *Quomodo uestimentum* was thus no doubt the reading of Tyconius' Bible. On the other hand the reading of V on p 77 does not make any sense:—"Iterum <in> corpus ipsius diaboli conuenit dicens: Quomodo uenisti sicut uestimentum sanguine consparsum non est mundum, ita nec tu eris mundus." There is nothing about 'coming' in the whole passage and *uenisti* and *uesti(mentum)* are evidently connected. Either 'uenistisicut' is a sort of rough doublet of 'uestimentum,' or more probably 'sicut' was in this place loosely substituted for 'quomodo' at this point by Tyconius on repeating his quotation[1]. The scribe of V (or an ancestor of V) began to write *quomodo uestimentum* as on p 70, but discovering his error wrote *sicut uestimentum,* leaving the letters "quomodo uenisti" (for "quomodo uesti-") imperfectly cancelled. The process is exactly similar to that by which *multa canta* p 46[17], which stands for πολλὰ ᾆσον Esai xxiii 16, became in V and the MSS which followed V *multa canticacanta.*

In Eze xxviii 9 λέγων ἐρεῖς is rendered "dicturus es" in the formal quotation p 77[29], and this is confirmed by *w,* which happens to be extant at this verse[2]. But when the verse is repeated on p 80[15] we find in V: "Numquid narrans narrabis in conspectu interficientium te, Deus sum ego?" Now if *narrans narrabis* were genuine it could only be regarded as a direct translation by Tyconius himself from the Greek. To this there are three objections. First, there is no other passage where he refers to the Greek. Secondly, the words λέγων ἐρεῖς are of no great importance in the sentence; Tyconius makes no remark on their special significance. Thirdly, *narrans narrabis* is not a translation of λέγων ἐρεῖς. The verb 'narrare' occurs 15 times in

[1] As *quoniam* 54[11, 12] for *quia* 54[3], *propterea* 79[35] for *propter hoc* 77[25], and *quoad usque* 74[28] for *donec* 52[9].

[2] *Cf k,* Mt ii 6, 13; Mc x 39.

the Vulgate N.T., and besides these places it occurs in Mt xiii 36 in various forms of the Old Latin, but it is never a rendering of λέγειν or εἰπεῖν. In Eze xxviii 9 Hier[loc] has *numquid loquens dices*, and in the Vulgate *numquid dicens loqueris*.

But if "narrans narrabis" cannot be a direct translation from the Greek still less can it be a paraphrase of "dicturus es." Tyconius would scarcely substitute for "dicturus es" an imperfectly naturalised Hebrew idiom, to which he himself attached a peculiar significance[1]. On the other hand the simple *narrabis* alone might very well be a paraphrase for *dicturus es*. I believe Tyconius was influenced (consciously or unconsciously) by the familiar verse Ps xxi 23: "narrabo nomen tuum fratribus meis." An exact parallel is afforded by his double quotation of 2 Regn vii 14, which is given on p 37 correctly, but repeated on the next page in a form influenced by Ps lxxxviii 33.

Finally we come to the variations in 2 The ii 7. On p 52 Tyconius, after quoting Ps cxxxvi 9 ("Felix est qui obtinebit, etc"), says: "Obtinet autem, sicut scriptum est: *Qui obtinet modo, donec de medio fiat.*" This is the reading of both MSS, except that R has *quod obt.* for *qui obt.* On p 74, but unfortunately after R has failed us, we find: "*Tantum ut quid detinens detinet modo, quoad usque de medio fiat.*" For *quid detinens detinet modo* V*corr* substituted *qui detinens est detineat modo.* The Greek is μόνον ὁ κατέχων ἄρτι ἕως ἐκ μέσου γένηται, and for ὁ κατέχων ἄρτι the extant Latin renderings are

qui nunc tenet teneat	d_2 *Tert de Res Carn* 24 *Ambst*
qui tenet nunc teneat	*Vg*
qui modo tenet teneat	*Aug* (*de Ciuit Dei*)
qui tenet modo teneat	*Hesych* (*ap Aug Ep* 198)

An improved text may shew that *teneat* was a later accretion in some of these authorities. But even if it be not so, it is noticeable that in none of them does 'nunc' or 'modo' occupy the last place, a fact which condemns the reading of V*corr* on p 74 and makes the 'detinens' of V* suspicious, while its presence is easily explained by the hypothesis of dittography. As between *obtinere* and *detinere*, it is worth remark that the quotation on p 52 is

[1] See his disquisition on "disrumpens disrumpam," p 39[4–15].

introduced for the sake of the word *obtinere*, to illustrate Ps cxxxvi 9. The quotation on p 74 is still further open to objection on the ground of the expression *quoad usque*, which though it has good African authority elsewhere[1] is here only found in Ambrosiaster$^{1}/_{2}$, while *donec* receives additional support from an allusion in Tyconius 8^{2}.

VIII. *The Latin Version used by Tyconius.*

The confusion and variety of text in the forms of the "Old Latin" has been a matter of common remark since the days of S. Augustine. Successive adaptation of the language of a primitive version to local dialects and irregular revision from Greek MSS were probably the causes which produced this variety, but we have hardly any historical traditions of the localities in which such changes took place or the men by whom they were made. In this confusion there is only one way out of the difficulty. Our MSS can give us no help alone, for they are not connected by sufficiently accurate traditions with local uses. It is only by carefully studying the quotations of Ecclesiastical writers, of whom we know where and when they wrote, that any fixed criteria can be found for assigning the continuous texts of the MSS to Africa, Gaul, or Italy. In all such investigations the quotations of S. Cyprian are the starting point. Except Tertullian he is the oldest African Father who quotes Scripture, and Tertullian's evidence in our present state of knowledge is rendered of doubtful value by his acquaintance with Greek and his habit of paraphrase. Cyprian on the other hand always uses a Latin Version and quotes accurately and consistently.

For the Gospels Prof. Sanday has definitely proved the African character of *k* (and in a less degree of *e*) by using the text of Cyprian as a working standard[2]. No such investigation has yet been made for any part of the Old Testament; I shall therefore begin by comparing the text of Tyconius with that of Cyprian. Each book of the Bible must be treated separately, for we have no reason to suppose that the original translation was all made at one

[1] *Cf k*, Mt ii 13, v 18 *bis*, x 11, xiii 13; Mc xii 36, xiii 30.

[2] O. L. Bibl. Texts (*k*), vol ii.

time or by the same hand; in extreme cases, such as the Book of Job on the one hand and the Book of Daniel on the other, it is at once seen that the literary fates of the various parts of the Bible have been quite independent.

In the Prophets the evidence is most full and clear in the Book of Isaiah. I shall therefore begin by treating that book separately.

For the sake of clearness it may be convenient to give at once the conclusions which I shall try to prove.

1. The text of Tyconius in the Prophets is from the same version as that used by S. Cyprian, slightly altered in the Latinity but presenting no clear traces of revision from the Greek.

2. This text is practically identical with that used by Habetdeus, the spokesman of the Donatists at the Council of Carthage.

3. The text of the Speculum (*m*) is of the same version, but greatly changed as to the Latinity.

Tyconius and S. Cyprian.

In the following extracts the references to S. Cyprian are by Hartel's pages, but in the *Testimonia*, unless otherwise stated, the text followed is not Hartel's but that of the MS called by him L. The pre-eminence of L in the *Testimonia* has been proved once for all by Prof. Sanday in O. Lat. Bibl. Texts (*k*) II lxii—lxiv, and his judgment has been confirmed by Dombart the editor of Commodian, and Brandt the editor of Lactantius, both of which authors regularly use the *Testimonia* for Biblical quotations.

Readings marked O_1 (following Prof. Sanday's notation) are from my collation of Bodl. Add. C 15, *saec.* x.

	Cyp 366	*Tyc* 50, 51
	Esai xiii	
6	Vlulate,	ululate,
	proximus est enim dies Domini	proximus est enim dies Domini,
	et *ob*tritio a Deo aderit.	et *con*tritio a Deo aderit...
9	ecce enim dies Domini	ecce enim dies Domini
	uenit* insanabilis	insanabilis* uenit
	indignationis et irae	indignationis et irae,
	ponere orbem terr*ae* desertum	ponere orbem terr*arum* desertum,
	et peccatores perdere ex eo.	et peccatores perdere ex eo.

Esai xiv

	Cyp 669	*Tyc* 70 (71, 72, 75)
13	Tu autem dixisti in animo tuo:	tu autem dixisti in animo tuo:
	in caelum ascendam,	In caelum ascendam,
	super stellas Dei	super stellas Dei
	ponam sedem meam,	ponam sedem meam,
	sedebo in monte alto	sedebo in monte alto
	super montes altos in Aquilonem,	super montes altos in Aquilonem,
14	ascendam super nubes,	ascendam super nubes,
	ero similis Altissimo...	ero similis Altissimo.
15	*tu uero* ad inferos descendes	*nunc autem* ad inferos descendes
	in fundamenta terrae,	in fundamenta terrae,
16	et qui uide*bunt* te	et qui uide*rint* te.
	mirabuntur super te.	mirabuntur super te.

ero] et ero *Tyc* 70 R
te uiderint] *Tyc* 70 R

Esai xiv

	Cyp 183	*Tyc* 70, 71, 75, 76
16	Hic homo qui concitat terram,	Hic *est* homo qui concitat terram,
	commouet reges;	[com]mouet reges:
17	qui ponit orbem terrae totum desertum.	qui ponit orbem terrae totum desertum.

(*Variants of Tyc*)
hic est] 70, 71, 75*bis; om* est 76
concitat] 70, $75^1/_2$; incitat 71, $75^1/_2$, 76
commouet] $75^2/_2$; mouet 70

[The quotations of S. Cyprian put down to Esai xxix 13 are really from Mc vii 6 seq. The reading of Tyconius will be noticed in the next section.]

Esai xlv

	Cyp 56	*Tyc* 3, 4
1	Sic dicit Dominus Deus	Sic dicit Dominus ʌ
	Christo meo Domino	Christo meo Domino
	cuius tenui dexteram	cuius *ego* tenui dexteram
	ut exaudiant eum gentes...	ut exaudiant eum gentes.

ut] et W; *om* B

Esai liii

	Cyp 77	*Tyc* 2
4	hic peccata nostra *portat*	Hic peccata nostra *feret*
	et pro nobis dolet...	et pro nobis dolet,
5	ipse *autem* uulneratus est	ipse uulneratus est
	propter facinora nostra...	propter facinora nostra,
6	et *Dominus* tradidit *illum*	et *Deus* tradidit *eum*
	pro peccatis nostris...	pro peccatis nostris.

ipse] et ipse VM
eum] RM; illum V

Esai lviii

Cyp 108	*Tyc* 76
3 *aut enim* sub*iectos* uobis	*Omnes* sub*ditos* uobis
*sub*pungitis...	*con*pungitis.

Esai lxiii

Cyp 72	*Tyc* 9, 10
9 Non senior *neque* angelus	Non senior *non* angelus,
sed ipse *Dominus liberabit* eos,	sed ipse *conseruauit* eos,
quia dilig*et* eos	*propter quod* dilig*eret* eos
et parc*et eis*,	et parc*eret illis*;
ipse redemit eos.	ipse redemit eos.
liberauit WO	conseruabit R, considerauit V
et ipse WMBO	parcet R

The above extracts may be analysed as follows. References in square brackets as [*m* 418] are to authorities not contained in Sabatier.

Readings in which *Cyp* and *Tyc* are agreed against other Latin authorities.	Readings in which *Cyp* and *Tyc* differ.
Esai xiii 6 [*m* 418]	
1. proximus *Cyp Tyc*	
prope *m*	2. contritio *Tyc m*
3. aderit *Cyp Tyc*	obtritio *Cyp*
ueniet *m*	
Esai xiii 9 [*m* 418]	
	4. insanabilis uenit (order) *Tyc Iren m*
5. insanabilis *Cyp Tyc Iren*	
sine refrigerio *m*	uenit insanabilis *Cyp*
6. uenit *Cyp Tyc Iren*	
adueniet *m*	
7. indignationis et irae *Cyp Tyc m*	
furore et ira plenus *Iren*	8. terrarum *Tyc*
	terrae *Cyp Iren m*
Esai xiv 13 [*Aug de Gen ad Lit* xi (*Eug* 180)]	
9. in animo tuo *Cyp Tyc*	
sensu tuo *Aug*	
10. stellas *Cyp Tyc*	
sidera *Ambr Aug Vig*	
11. Dei *Cyp Tyc* (=Heb!)	
caeli *Ambr Aug Vig*	
12. sedem meam *Cyp Tyc Ambr* $^1/_2$ *Aug-Ps* 59	
thronum meum *Aug* (*Tert Ambr* $^1/_2$)	

Readings in which *Cyp* and *Tyc* are agreed against other Latin authorities. | Readings in which *Cyp* and *Tyc* differ.

13. in monte alto *Cyp Tyc*
in monte excelso *Ambr Aug*

14. super montes altos *Cyp Tyc Ambr*
super montes excelsos *Aug*

15. in Aquilonem *Cyp Tyc*
qui sunt ad Aquilonem *Aug*
qui sunt ab Aquilone *Ambr*

Esai xiv 15 [*Aug* (*Eug* 180)]

16. nunc autem *Tyc Aug* (=LXX)
tu uero *Cyp*

Esai xiv 16

18. qui uiderint *Tyc*
qui uidebunt *Cyp*

19. hic est homo *Tyc* 4/5
hic homo *Cyp*

Esai xlv 1

20. Dominus *Tyc Tert*[prax] 11 *Vig* (*Barn* 12)
Dominus Deus *Cyp* '*Tert*' *adv Iud* 7

21. ego tenui *Tyc*
om ego *Cyp rell*

22. ut exaudiant eum *Cyp Tyc* '*Tert*' *adv Iud* (illum)
exaudient illum *Barn*[lat]
ut obaudiant eum *Vig* 1/2
et obedire faciam ante eum *Vig* 1/2
obaudire ante eum *Lact*

Esai liii 4, 5, 6

23. feret[1] *Tyc Faustin* (fert)
portat *Cyp Hil Ambr Fulg*

24. facinora *Cyp Tyc*
iniquitates *Hil Ambr Aug Fulg Faustin*

25. Deus *Tyc*
Dominus *Cyp Aug Fulg*

26. eum *Tyc Aug* 1/3 *Fulg*
illum *Cyp Aug* [illegible]

Esai lviii 3 [*m* 592]

27. et omnes *Tyc m Tert*[illegible] *Ambr* (=LXX)
aut enim *Cyp*

28. subditos *Tyc Ambr m*
subiectos *Cyp Tert*

[1] Possibly *feret=fert*. See esp. Ioh xv 5 *e* (*d*); *Rönsch* 286.

Readings in which *Cyp* and *Tyc* are agreed against other Latin authorities.	Readings in which *Cyp* and *Tyc* differ.
29. (compound of *pungere*) *Cyp Tyc m* succutitis *Tert* stimulatis *Ambr*	29. conpungitis *Tyc m*^{codd} (-etis *m*^{txt}) subpungitis *Cyp* succutitis *Tyc* stimulatis *Ambr*
Esai lxiii 9 [*Priscillian* 31]	
30. non *Cyp Tyc Vig Taps*$^2/_2$ (*Tert*$^2/_2$) neque *Iren Priscill*	
31. senior...angelus *Cyp Tyc Iren* (πρέσβυς...ἄγγελος LXX) legatus...angelus *Vig Taps*$^2/_2$ nuntius...angelus *Priscill* angelus...legatus *Tert de Carn Chr* 11 legatus...nuntius *Tert adv Marc* iv 22	32. non angelus *Tyc* neque ang. *Cyp Vig Taps*$^2/_2$ *Iren*
	33. ipse *Tyc Vig*$^1/_2$ (=LXX B memph *Hieron*) ipse Dominus *Cyp Tert*$^1/_2$ *Iren Vig*$^1/_2$ (=LXX ℵA λ *rell*) ipse Deus *Tert adv Marc*
34. ipse [Dominus] *Cyp Tyc Tert*$^2/_2$ *Iren Vig*$^1/_2$ ipse Dominus ueniet et *Vig*$^1/_2$ *Priscill*	35. conseruauit eos *Tyc* liberabit (-uit) eos *Cyp* saluos eos fecit *Tert*$^2/_2$(*Priscill*) saluabit (-uit) eos *Vig*$^2/_2$
	36. proper quod diligeret *Tyc* quia diliget *Cyp* quoniam diligit *Iren* eo quod diligeret *Vig*
38. redemit *Cyp Tyc* liberauit (-bit) *Iren*	37. parceret illis *Tyc* parcet eis *Cyp*

These 38 readings are not enough by themselves to enable us to form a perfect estimate of the relation of the text of Isaiah in Tyconius to that in Cyprian, but the general character of the text does, I think, sufficiently appear.

In the first place the agreement of Cyp. and Tyc. is greatest in the long quotations. Now the quotations of S. Cyprian are of almost uniform quality, and reach the same standard of accuracy whether they be long or short. But we have seen reason to believe that the casual quotations of Tyconius are by no means always to be relied on, while on the other hand the longer quotations are very faithful to the LXX. It is therefore not unlikely that some of the differences between Cyp. and the shorter quotations of Tyconius may be due to inaccuracy in the latter. Such for instance would be the unsupported insertion of *ego* in 21, *d̅s* for *d̅n̅s* in 25, and possibly *non* for *neque* in 30. It is interesting also to notice that the text of Tyconius has escaped the blunders *tu uero* for *nunc autem* (νῦν δὲ) in 16, and *aut enim* for *et omnes* in 27; these are found in no text independent of S. Cyprian.

Some of the nineteen readings where Cyp. and Tyc. agree against other Latin authorities are expressions really characteristic of the African version, and go far to prove the genuinely African tenour of the text of Tyconius. They are as follows.

1. proximus (ἐγγὺς) *for* prope. So Ioh ii 13 *e*.

7. indignatio (θυμὸς) *for* furor. 'Furor,' so far as I know, never occurs in any African quotation, but it is the general O. T. rendering of θυμὸς in *Iren* and *Ambr*. *Cf* Lc iv 28 ira *a b e ff q* vg *Ambr*, 'iracundia' *c*, but 'furore' *d f*.

9. animus (διάνοια) *for* sensus, mens, etc. *Cf* Esai xxxv 4 οἱ ὀλιγόψυχοι τῇ διανοίᾳ, "qui estis pusill(i)animes" *Cyp* 71 *Habetdeus* 313, but "pusillanimes sensu" *Iren Nouat*, and "modici animi sensu" *Hil* $^2/_2$

13, 14 altus (ὑψηλὸς) *for* excelsus. Predominantly African; 'altus' is found in the Gospels in *k* $^2/_2$ *e* $^1/_2$ *d* $^3/_5$ *a* $^1/_5$ and *f* vg $^1/_5$

24. facinus (ἀνομία) *for* iniquitas. Again in Tyconius Esai xliv 22, and Cyp. in Isaiah $^7/_7$. In the Gospels the only instance of 'facinus' is Mt xxiv 12 *Cyp* 335.

These five renderings are by themselves sufficient to shew the near relation of the text of Tyconius in Isaiah at least to that of Cyprian. The two texts chiefly differ in points of Latinity, that of Cyprian being as a rule more literally in agreement with the Greek. Instances of this are: 2. contritio *Tyc m*, but obtritio *Cyp* (συντριβὴ); 29. conpungitis *Tyc* (*m*), but subpungitis *Cyp* (ὑπονύσσετε)[1].

[1] An exception is 35—37, where we find for

ἔσωσεν αὐτοὺς, διὰ τὸ ἀγαπᾷν αὐτοὺς καὶ φείδεσθαι αὐτῶν. Esai lxiii 9
liberabit illos quia diliget eos, et parcet eis. *Cyp*
conseruauit eos, propter quod diligeret eos et parceret illis. *Tyc*

Cod. R of Tyconius however reads

The 'est' in 19 is characteristic of all forms of the Old Latin except the earliest stage of the African text[1].

When we turn to readings involving variation in the Greek, we find the same marks of fundamental agreement between S. Cyprian and Tyconius as in the renderings. In estimating the differences between two Latin authorities in matters which can be represented in Greek it is of course necessary to be careful to avoid assuming that all these differences actually correspond to real Greek variants; for instance it is most improbable that No. 4 "insanabilis uenit" for "uenit insanabilis" was produced by revision from the Greek, though there are Greek MSS in which this change of order is found. Again the Latin contractions for 'God' and 'Lord' are more often confused than those used in Greek; Latin evidence in fact for $\overline{\text{dns}}$ or $\overline{\text{dms}}$ against $\overline{\text{ds}}$, and *vice versa*, is worth very little.

The only difference in these thirty-eight readings which corresponds to a Greek variant is No. 33, where Tyc and Vig-Taps$^{1}/_{2}$ unite in resisting the temptation to add 'Dominus' to 'ipse' (*αὐτὸς* = פניו). In the Greek *αὐτὸς* alone is the reading of B memph *Hieron*, but [ὁ] Κύριος is added by א A Lucian, the Syr-Hex, and nearly all other MSS. '*Dominus*' is found in Cyprian and also in Irenaeus and Tertullian$^{1}/_{2}$, but "*ipse Deus*" is the reading of Tert adv Marc iv 22, while Priscillian and Vig-Taps$^{1}/_{2}$ read "*ipse Dominus uenit et.*" Possibly all these additions may be independent.

In the earlier part of the same verse, Tyconius and Cyprian agree in a noteworthy rendering. The Latin variations in Esai lxiii 9 between 'senior' and 'legatus' evidently go back to meanings of the Greek *πρέσβυς*: *Cyp Tyc* and *Iren* have 'senior,' but *Tert*$^{2}/_{2}$ *Vig-Taps*$^{2}/_{2}$ and *Priscillian* have 'legatus.'

Two other striking agreements of Cyp. and Tyc. in matters affecting the Greek are Nos. 10–11 and 22. No. 10–11 is *stellas Dei* in Esai xiv 13, supported by S. Cyprian and Tyconius alone. The reading is absolutely certain in Tyconius, as he afterwards quotes the verse again in the same words, saying "*stellarum Dei*, id est sanctorum." All other authorities for the LXX have

conseruabit eos propter quod diligeret eos, et parcet illis,

thus producing a text with nearly the same tenses as Cyprian.

[1] *Cf* *k*. lii.

τῶν ἀστ[έ]ρων τοῦ οὐρανοῦ. But the Hebrew is כוכבי אל. Is it possible that $\overline{ουνου}$ of the MSS is a corruption of $\overline{θυ}$, and that the original literal rendering of the LXX has been preserved only in the African Latin[1]? At least this reading shews the intimate connection of the texts of S. Cyprian and Tyconius.

No. 22 affords another instance of agreement between Cyp. and Tyc., this time in what appears to be a correction of the originally literal Latin version by one who was not familiar with the Greek. In Esai xlv 1 a consensus of Latin authorities read τῷ χριστῷ μου Κυρίῳ for τῷ χριστῷ μου Κύρῳ, for which no real Greek authority can be found[2]. But there are noteworthy Latin variants in the rendering of the latter part of the verse. The Greek is

ἐπακοῦσαι ἔμπροσθεν αὐτοῦ ἔθνη,

the Latin renderings being

obaudire ante eum gentes *Lact* (for once deserting *Cyp*)
et obedire faciam ante eum gentes *Vig* $^1/_2$
ut obaudiant eum *Vig* $^1/_2$
exaudient illum *Barn*^{lat}

but ut exaudiant eum *Cyp Tyc* '*Tert*' *advIud* (illum)
(one MS of Cyp. omits *ut*, another reads *et exaudiant*)

Does it not appear as if *ut exaudiant eum* was an early Latin correction of *exaudire ante eum*? In any case the rendering of both S. Cyprian and Tyconius is sufficiently eccentric to demand a common origin for the texts used by these Fathers.

Tyconius and Habetdeus.

At the *Collatio Carthaginiensis* held in 411 A.D. between the Catholics and Donatists a statement of Donatist doctrine illustrated by Scriptural proofs was read by Habetdeus a Donatist Bishop. The text used by him is thus both localised and dated. Most fortunately one of the quotations of Habetdeus coincides with the end of one of Tyconius' longer quotations; it will not be

[1] For a parallel instance see next section, p cx.

[2] *Barn*^{gr} 12 is wholly assimilated to Ps cix in the best text (*codd.* ℵ*I).

necessary to do more than quote the two passages in parallel columns to shew the essential identity of the versions[1].

Habetdeus (Du Pin's *Optatus* AD 1702, p 315)	Tyconius 71 (77).
	Esai xiv
20 quomodo uestimentum	quomodo uestimentum
conspersum* *in* sanguine	sanguine* consparsum
non erit mundum,	non erit mundum,
ita nec tu eris mundus,	ita nec tu eris mundus,
quia terram meam perdidisti	quia terram meam perdidisti
et plebem meam occidisti.	et plebem meam occidisti.
non *manebis* in aeternum tempus	non *eris* in aeternum tempus
semen nequam;	semen nequam;
21 para filios tuos interfici	para filios tuos interfici
peccatis patris *s*ui,	peccatis patris *t*ui,
ut non *ex*surgant.	ut non *r*esurgant.

Tyconius and the 'Speculum' (m).

The Old Latin Speculum (*m*), the second of those edited by Weihrich in vol. xii of the *Corpus Scriptorum Ecclesiasticorum Latinorum*, is generally considered to contain a "degenerate African" text[2]. The passages quoted in it from Isaiah in common with Tyconius are given below.

m 646	*Tyc* 73
	Esai v
6 *et* nubibus mandabo	Nubibus mandabo
ne pluant super eam *pluuiam*.	ne pluant super eam *imbrem*.

m 418	*Tyc* 50, 51
	Esai xiii
6 Vlulate,	ululate,
prope est enim dies Domini,	*proximus* est enim dies Domini,
et contritio a Deo *ueniet*	et contritio a Deo *aderit*....

[1] The language of the other quotations of Habetdeus from Isaiah would lead to a similar result. Among the characteristic 'African' expressions are *facinorosus* (ἄνομος) Esai lxvi 3; *fortitudo* (ἰσχὺς) Esai lii 1; *illic* (ἐκεῖ) Esai xxxv 8 *ter*, 9 *bis*; *iste* (οὗτος) Esai i 13; *quasi* (ὡς) Esai lxvi 3 *ter*.

[2] Prof. Sanday in *Stud. Bibl.* i 249; S. Berger, *Vulgate* 86 (where the *fragment de Fleury* is Weihrich's F of the *Speculum*). The connection between *m* and Priscillian does not seem so close in the Prophets as in the book of Job and the Epistle of S. James.

(*Item illic:*)

9 Ecce enim dies Domini	ecce enim dies Domini
*sine refrigerio adu*eniet	*insanabilis u*enit
indignationis et irae,	indignationis et irae,
ponere orbem terr*ae* desertum,	ponere orbem terr*arum* desertum,
et peccatores perdere ex eo.	et peccatores perdere ex eo.
10 *nam* stellae caeli et *lucifer*	Stellae *enim* caeli et *Orion*
et omn*e* orna*mentum* caeli	et omn*is* orna*tura* caeli
lumen non dabunt,	lumen non dabunt,
et *obscurabuntur* sole* oriente	et *tenebrescet* oriente* sole
et* lu*nae* non permanebit lumen	†lu*men** et† non permanebit lumen *eius.*
11 et *mandabo uniuerso* orbi mala	et *infligam* orbi *terrae* mala
et *impiis* peccata eorum,	et *iniustis* peccata eorum,
et perdam *contumeliam iniquorum*	et perdam *iniuriam scelestorum*
et *contumeliam* superborum	et *iniuriam* superborum
humiliabo.	humiliabo.
12 et erunt qui *derelicti sunt pretiosi*	et erunt qui *remanserint honorati*
magis quam aurum,	magis quam aurum
∧	*quod non tetigit ignem,*
et homo *pretiosus*	et homo *honoratus erit*
magis quam lapis ex ˢ*a*ffyr.	magis quam lapis ex *Su*fir.

omnis ornatura] *conieci*: omnis creatura R; omnes ex ea rura V
oriente sole lumen] *om* V (*spatio relicto*)

m 675	*Tyc* 70̇ (71)
	Esai xiv
12 Quomodo cecidit de caelo	Quomodo cecidit de caelo
lucifer *qui* mane ori*ebatur*!	lucifer mane ori*ens*!

m 459	*Tyc* 47
	Esai xxiv
8 Cessauit *superbia*	cessauit *inpudicitia*
et diuitiae impiorum.	et diuitiae impiorum.

m 692	*Tyc* 10
	Esai xxxiii
20 Tabernacula *tua*	tabernacula
∧ non commouebuntur,	*quae* non commouebuntur,
neque *fatigabuntur*	neque *agitabuntur*
pali tabernaculi *eius*	pali tabernaculi *tui*
in aeternum tempus,	in aeternum tempus
neque funes eius *dis*rumpentur.	neque funes eius *r*umpentur.

Esai xlii

m 673	*Tyc* 9
16 *et ad*ducam caecos	Ducam caecos
in ui*a* qu*a* *ignorabant*	in ui*am* qu*am* *non nouerunt*,
et semitas quas *nesciebant*	et semitas quas *non nouerunt*
calc*are* *faciam*,	calc*abunt*,
et faciam illis tenebras in lucem	et faciam illis tenebras in lucem
et *quae* praua *sunt dirigam.*	et praua *in directum.*
haec uerba faciam,	haec uerba faciam,
et non derelinquam eos.	et non derelinquam eos.

calcare faciam] faciam illos calcare *sess.*
eos] illos *sess.*

Esai xliv

m 491	*Tyc* 9
21 ...*et Israhel quia puer* meus es tu,	*Finxi te puerum meum*, meus es tu,
et Israhel *ne* obliuisc*aris* mei.	∧ Israhel noli obliuisc*i* mei.
ecce enim deleui	ecce enim deleui
ut niuem iniquitates tu*as*	*uelut nubem facinora* tua
et *ut caliginem* peccata tua.	et *sicut nimbum* peccata tua.

Esai lviii

m 592	*Tyc* 76
3 *et* omnes subditos uobis	Omnes subditos uobis
conpungitis.	conpungitis.

conpungetis *sess* al

Esai lviii

m 593	*Tyc* 57
10 *et* tenebrae *tibi*	Tenebrae *tuae*
erunt* *ut* meridies.	*sicut* meridies* erunt.

It will not be necessary to analyse these passages in detail. The amount of divergence is much greater than in the case of Tyconius and S. Cyprian, who only differ 19 times in 14 verses, while Tyconius and *m* differ 46 times in 13 verses. The Cyprianic text being our working standard, these figures alone shew that *m* has suffered much more change than Tyconius. At the same time Tyconius and *m* agree in peculiar expressions which can only be explained on the assumption that their texts go back to one original version. A clear illustration of this is Esai xiii 10,

> *οἱ γὰρ ἀστέρες τοῦ οὐρανοῦ καὶ ὁ Ὠρίων*
> *καὶ πᾶς ὁ κόσμος τοῦ οὐρανοῦ τὸ φῶς οὐ δώσουσι·*
> *καὶ σκοτισθήσεται τοῦ ἡλίου ἀνατέλλοντος*
> *καὶ ἡ σελήνη οὐ δώσει τὸ φῶς αὐτῆς.*

Here cod. ℵ has οικος for κοσμος and several MSS have *φέγγος* for the second *φῶς*; otherwise there is no variation. The only Latin writer besides Tyconius and *m* who quotes the verse is S. Jerome, who twice gives the verse literally from the LXX[1]. Now although *m* and Tyconius differ no less than seven times in their rendering of Esai xiii 10, they agree in reading *non permanebit lumen* [*eius*] for *οὐ δώσει τὸ φῶς αὐτῆς*, a coincidence still further extended if we may regard the preceding words in Tyconius which correspond to *καὶ ἡ σελήνη*, viz "*lumen et,*" as a corruption of "*et lunae*" as found in *m*. This paraphrase of the Greek is the more striking, seeing that in the former part of the verse both *m* and Tyconius have *lumen non dabunt* for *τὸ φῶς οὐ δώσουσι*.

A point of contact such as this between Tyconius and the Speculum is most important, more especially for the criticism of the latter. It seems to shew that the constant departures from the text of S. Cyprian and Tyconius found in *m* were not due to an attempt to bring *m* into more literal accordance with the Greek. Most of these variants from the Cyprianic standard consist of synonyms, more or less accurate, such as *iniquitas* for *facinus*, *lucifer* for *Orion*, *contumelia* for *iniuria*. These are extremely instructive for the criticism of the Latin text, while on the other hand the value of the Speculum for the criticism of the LXX is enhanced, if we have grounds for believing that most of the late character of its text is due not to correction from the Greek but to literary revision of the Latinity[2].

A parallel instance of real agreement with the old African text in *m*, side by side with superficial variation, is found in Esai v 26, where *Cyp* 56 and 57 has *et adtrahet illos*, but in *m* 657 we find *et trahet eas*. In both cases however the renderings point to *καὶ συρεῖ αὐτούς*, which is otherwise absolutely unattested. Cod. B has *καὶ συριεῖ αὐτούς*, and cod. A *καὶ συριεῖ αὐτοῖς* (ושרק לו).

[1] See Sabatier *ad loc.* S. Jerome's words are: Stellae enim caeli et omnis ornatus caeli lumen suum (*v.* lucem) non dabunt: et obtenebrabuntur sole oriente (*v.* tenebrabuntur orto sole), et luna non dabit lumen suum (*v.* lucem).

[2] There are a few cases where *m* deserts the older African Fathers in widely spread distinctively Greek variations: e.g. Esai lviii 8 *ἰάματα* is rendered by '*sanitates*' in Irenaeus, Lucifer, Ambrose and *m* 593; but *Tert de Res Carn* 27, *Cyp* 108, 291, 376, Latin MSS known to *Hieron*, and *Barn*[lat] 3 have '*uestimenta,*' corresponding to the Greek *ἱμάτια*, which is read by *Barn*[gr] 3, *Iust-Tr* 15, and codd. 147 91 106.

In other prophetical books than that of Isaiah the evidence is at once less in amount and more conflicting in character; direct comparison with the text of S. Cyprian for the most part fails us. In the Minor Prophets Tyconius and S. Cyprian have in common only the two verses Amos viii 9 and Mal iv 2, the latter being a mere allusion in Tyconius. In Jeremiah there is only a reference of no textual value to Hier ix 23, shared also by the Speculum. In Daniel there is nothing. Indeed the quotations of Tyconius from Daniel are so few, that it is impossible to discover whether the version he used was translated from Theodotion or whether it resembled the curious mixed text found in S. Cyprian[1]. Finally, out of the long passages from Ezekiel found in Tyconius, only five verses are shared with S. Cyprian. These are given below.

Eze xxxvi

	Cyp 761, 767	*Tyc* 33
25	et aspargam *super uos*	et aspergam *uos*
	aquam mundam	aquam mundam
	et mundabimini	et mundabimini
	ab omnibus *inmunditiis uestris*,	ab omnibus ∧ ∧
	et ab omnibus simulacris uestris,	∧ ∧ simulacris uestris,
26	et mundabo uos	et mundabo uos
	et dabo uobis cor nouum,	et dabo uobis cor nouum,
	et spiritum nouum dabo in uobis	et spiritum nouum dabo in uobis
	in uobis] in uos 761^{cod}, 767^{cod}; uobis $767^{codd\ mult}$	aqua munda R in uobis] in uos V

Eze xxxvii

	Cyp 158	*Tyc* 36
11	dicunt:	*ipsi* dicunt:
	arida facta sunt ossa nostra,	arida facta sunt ossa nostra,
	periit spes nostra	*interiit* spes nostra,
	expirauimus.	expirauimus.
12	propterea prophe*ta* et dic:	propterea profe*tare* et dic:
	haec dicit Dominus,	haec dicit Dominus,
	Ecce ego aperi*o*	Ecce ego aperi*am*
	monumenta uestra	monumenta uestra
	et educam uos	et educam uos
	de monumentis uestris	de monumentis uestris

[1] Whatever may be the connection between the *Testimonia* and the early forms of the *Altercatio Simonis et Theophili* (Harnack, *Texte und Unters.* I), it is at least clear that S. Cyprian did not exclusively derive his knowledge of the LXX of Daniel thence; e.g. the quotation from Dan ix 4 ff in *Cyp*260 is not likely ever to have found a place in the *Altercatio*.

14 et inducam uos in terram Israhel. ∧
dabo Spiritum meum in uos
et uiuetis,
et ponam uos *in* terr*a* uestr*a*
et *cognoscetis quoniam* ego Dominus
locutus sum, etc.
perit LO$_1$WM*

et inducam uos in terram Israhel,...
et dabo Spiritum meum in uos
et uiuetis,
et ponam uos *super* terr*am* uestr*am*
et *scietis quia* ego *sum* Dominus.

The readings in these five verses which bear on the Old Latin version are as follows.

Readings where *Cyp* and *Tyc* agree against other Latin authorities.

Eze xxxvi 25

2. simulacris *Cyp*$^2/_2$ *Tyc*
   idolis *Aug*

Eze xxxvii 11, 12 [*m* 424]

3. facta *Cyp Tyc Ambr*
   effecta *m*
5. expirauimus *Cyp Tyc*
   interibimus (-iuimus) *Ambr*
   om. m

Eze xxxvii 14 [*m* 424]

8. spiritum meum in uos *Cyp Tyc m*
   spiritum in uobis *Iren*
   spiritum meum in uobis *Ambr*

Readings where *Cyp* and *Tyc* differ.

1. aspargam super uos aquam mundam *Cyp*$^2/_2$ *Aug*$^1/_2$
   asp. uos aqua munda *Tyc* cod R *Aug*$^1/_2$
   asp. uos aquam mundam *Tyc* cod V
4. periit *Cyp Ambr*
   interiit *Tyc m*
6. propheta *Cyp*
   profetare *Tyc m*
   prophetiza *Ambr*
7. aperio *Cyp* (aperio uobis *Ambr*)
   aperiam *Tyc Iren m*
9. in terra uestra *Cyp* (in terram uestram *m*)
   super terram uestram *Tyc Iren Ambr*
10. cognoscetis *Cyp Iren*
    scietis *Tyc Ambr m*
11. quoniam *Cyp Iren m*
    quia *Tyc Ambr*
12. ego Dominus *Cyp Ambr*^{codd}
    ego sum Dominus *Tyc Iren Ambr*^{codd} *m*

These twelve variants for the most part relate rather to matters of accuracy than to recensional varieties[1]; none of the characteristic common words (such as *δόξα*) occur, in rendering which 'African' authorities generally differ from the rest. This is the more unfortunate, as the history of the text of Ezekiel in Africa is most obscure. The ample quotations of Tyconius agree closely with the fragments of the Weingarten MS of the Prophets (*w*); in the long quotation from Eze xxviii I can only count 23 variations in 16 continuous verses, and these mostly relate to minor matters. But the text of *w* comes to us without a character; it may be African, Gallican or Italian, revised or unrevised, and no leaf is preserved in it from Isaiah, the book in which the geographical affinities of text are most clear. On the other hand, against the agreement of Tyconius and *w* stand in sharp relief the quotations of Tertullian. In *adv Marc* ii 10 he quotes Eze xxviii 11—16, differing from Tyconius in these six verses at least 17 times, three of these being crucial various readings in the Greek. Yet we cannot at once put down the whole of this variation to Tertullian's habit of quoting directly from the Greek, for he renders *ἀποσφράγισμα* by *resignaculum*, as opposed to *signaculum* (*Tyc m*) and *consignatio* (*Arnob-jun w*). 'Resignaculum' in this passage is especially singled out in Hieron[loc]: "Et quia in Latinis codicibus pro *signaculo* '*resignaculum*' legitur, dum *κακοζήλως* uerbum e uerbo exprimens qui interpretatus est iuxta LXX translationem *ἀποσφράγισμα*, id est resignaculum, posuit[2]." No better evidence could be given that *resignaculum* was a genuine Latin rendering and not an eccentricity of Tertullian. Yet the text of Tyconius contains many ancient readings opposed to the post-Hexaplar tradition of the LXX[3]; it can hardly be the result of a late revision from the Greek. The whole question is evidently most complicated, and needs a thorough investigation not from the points of view of the text of Tyconius alone; the safest working hypothesis in the meanwhile I suppose to be the recognition of the fact that in the text of Tertullian everything is possible. Side by side with Tertullian's own paraphrases and translations we no

[1] Compare on the other hand the same passage in Tertullian *de Res Carn* 29.

[2] From Sabatier *ad loc.*

[3] See pp cviii—cx.

doubt often meet with genuine fragments of the oldest forms of the Latin version.

One fact more remains to be noticed in connection with the Old Latin of Ezekiel, which seems to suggest that that book underwent a revision of its Latinity in very early times. In 'Tert' *adv Iud* 11, a work which at least contains very ancient elements, there is a long quotation extending from Eze viii 12 to ix 6. The language of this extract recalls the peculiarities of S. Cyprian's quotations from Isaiah, for we find *claritas* = *δόξα* Eze ix 3 and *facinus* = *ἀνομία* Eze ix 4, though *Cyp* 90, 367 quotes the latter verses with the rendering *iniquitas*. The only various reading however between this quotation and *Cyp* concerning the Greek is the curious phrase *Tau signum* for *τὸ σημεῖον* in Eze ix 6[1]. 'Tau' is omitted by S. Cyprian, but it may have stood in his version, for the title of *Test* ii 22, in which one of his citations of the verse occurs, is "Quod in hoc signo *crucis* salus sit omnibus qui in frontibus notentur." The reading of *τὸ* as *ταῦ* or Τ is unattested by any Greek MS, but it is evident how easily ΤΟ СΗΜΕΙΟΝ could be read Τ· СΗΜΕΙΟΝ[2].

Style and Vocabulary.

Direct comparison will not carry us farther with the text of Tyconius, but in so literal a version as the Old Latin much can be done by a comparison of the usage of rendering in different passages. In this department it is especially necessary to avoid premature theorising. Judging by the results already attained in the study of the Old Latin Gospels there are no general principles to guide the student. Neither literal rendering of the Greek, nor systematic transliteration of Greek words, nor the reverse of these, is specially characteristic of the African version. The only method which does not mislead is actually to catalogue all peculiarities, trusting that on further knowledge we shall find some to be really

[1] In *ver* 4 the *Tau* does not seem to be genuine in *adv Iud* 11, as it is omitted by cod. λ (Oehler ii 732).

[2] Comp. Barn ix ἐν τῷ ἑνὶ τὸν σταυρόν, which becomes in the Latin *habes in una littera Tau crucem*. Possibly the text of *adv Iud* may have been influenced by Tert *adv Marc* iii 22. The verses are also quoted in the *Altercatio Simonis*, p 33. See addl. note, p cxix.

characteristic. Thus *k*, the best representative of the African text, has many Greek transliterations such as *eremum* for *desertum* Mt xi 7, *anastasis* for *resurrectio* Mc xii 23, yet the same MS is our principal authority in S. Matthew for *similitudo* instead of *parabola*. Nothing but actually collecting the facts and grouping them, and then taking the evidence of the groups, will reveal to us the true literary history of the Old Latin Bible[1].

In the following glossary most of the words used in the quotations of Tyconius are included, except such terms as do not admit of variation in translation from Latin into Greek. Besides giving the words and their Greek equivalents I have added some illustrations of their use in other 'African' authorities, especially codd. *k e* and the quotations of S. Cyprian. Asterisks denote that all examples of a word in Tyconius have not been collected.

abiectus (ἐξουθενημένος) 1 Co i 28, **20**
contemptibilis *r m*567 d_2 vg *Tert adv Marc* v 5 *Aug.*

ablative absolute (=*Gk gen. abs.*)
Zech xiv 12, **49**
[*see* dum].

abominatio (βδέλυγμα) Mt xxiv 15, **5.**
The phrase τὸ βδέλυγμα τῆς ἐρημώσεως (Mt xxiv 15, Mc xiii 14) *is rendered as follows:*
abominationem uastationis *e Cyp* 335 *Tyc* (Mt)
exsecrationem desol*u*tionis *k* (Mc)
aspernationem desolationis *i* (Mc)
abom. desolationis *a b c d f h q* vg *Iren*$^2/_2$ *Hil Aug* (Mt)
a c ff n q vg [*hiant b f*] (Mc);
Dan ix 27
execratio uastationum *de Pasch Comp* 261, 262
exsecr. uastationis '*Tert*' *adv Iud* 8
abom. desolationis *Iren*
desolationis interitus *w Hesych ap Aug.*

abstinere se (φυλάσσεσθαι *with* ἀπὸ)
1 Ioh v 21, **70**
cf Ac xxi 25 vg.

acceptabilis (δεκτὸς) Lc iv 19 (=Esai lxi 2), **60, 65**
acceptabilem *e Cyp* 75 (Esai)
acceptum *rell* (*incl m*399).

accipere (δέχεσθαι) Hier xxxii 28, **54.**
* (λαμβάνειν) Hier xxxii 15, 17, **53** *and a dozen times elsewhere.*

adesse (ἐπέρχεσθαι) Esai xiii 13, **51.**

[1] See especially Koffmane, *Gesch. des Kirchenlateins*, 39, 40.

(ἥκειν) Esai xiii 6, **50** (=*Cyp* 366).

adhuc (ἔτι) Soph ii 15, **42** (*in a neg. sentence*)
Eze xxxvii 23, **34** (*in a neg. sentence*)
Ioh xx 1, **57** (=*rell*)
[*see* iam, ultra].

(ἄρτι) 1 Ioh ii 9, **68** (=*Cyp* 116 *rell*)
[*see* modo, nunc].

adicere (συνεπιτίθεσθαι) Zech i 15, **76**.

adimplere (ἐμπιπλάναι) Ps xc 16, **3**.

adire (ἐντυγχάνειν) Sap viii 21, **20**.

admittere (*see* facinus adm.).

adnuntiare (διαγγέλλειν) Ps ii 6, **72**.
(καταγγέλλειν) Phil i 18, **70** (=*Cyp* vg *rell*).

adpropinquare (ἐγγίζειν) Soph iii 2, **42**
Esai xxxix 13, **8**
Eze xxxvi 8, **36** (ἐλπίζουσιν *Gk* MSS)
Ro xiii 12, **57** (=*Cyp*425 vg)
On Eze xxxvi 8 *see p* cx.

aeternum—in aeternum (εἰς τὸν αἰῶνα, ἕως αἰῶνος)
Gen iii 22, **81**
2 Regn vii 13, 16 *bis*, **37**
Ps xvii 51, **5** (usq. in saeculum *V*,=vg)
Esai xiv 20, **71**, **77** ; xix 20, **43** ; xxxiii 20, **10**
Hier xvii 25, **62**
Eze xxvii 36, **46** ; xxviii 19, **78**, **85**
[*see* saeculum].

alienatio (ἔκστασις) Zech xiv 13, **49**
mentis alienatione (ἐκστάσει)
Eze xxvii 35, **46** ; xxxii 10, **44**
[*cf* in stupore mentis].

alligatus—habe[n]s in te alligatum (ἐνδέδεσαι)
Eze xxviii 13, **78**, **81** (=*w* [*Arnob-jun*]).
but indutus es (ἐνδέδυσαι) *Tert adv Marc* ii 10 *Hier*$^1/_2$.

altus (ὑψηλὸς) Esai xiv 13 *bis*, **70**, **72** ; xiv 26, **52** ; xxiv 4, **47**
so Cyp in Isaiah$^5/_5$
(excelsus *rell*)
[*see* excelsus].

ambo (ἀμφότεροι) Mt xiii 30, **29** (=*k*)
Lc i 6, **13** (=*rell*)
utraque Mt xiii 30 *rell* (*hiat e*).

animatio (θυμὸς) Esai xiii 13, **51**
'propter animationem irae (θυμὸν ὀργῆς) Domini, in die qua aderit indignatio (θυμὸς) eius'
θυμὸς=animatio (Esai xlii 25) *Cyp* 253, 286, *also joined with* ira
[*see* indignatio, ira].

animus (διάνοια) Esai xiv 13, **70**, **71** (=*Cyp* 669)
in Lc i 51 διανοίᾳ=sensu *e*, mente *rell* (cogitatione *d*).

apotheca (ἀποθήκη) Eze xxviii 13, **78**, **81** (=*w*)
horrea *Tert adv Marc* ii 10
cf Lc xii 18, 24 *d e* (apotheca)
elsewhere always horrea *in* NT *in all* MSS *except d* Lc iii 17 (repositio).

apparere (λειτουργεῖν) Dan vii 10, **60**
cf Tert adv Prax 3 (*edd*)
and Ps ciii 4, *where* apparitores=λειτουργοὺς *adv Marc* ii 8, iii 9.

arbor (ξύλον) Ge ii 17, **61**
cf Cyp 158, 405
elsewh. lignum, *e.g.* Eze xx 32, **35.**
arbor nauis (ἱστὸς) Esai xxxiii 23, **10.**

arguere (παιδεύειν) Eze xxviii 3, **77**, **79**
erudierunt *w.*
emendare=παιδεύειν *Cyp* (157,) 181
arguere=ἐλέγχειν, *but it is used for* παιδεύειν *as here in* Ps xciii 12 *Op Imp in Mt* iii 39.

aspergere *with double acc.* Eze xxxvi 25, **33**
ῥανῶ ἐφ' ὑμᾶς καθαρὸν ὕδωρ LXX
aspargam super uos aquam mundam $Cyp^2/_2$ $Aug^1/_2$
asp. uos aqua munda $Aug^1/_2$ *Tyc cod* R
asp. uos aquam mundam *Tyc cod* V.
cf Lev v 9 ῥανεῖ ἀπὸ τοῦ αἵματος......ἐπὶ τὸν τοῖχον
asparget sanguinem......parietem *cod Lugd.*

assumere (ἀναλαμβάνειν) Esai lxiii 9, **10.**
(προσδέχεσθαι) Esai xlv 4, **8.**

astrum (ἄστρον) Nah iii 16, **42**
Eze xxxii 7, **44**, **45**
cf sideribus Lc xxi 25 *d e* ($Tert^1/_2$), stellis *rell*
[*see* stella (ἀστὴρ)].

auaritia (πλεονεξία) Col iii 5, **83** (=d_2 vg *Iren Hil Aug*)
cupiditas *Cyp* 645 [*cf* Lc xii 15 *c d e*].

audire (εἰσακούειν) Ex xvi 28, **26**
Soph iii 2, **42.**

auersari (ἀποστρέφεσθαι *w. acc.*)
Am i 3, 11, **53**
cf Mt v 32 auersatus fueris *k Cyp*
auertaris, auerteris te *rell.*

auertere (ἀποστρέφειν) Esai xiv 27, **52**
Hier xxv 39, **50.**
(ἐπιστρέφειν) Ps cxxv 1, **67**
[*comp* conuerti].

aues (πετεινὰ) Eze xxxii 4, **44**
In the Gospels aues=πετεινὰ $^3/_8$ *viz*

Mc iv 4 *b c ff*
iv 32 *b c d f ff i q* vg (*hiat a*), uolatilia *e*
Lc xii 24 *b f q*.

auferre* (αἴρειν) Esai x 14, **75**
[*see* extollere, ferre, tollere].
(ἀποστρέφειν) Ro xi 26, **34**.
(ἀφαίρειν) Esai x 13, **75**; xiv 25 *bis*, **52**; liii 11, **2**
Eze xxvi 16, **45**; xxxvi 26, **33**.
(ἀφιστάναι) 2 Regn vii 15 *ter*, **37**.

beatus (μακάριος) Mt xxiv 46, **11** (= MSS *incl e*)
Ioh xiii 17, **26** (= MSS *incl e*), *but* felices *Cyp* 118
[*see* felix].

bellator, -trix (ὁπλομάχος) Esai xiii 4, 5, **50**.

bonitas (χρηστότης) Ps lxiv 12, **60**.

cadere
cadent = ῥάξουσιν Esai xiii 16, **51**
? *read by Tyconius for* elident
cf Mt vii 6 *k Cyp* 154.
qui ceciderunt = τεθνηκότες Esai xiv 19, **71, 76**.

caedere (κόπτειν) Zech xiv 12, **49**.

cardines caeli (τὰ ἄκρα τοῦ οὐρανοῦ)
Hier xxv 36, **49**
elsewh. summum (a summo terrae, **9**).

The rendering cardines *in this place was probably suggested by the preceding* quattuor. *cf* exoriri *for* ἐξέρχεσθαι *used of the sun* Gen xix 23, **85**.

cauere (βλέπειν) Mt xxiv 4, **5** (= *e Cyp* 335), uidere *rell*.

cena pura (παρασκευή) Ioh xix 42, **59** (= *e gat*), parasceue *rell*.
see Rönsch, *It und Vg* 307, *to which we may add* Mc xv 47 *k*.

ceruix (τράχηλος) Hier xvii 23, **62**
[*see* collum].

charisma (χάρισμα) 1 Co xii 4, **69** (= *Iren* $^1/_2$)
gratia *Iren* $^1/_2$
donum *Hil* $^1/_2$ *Vig* $^1/_2$
donatio d_2 *m*310, 324 vg *Hil* $^1/_2$ *Aug Vig* $^2/_3$.

cibus (βρῶσις) Col ii 16, **64** (= *Tert rell*).

circumstantia—circumstantiam pati (συμφοραίνειν)
Esai xiii 8, **51**.

circumuenire (κατασοφίζεσθαι) Ex i 10, **55**.

clamare (κράζειν) Eze xxvii 30, **45**.

claritas (δόξα) Esai x 16, **48**; lxii 2, **81**
Ioh xvii 5, **2, 37** (= *Cyp rell, exc a f*)
2 Co iii 18^b, **19** (*but cf* **21**).

In Cyprian's quotations from Isaiah claritas = δόξα $^8/_{10}$
[*see* gloria].

cogitatio (βουλὴ) Sap vi 3, **72**
Esai xiv 26, **52**; xix 3, **43**.
(διαλογισμὸς) Ro i 21, **84**.
cogitationes = ἐπιτηδεύματα
Eze xxxvi 31, **33**
[*see* studia].

colligere (συνάγειν) Zech xiv 14, **49**
Esai xiii 4, **50**, 14, 15, **51**; xxiii 18, **46**; xliii 5, **9**; xlix 18, **82**
so k e Cyp constantly in the Gospels
[*see* congregare].

collum (τράχηλος) Ac xv 10, **12** (= *Hil Aug*)
ceruix *d* e_2 vg *Iren.*
collum *occurs in all* MSS *in the Gospels* $^4/_4$; *in most other books it is characteristically African.*
cf e.g. Esai lviii 5 collum *Cyp*108 *Barn*[lat]3 (*Ambr*) *but* ceruicem *Lucif* 141 *m*593
[*see* ceruix].

comedere (ἐσθίειν) Esai xxiv 6, **47**.
(κατεσθίειν) Abd 18, **83**, **85**
Eze xx 47, **40**
[*see* consumere, deuorare].

commemorari (μνησθῆναι) Ge xix 29, **85**
Mt v 23 commemoratus *k*
recordatus *Cyp ff f* vg
rememoratus *a b c g h q*
[*see* reminisci].

commemoratio (μνεία) Esai xxiii 16, **46**.

commercia, -orum (ἐμπόριον) (Esai xxiii 17), **46**[22]
cf domum commercatorum Ioh ii 16 *e*.

comminuere (σείειν) Esai x 13, **75**; xix 1, **43**
commouere Agg ii 22, **80**; Esai xiv 16, **75** (mouet, **70**).

comminutio (συντριβὴ) Prov xiv 28, **76**.

commixticius (ἐπίμικτος) Eze xxx 5, **43**.

commixtio (σύμμικτος) Eze xxvii 33, 34, **46**
[*see* promiscuus].

commutari (μεταμορφοῦσθαι) 2 Co iii 18, **19**
transformari *m*375 vg *Aug* (*cf Tyc* **21**)
transfigurari *Tert adv Marc* v 11
reformari d_2 *Ambr*
transferri *Hil*
cf Mc ix 2 commutata est *figura* eius *k*, transfiguratus est *rell.*

conburere (κατακαίειν) Eze xx 47, **40**.

concisor (κόπτων) Esai x 15, **79**.

concitare (παροξύνειν) Esai xiv 16, **70**, **75** (= *Cyp* 183)
[*see* exacerbare, incitare].

conexus *see* constructus.
confidere (πεποιθέναι) Soph iii 2, **42**
Zech xiv 11, **48**.
confirmare (ἀνορθοῦν) 2 Regn vii 16, **37**.
(στηρίζειν) Eze xx 46, **40**; xxi 2, **41**
cf Lc ix 51 *c e*.
confringere (συντρίβειν) Esai xiii 18, **52**; xiv 12, **71**
Hier xxv 35, **49**.
conterere Esai xiv 12, **70**
(*cf esp.* Lc ix 39 *e*)
[*see* conterere].
congregare (ἀθροίζειν) Eze xxxvi 24, **33**.
(συνάγειν) Eze xxxvii 21, **34**; xxxix 2, **74**
[*see* colligere].
conlidere (ἐδαφίζειν) Ps cxxxvi 9, **52**.
conpungere (ὑπονύσσειν) Esai lviii 3, **76** (=*m*592)
but subpungere *Cyp* 108.
conroborare (κραταιοῦν) Ps lxxix 16, **6** (confirmasti V)
=*e* Lc i 80, ii 40; confortare, confirmare, *a b rell.*
conscelerare (ἀσεβεῖν *followed by acc.*)
Soph iii 4, **42**
impie agunt (*om* legem) *Lucif*
reprobant *legem m*500.
conseruare (σῴζειν) Esai lxiii 9, **9**.
consolari (παρακαλεῖσθαι) Ps cxxv 1, **67**
[*see* exhortari].
consparsus (πεφυρμένος) Esai xiv 20, **71**, **77**
=*Habetdeus* 315.
constitutio mundi (καταβολὴ κόσμου)
Ioh xvii 24, **2**, **37** (=*rell incl Cyp* 159).
constructus—(omne corpus) constructum et conexum = συναρμολογούμενον καὶ συνβιβαζόμενον Eph iv 16, **3**
constructum et subministratum = ἐπιχορηγούμενον καὶ συνβιβαζόμενον Col ii 19, **3**.
Thus in each case the words are transposed: so that constructus = συνβιβαζόμενος, conexus = συναρμολογούμενος.
The other Latin renderings are
Eph iv 16 compactum et conexum d_2 vg *Iren Lucif Ambr Ambst*
conexum et compactum *Aug*$^2/_2$
Col ii 19 subministratum et constructum vg
subm. et copulatum *Ambr*
subm. et compaginatum *Ambst* (*Iren*)
compactum et conexum *Aug*
productum et porrectum *m*514 (*Lucif*)
subministratum et prouectum d_2.

consumere (ἐξαναλίσκειν) Hier xxv 38, **49**.
(κατεσθίειν) Hier xvii 27, **62**
[*see* comedere, deuorare].

consummatus (τέλειος) 1 Ioh iv 18, **25** (= $Aug^2/_6$)
perfectus $Tert^2/_2$ $Aug^4/_6$ *Ambr Fulg q* vg
cf τετελειωμένοι Ioh xvii 23
perfecti *a e f Hil*
consummati *b* vg *Ambr*
perfecti consummati *d*.

contaminare (βεβηλοῦν) Eze xxviii 18, **78**, **84**
[*see* polluere, profanare].
(μιαίνειν) Eze xxxvii 23, **34**
[*see* inquinare, polluere].

contegere (καλύπτειν) Eze xxxii 7, **44**, **45**
= Ps liv 6 *latt*[omn] *exc Heb*.

contemnens (φαυλίστρια) Soph ii 15, **42**.

conterere (ἐκτρίβειν) Ge xix 29, **85**.
(συντρίβειν) Esai xiv 12, **70**
Eze xxvii 26, **74**, **78** ; xxvii 34, **46** ; xxxii 12, **44**
but confringere Esai xiv 12, **71**
[*see* confringere].

continere (κρατεῖν) Sap vi 2, **72**
[*see* obtinere].

contritio (συντριβὴ) Esai xiii 6, **50** (= *m*418)
but obtritio *Cyp* 366.

contumax esse (ἀπείθειν) Esai lxiii 10, **10**
cf Esai l 5 ; lxv 2 *Cyp*.

contumelia (ὕβρις) Eze xxxii 12, **44**
[*see* iniuria].
(ἀτιμία) Ro ix 21, **82** ; 2 Tim ii 20, **82**
2 Tim ii 20 in contumelia V (*hiat* R) = εἰς ἀτιμίαν, inhonorata *Cyp* 623
[*see* ignominia, iniuria].

conuertere (ἐπιστρέφειν) Esai xlix 6, **38**.
(καταστρέφειν) Agg ii 23, **80**
but subuertere Ge xix 29, **85**.

conuerti (ἀποστρέφεσθαι) Esai xiii 14, **51** ; xlii 17, **9**.
(ἐπιστρέφεσθαι) Ps lxxix 15, **6**
Esai xliv 22, **9**
Hier iii 12, **75**
[*comp* auertere].

cooperire (κατακαλύπτειν) Eze xxxii 7, **44**
but operiam **45**.

coram (ἐνώπιον) Ps cxlii 2, **20**.
(ἐναντίον) Hier xxv 37, **49**.

creare (κτίζειν) Eze xxviii 14, 15, **78**, **83** (= *w*)

Eph ii 10, **20** (=*rell*)
but condere *Tert adv Marc* ii 10 *and* v 17.

cubiculum (ταμεῖον)
'cubiculorum opera Christum esse,' **70**
cf Mt xxiv 26, ecce in cubiculis *Cyp* 336 *c* (*d*)
[*see* promptuarium].

custodire—custodiamus 1 Ioh ii 3, **68** (=*Cyp* 546) *stands for* φυλάξωμεν ℵ*.
All other documents, incl h Aug Lucif, have τηρῶμεν, (ob)seruamus.
cf e.g. Eze xxxvi 27, **33**.

cydaeus (χυδαῖος) Ex i 7, **55**.

debellare (πολεμεῖν) Ps cxix 6, **10**
[*see* expugnare].

decenter (εὐσχημόνως) Ro xiii 13, **57** (=*Cyp* 425 *Hil*)
honeste *m*528 d_2 vg *Aug Ambr*.

decor (κάλλος) Eze xxviii 7 *bis*, **77**, **80**; xxviii 12, **78**, **80** (=*Tert*);
xxviii 17 *bis*, **78**, **83** (=$w^4/_4$)
[*see* species].

deformatio (μόρφωσις) 2 Tim iii 5, **69** (=*Cyp* 224)
forma *m*515 d_2 vg *Lucif Aug*.

dehonestari (παραδειγματίζεσθαι)
Eze xxviii 17, [**78**,] **84** (=*Hieron*[loc])
in traductionem *m*675 *Arnob-jun*.

deicere (καταρρίπτειν) Thren ii 1, **84**.
(καταβάλλειν) Eze xxxii 12, **44**; xxxix 3, **74**.

deliciae (τρυφή) Eze xxviii 13, **78**, **80** (=*rell*); xxxvi 35, **34**.

delictum 2 Regn vii 14 (Ps lxxxviii 33), **38** R, *not* V
[*elsewhere* peccatum].

delinquere (ἁμαρτάνειν) Ps l 6, **20** V, *not* R
[*elsewhere* peccare].

demolitus (καθῃρημένος) Eze xxxvi 36, **34**.
(κατεσκαμμένος) Eze xxxvi 35, **34**.

deputari (λογίζεσθαι) Ro iv 3, **19**; ix 8, **27** (=*Hil Aug*)
aestimantur Ro ix 8 d_2 vg.

desertor (ἀφεστηκώς) Eze xx 38, **35** (=*m*455).

desolari (ἐρημοῦσθαι) Eze xxxii 15, **45**; (xxxv 14, **73**;) xxxvi 10, **36**.

desolatio (ἐρήμωσις) Hier xxxii 18, **53**
[*see* uastatio *and* abominatio].

despoliare se (ἐκδύεσθαι) Eze xxvi 16, **45** (=*h w*).

destruere (καταργεῖν) Ro iii 31, **14** (=*rell*, *exc* euacuare *Tert*)
[*see* euacuare].

detegere (ἀποκαλύπτειν) 2 The ii 6, **74** (V, *hiat* R)
but reuelabitur *ver*. 8, **75**
cf **74**[25]

detinere (κατέχειν) 2 The ii 6, 7, **74**
[*see* obtinere *and p* li].

deuastatio (*ἄβατος*) Hier xxxii 18, **53.**
deuorare (*κατεσθίειν*) Eze xxviii 18, **78, 84**
[*see* comedere, consumere].
dicturus—dicturus es (*λέγων ἐρεῖς*)
Eze xxviii 9, **77** (= *w*)
[*see* narrare *and p* l].
dignitas—tibi dignitatem *read by Tyconius* **9,** *for* tibi indignationem (*δείξω σοι τὸν θυμόν μου* Esai xlviii 9).
dilectio (*ἀγάπη*) 1 Ioh iv 18 *ter*, **25** (= *Tert* $^2/_2$ *Aug* $^3/_6$)
caritas *q* vg *Aug* $^3/_6$ *Ambr.*
diligere (*ἀγαπᾶν*) Esai lxiii 9, **10**
1 Ioh iii 14, **68**; iv 20, **68**
diluculo (*ὄρθρου*) Lc xxiv 1, **57** (= *c ff i* vg)
tempore *e b g r* rhe*
ante lucem *a*
but deluculo Os vi 4 *h*, [Ioh] viii 2 *e*
cf diluculo uigilabunt (= *ὀρθριοῦσι*) Os vi 1 *h* *Cyp* 293.
dirigere (*ἀνορθοῦν*) 1 Regn vii 13, **37**
[*see* confirmare].
diripere (*προνομεύειν*) Esai xiii 16, **51.**
dirutus (*κατεφθαρμένος*) Esai xlix 19, **82.**
discens (*μαθητής*) Ac xv 10, **12**
discipulorum *d* e_2 vg *Iren Hil Aug*
discens *in the Acts h* $^6/_7$ (discipulorum Ac vi 2)
" *in* Mt Mc *k* $^8/_{24}$
[*see* discipulus].
discipulus (*μαθητής*) Mt x 25, **6** (= MSS *incl k*)
[*see* discens].
disponere (*συντάσσειν*) Ge xviii 19, **24.**
(*διατιθέναι*) Ies Naue vii 11, **39**
Eze xxxvii 26, **35.**
dissoluere (*καταλύειν*) Mt xxvii 40, **75**
destruere MSS, *but hiant e k*
cf Mc xiii 2 *e* *Cyp* 49 (resoluatur *k*).
[*in* Mt xxiv 2 *Tyc* **7**[27] *seems to support* destruere (= *e rell*)].
doctrina (*ἐπιστήμη*) Eze xxviii 4[b], 5, 7, **77**; xxviii 17, **78** (= *m*675)
doctrina *also occurs in* cod *w* Eze xxviii 3, 4 *ter*, 5, 7
[*see* sapientia, scientia, *and Introd p* xlvii].
domus (*κατοικία*) Hier iii 12, **75**
(*a careless or corrupt* q^n—*hiat* R; *Ps-Cyp de Paenitentia* 16 *has* habitatio).
donec (*ἄχρι οὗ, ἄχρις ἂν*) Ro xi 25, **34**; Gal iii 19, **17.**
(*ἕως*) Esai xxxiii 23, **10**
Hier xxv 38, **49**
Eze xxviii 15, **78, 83**

2 The ii 7, **8**, **52** (*not* **74**)

[*see* quoad usque].

dum (ἐν *with infin.*) Eze xxvi 15, **45**; xxxvi 20, 23, **32**, **33**; xxxvii 28, **35**.

(*with indic. for abl. abs.*) Esai lix 9[a], **74**.

(*with indic. for pres. part.*) Esai lix 9[b], **74**.

edere (ἐσθίειν) Esai xxiii 18, **46**, **47**

[*see* manducare].

egens (πτωχὸς) Esai xxiv 6, **47**

cf Lc xvi 20 *e*

(egenus *and* egens *are characteristically African for* pauper: *e.g.* Esai lviii 8 *Cyp* 108, *m*592).

egredi (ἀποστρέφειν) Eze xxi 5, **41**, *perh. for* regredi.

(ἐκπορεύεσθαι) Hier xvii 19, **62**, *but* exire *in v.* 21.

(ἐξέρχεσθαι) Eze xxxvi 20, **32**

[*see* prodire, *which occurs once* (1 Ioh iv 1, **67**), *elsewhere* ἐξέρχεσθαι = exire. *comp k* lxxviii].

eligere (ἐκλέγειν) Eze xx 38, **35**.

emittere (ἐκβάλλειν) Mt xii 35, **84** (= *k Cyp* 670).

(ἐκσπᾶν) Eze xxi 5, **41**.

(ἐξαποστέλλειν) Ge xix 29, **85**.

emundare (καθαρίζειν) Eze xxxvii 23, **34**

elsewh. mundare

cf Mt viii 2, 3 *bis*, x 8, xi 5 *k*

[*see* mundare].

ensis (ῥομφαία) Ge iii 24, **81**

elsewh. gladius.

cf Ps xliv 4 *Cyp* 98.

eram, erat (ἤμην, ἦν) Ps cxix 7, **10**; Sap viii 21, **20**

Ion iii 3, **41**; Nah iii 3, **42**

Lc i 6, **13** (= MSS *exc e*); Ioh vii 39, **22** (= MSS)

e Lc i 6 *has* fuerunt.

fuit *occurs in k about* 30 *times where the other* MSS *have* erat.

fuit *etc in Tyc is used to render*

ἐγένοντο Ex i 7, **55**

ἐγενήθη Eze xxviii 13, 14, **78**; xxxvi 34, **34**

γέγονεν Gal iii 24, **18** (= *rell*)

cf also contumaces fuerunt (ἠπείθησαν) Esai lxiii 10, **10**.

ergo (ἄρα) Gal iii 29, **7** (= *rell*)

propterea ergo maledictio Esai xxiv 6, **47** *must stand for* διὰ τοῦτο ἄρα ἀρὰ, *but the first* ΑΡΑ *is found in no other authority.*

(οὖν) Ioh xix 42, **59**; Col ii 16, **64**, *and elsewhere.*

[*see* itaque].

eripere (ἐξαιρεῖν) Ps xc 15, **3**.

(ῥύεσθαι) Ps xc 14, **3.**

esse (μένειν) non eris = οὐ μὴ μείνῃς
Esai xiv 20, **71, 77**
non manebis *Habetdeus* 315.

est *etc is regularly supplied where the copula is not expressed in the Greek except in the following places:*
after ecce, Ex i 9, **55**
after haec, Esai xiv 26, **52**
after qui, Hier xvii 26, **62**; xxxii 21, **53**
Eph i 10, ii 17, **18**
cf also 3 Regn xiii 2, **41.**

euacuare (καταργεῖν) 1 Co i 28, **20** (*cf r m*567 *Aug*)
[*see* destruere].

euacuari (κενοῦσθαι) Ro iv 14, **13** (= '*Iulianus*' *ap Aug*)
exinaniri d_2 vg *Aug*
[*see* inanis fieri].

euangelizare (εὐαγγελίζεσθαι)
Eph ii 17, **18** (= d_2 vg *rell*)
adnuntiare *Cyp* 94 *Tert.*

euenire (ἐπέρχεσθαι) Nah iii 18, **42.**

exacerbare (παροξύνειν) Esai lxiii 10, **10**
[*see* concitare, incitare].

exardescere (ἐκκαίεσθαι) Abd 18, **83, 85**
[*cf* succendere].

exasperare (παροργίζειν) Eze xxxii 9, **44.**

exaudire (ἐπακούειν) Ps cx 15, **3** [εἰσακ- ℵ*B]
Esai xlv 1, **4**
2 Co vi 2, **60** (= *rell*).

excelsus (ὑψηλὸς) Eze xx 33, 34, **35**
[*see* altus].

excitare (ἐπεγείρειν) Esai xiii 17, **51**
ἐπεγείρειν occurs in NT Ac xiii 50, xiv 2
the renderings are
excitare Ac xiii 50 vg
incitare Ac xiv 2 *d*
suscitare Ac xiii 50 *d* ,, xiv 2 e_2 vg.

(**excludere** = [ἐκ]βάλλειν)
qui...*uestitum nuptialem* non habet...excluditur **83,** *cf* Mt xxii 13, *where however latt*^{min} *incl Habetdeus* 31 i *hace* mittete (βάλετε D 28 13–69 *etc*)
[*see* expellere].

execratio (βδέλυγμα) Ap xvii 4, **82** (= *Cyp* 148, 196)
abominatio *Prms* vg
cf Lc xvi 15 *e* *Cyp* 748
[*see* abominatio].

exhortari (παρακαλεῖσθαι) Esai xiii 2, **50**
[*see* consolari].

exinanire (ἐκκενοῦν) Eze xxviii 7, **77**, **80** (=*w*)
exinanire=κενοῦν *is avoided by Tyc in* NT
[Phil ii 7 se inaniuit *Cyp* 79 *codd* MB, 149 *codd* LMB semetipsum exinaniuit, 79 *cod* L=vg, se exinaniuit *sess Hartel* $^2/_2$]
[*cf* euacuari, inanis fieri].

expauescere (ἐξιστάναι) Esai xiii 8, **51**
[*see* stupere].

expellere (ἐκβάλλειν) Gal iv 30, **30**
cf k, e.g. Mt x 1
(eicere *lat*$^{eur\text{-}it\text{-}vg}$)
[*comp* excludere].

(ἐξωθεῖν) Ioel ii 20, **73**
Hier xxv 36, **49** (=*d* vg Ac vii 45).

expirare (διαφωνεῖν) Eze xxxvii 11, **36** (=*Cyp* 148)
*om m*424
exsperauimus *Cyp cod* O_1
desperauimus *Hieron*
interiuimus *Amb*
auulsi sumus in eis *Tert Res Carn* 29.

expugnare (πολεμεῖν) Esai xix 2, **43**
[*see* debellare].

exterminium (ἀπώλεια) 2 The ii 3, **30**
perditio *Tert*$^2/_2$ *Iren* d_2 vg
interitus *Ambr Aug*$^2/_2$
[*see* interitus, perditio].

(ἀφανισμὸς) Soph ii 13, 15, **42**.

extollere (αἴρειν) Esai xlix 18, **81**
[*see* auferre, ferre, tollere].

exurgere, *perf.* **exsurrexit** (ἀνιστάναι)
Ex i 8, **55**.
(ἐξεγείρειν)
Cant iv 16, **74**
Zech ii 13, **73**.
(ἐπεγείρειν)
Esai xix 2, **43**.

facinus (ἀνομία) Esai xliv 22, **9**; liii 5, **2** (=*Cyp*)
2 The ii 7, **30**, **74**, **84** (iniq. *Tert rell*)
so also Mt xxiv 12 *Cyp* 335 *and* $^7/_7$ *in Isaiah*
[*see* iniquitas].

facinus admittere (ἀνομεῖν) Esai xxiv 5, **47**; xliii 27, **9**
cf Dan ix 5, *Cyp* 260
(*cf also* ......-misit Ex xxxii 7 *r*, *but* ......-tem fecisti Eze xvi 52 *w*).

famulus (παῖς) Esai xxiv 2, **47**
elsewh. puer, *e.g.* Esai xliv 1, **9**.

felix (μακάριος) Ps cxxxvi 9, **52**
[*see* beatus].

ferre (αἴρειν) Ps xc 12, **3**
[*see* auferre, extollere, tollere].
(φέρειν) Esai liii 4, **2**
Hier xvii 26, **62**
[*see* portare].
festinare
uenire......festinet (διώξεται) Esai xiii 14, **51.**
fidelis fieri (πιστοῦσθαι) 2 Regn vii 16, **37.**
fiens fiet et erit (γινόμενος ἔσται)
Ge xviii 18, **24.**
Probably derived from a conflation of fiens erit *and* fiet et erit. *For the latter construction see k* ciii.
figmentum (ποίημα) Eph ii 10, **20** (= *r* d_2 *Aug*)
factura *Tert* vg.
fingere (πλάσσειν) Esai xliii 7, **9**; xliv 21, **9.**
fornicaria (πόρνη) Esai xxiii 15, 16, **46**
[*comp* meretrix].
fortitudo (ἰσχὺς) Esai x 13 *bis*, **75** (= *Cyp* Esai xi 2; xxxiii 11 *etc*)
[*see* uires, uirtus].
fructum afferre (καρποφορεῖν) Ro vii 5, **12** (= Mt xiii 23 MSS)
fructicare d_2 vg
fructum ferre *Tert Aug.*
fulgere (λάμπειν) 2 Co iv 6 *bis*, **57**
fulgere, fulsit *Tyc*
fulgere, illuxit d_2 *Ambst*
clarescere, claruit *r Aug*
splendescere, illuxit vg *Ambr Vig*
cf Mt xvii 2 *e.*
fulgor (αὐγὴ) Esai lix 9, **74**
cf Mc xiii 24 *k* (= φέγγος), splendor *rell.*
funis (σχοινίον) Esai xxxiii 20, 23, **10.**
generare (γεννᾶν) Lc iii 22, **7**
(genuit *a b c d ff* r rhe Hil*[ter] *Faust ap Aug codd latt ap Aug*)
Gal iv 24, **13**, **29** (= *Tert rell*).
generare *for* gignere (*except in genealogies*) *is predominantly African*
e.g. Esai i 2 *Cyp* 40, 273, 430
(*each time with a various reading in the inferior codices*).
generatio (γενεὰ) Ge xv 16, **61**; Ex xiii 18, **61**
Eccl i 4 *bis*, **4**
Baruch vi 2, **61**
[*see* saeculum].
gentiles (ἔθνη) Nah iii 3, **42**
gentilibus V, gentigentibus R; *possibly only a corruption of* gentibus, *yet cf Cyp Test* III 34 (Hier x 2)
[*see* natio].

germinare (ἀνατέλλειν) Iob xi 17, **75**
cf k Mc xiii 28 (=ἐκφύειν).
gerund *in* **-dum** Gal ii 4, **30.**
-do Ps liv 21, **76.**
gladius (ἐγχειρίδιον) Eze xxi 3, 4, 5, **41**
*gladius=μαχαίρα and ῥομφαία *passim*
e.g. Eze xxxii 11 *bis*, **44**
[*see* ensis].
gloria (δόξα) Esai xliii 7, **9**
2 Co iii 18 *ter*, **19, 21**
[*see* claritas].
(δόξασμα) Thren ii 1, **84.**
(κῦδος) Esai xiv 25, **52.**
glorificare (δοξάζειν) Ps xc 15, **3**
Dan xi 38, **5**
[*see* magnificare].
habitare (ἐνοικεῖν, κατοικεῖν) Ge xix 29, **85**
Soph ii 15, **42**; Zech xiv 11, **48**
Esai xxiii 18, **46**; xxiv 5, **47**
Hier xvii 25, **62**
Eze xxxvi 10, **36**; xxxvi 17, **32**; xxxvi 28, **33**; xxxvii 25[b], **34**; xxviii 2, **77, 78** (=*w*)
[*see* inhabitare].

N.B. habitare *is never a transitive verb in Tyconius exc* Eze xxviii 2, *but it is used in the passive twice* (Hier xvii 25; Eze xxxvi 10).

(κατασκηνοῦν) Ps cxix 5, **10**
Ioel iii 17, **73.**
ciuitates cum habitantibus (πόλεις κατοικουμένας)
Esai x 13, **75.**
hic (= *art.*)
hoc donum=ἡ χάρις Sap viii 21, **20** (=*Aug Arnob-jun* vg)
in hunc mundum=εἰς τὸν κόσμον Ioh i 9, **4** (=*rell incl Cyp*)
in hoc mundo=εἰς τὸν κόσμον 1 Ioh iv 1, **67**
(in hoc saeculo *q*, in saeculo *Lucif* 261)
e Ioh i 9 *has* in hoc mundo
[*see* ille, iste].
holocausta (ὁλοκαυτώματα) Hier xvii 26, **62.**
honoratus (ἔντιμος) Esai xiii 12 *bis*, **51**
pretiosus *m*418.
iam (ἔτι *in negative sentences*) Ro vii 17, **15**; Gal iii 18, **14**
[*see* adhuc, ultra].
(ἤδη) 2 The ii 7, **74** (=*rell*).
(**ibi** *never occurs.*
It is however twice brought into the text by Vcorr *pp* 48 *and* 75)
[*see* illic].

idolorum seruitus (εἰδωλολατρεία)
Col iii 5, **83** (= d_2 *Cyp Aug*)
idololotria *Iren*[ed]
simulachrorum seruitus vg.

idolum (εἴδωλον) Eze xxxvi 17, **32**
cf Ap ix 20 et idola, id est simulacra, aurea et......'*Cyp*' [Test III 59 W]
Ps cxxxiv 15 idola *Cyp* 160, 321 *Aug*[loc]
simulacra *Cyp* 160[sess] *Hil and the Psalters*
[*see* simulacrum].

ignifer (πυρφόρος) Abd 18, **83**, **85**.

ignominia (ἀτιμία) Esai x 16, **48**
cf 1 Co xv 43, *where also there is a rhetorical contrast, as here, between* ἀτιμία *and* δόξα
ignominia *Cyp* 159 *Hil*
contumelia d_2 *m*429 *Aug*
ignobilitas *Iren Amb* vg
dedecoratio *Tert*
[*see* contumelia, iniuria].

ignorare (οὐκ ἴδειν) Ex i 8, **55**
[*see* non].

ille (= *article*)
1. *with adj. or part.* Ioel ii 20, **73**
Esai xiv 27, **52**; xxiv 2 *bis*, **47**
Eze xxvi 17, **45** (= *h w*); xxxvi 23, **33**.
2. *with proper names* Soph ii 13, **42**.
3. *with a simple noun* 2 Mach vii 29, **21** (= *Cyp Lucif* vg)
[*for* 3, *see* hic, iste].

illic (ἐκεῖ) Eze xx 35, **35**; xxxvi 20, 21, 22, **32**, **33**; xxxvii 21, **34**
Mt vi 21, **82** (= *k* $Cyp^2/_2$)
Ioh xix 42, **59** (= *e*)
[*cf* ibi].

illuc (ἐκεῖ) Hier xxv 36, **49**.

imber (ὑετὸς) Esai v 6, **73** (= *Cyp* 387 3 Regn xvii 14)
[*but* pluuiam *h* Ac xiv 17].

imperium (πρόσταγμα) Ps ii 6, **72** (= *Cyp Hil etc, not Aug*)
[*see* iussum, praeceptum].

impietas (ἀσέβεια) Am i 3, 11, **53**
Ro xi 26, **34**.

impius (ἀσεβὴς) Esai xxiv 8, **47**
Eze xx 38, **35**
? 2 The ii 8, **75** (ὁ ἄνομος MSS, *but cf* Esai xi 4)
[*see* iniustus].

implere (ἐμπιπλάναι) Eze xxxii 6, **44**
[*see* replere, satiare].

(πιμπλάναι) Eze xxviii 16, **78**

[*see* replere].

inanis fieri (κενοῦσθαι) 1 Co i 17, **31** (= *Cyp* 169 *Hil*)
euacuari d_2

[*see* euacuari].

incendere (ἀνάπτειν) Eze xx 47, **40**

[*see* succendere].

flamma incensa (ἡ φλὸξ ἡ ἐξαφθεῖσα)
Eze xx 47, **40.**

incidere (ἁλίσκεσθαι) Esai xiii 15, **52.**

incitare (παροξύνειν) Esai xiv 16, **71, 75, 76**

In the two longer and more formal quotations of the passage, **70** *and* **75**, *Tyconius has* concitare *like Cyprian* 183

[*see* concitare, exacerbare].

incrementum (αὔξησις) Eph iv 16, **3**; Col ii 19, **3** (= d_2 1/2 *Iren* 1/1 *Lucif* 1/2 *Ambr* 1/2 *Aug* 2/2)
augmentum vg 2/2 *m*514 *Lucif* 1/2 *Ambr* 1/2.

indignari (θυμοῦσθαι) Esai xiii 13, **51** (= *k* Mt ii 16)
(irasci *rell*).

indignatio (θυμὸς) Esai xiii 9, 13, **51**
Hier xxv 37, **49.**

θυμὸς = indignatio *Cyp* Esai xii 9
= ira *Cyp* Esai lxvi 15

[*see* animatio, ira].

indui (ἐνδύεσθαι) Esai xlix 18, **82.**

inferi (ᾅδης) Esai xiv 15, **70, 75**; xiv 19, **71, 76**
portas inferorum, *cf* Mt xvi 18, **63**
(infernus *is confined to European texts*).

infligere (ἐντέλλεσθαι) Esai xii 11, **51**
elsewh. praecipere (*e.g.* Esai xiii 4, **50**) *and* mandare (*e.g.* Hier xvii 22, **62**).

ingredi (εἰσέρχεσθαι) Eze xxxvi 20 *bis*, **32**, 21, 22, **33**; xxxviii 21, **34.**
(εἰσπορεύεσθαι) Hier xvii 19, **62**

[*elsewh. see* intrare, introire].

inhabitans (καθημένος) Hier xxxii 29, **54.**
(ἐνοικῶν) Esai xlix 19, **82.**

inhabitare (ἐνοικεῖν, κατοικεῖν)
with acc. Esai xxiv 6[b], **47**
Hier xvii 25, **62**
Eze xxvii 35, **46**; xxxii 15, **45**
with in Esai xiv 23, **52**; xxiv 1, 6[a], **47**
Eze xxvi 17, **45**; xxxvii 25[a, c], **34**

[*see* habitare].

inhabitari facere (κατοικεῖν) Eze xxxvi 33, **33.**

iniquitas (ἀδίκημα) Eze xxviii 15, **78, 83** (= *w*)
cf Ap xviii 5 *Cyp Prms* vg

Ac xviii 14 *h e* [iniuria *d*].
(ἀδικία) Eze xxviii 18, **78**, **84** *bis*
[*see* iniustitia].
(ἀνομία) Eze xxviii 16, **78** (=*w*); xxxvi 31, 33, **33**; xxxvii 23, **34**
[*cf* facinus].

iniquus (ἄνομος) Eze xxi 3, **41**
[*see* scelestus].

iniuria (ἀτιμία) Eze xxxvi 7, **36**
[*see* contumelia, ignominia].
(ὕβρις) Esai xiii 11 *bis*, **51**=*Cyp* Zech x 11; *h* vg Ac xxvii 10
cf iniuriosus (ὑβριστὴς) *Cyp* Esai ii 12
(contumelia *m*418)
[*see* contumelia].

iniuriam facere (ὑβρίζειν) Esai xiii 3, **50**.

iniustitia (ἀδικία) 2 Regn vii 14, **37**
[*see* iniquitas].

iniustus (ἄδικος) Soph iii 5, **42**
Eze xxi 3, **41**.
(ἀσεβὴς) Esai xiii 11, **51**
[*see* impius].

inlustris (ἐπιφανὴς) Soph iii 1
=*Cyp* Mal i 14
Tert Ac ii 20.
other renderings are
praeclarus *Auct ad Novat* (Soph iii 1), e_2 (Ac ii 20) [*om d*]
splendidus *Lucif* (Soph iii 1).

inponere (ἐπιτιθέναι) Eze xxvii 30, **45**
Ac xv 10, **12** (=*rell*).
(περιτιθέναι) Esai lxi 10, **3**.

inpudicitia (αὐθαδία) Esai xxiv 8, **47**.

inquinare (μιαίνειν) Esai xliii 28, **9**
cf Ag ii 14 *Habetdeus* 314 *and contr Fulg Donat.*
Ioh xviii 28 inquinarentur *e* (coinquinarentur *q*)
contaminarentur *b c f* vg
polluerentur *a ff*
[*see* contaminare, polluere].

insanabilis (ἀνίατος) Esai xiii 9, **51** (=*Cyp* 366)
(sine refrigerio *m*418)
[*see* sine].

insertus (ἐκκεκεντημένος) Esai xiv 19, **71**, **76**.

intellectus (σύνεσις) Esai x 13, **75**
[*see* prudentia].

interest—quid interest (τί γάρ;) Phil i 18, **70**
[nihil mea *Tert adv Marc* v 20, quid enim d_2 vg].

interficere (ἀναιρεῖν) Eze xxviii 9, **77**, **80**

2 The ii 8, **31** (=*Tert Iren rell*).
(ἀποκτείνειν) Mt xxiii 37, **63** (=*e Cyp* 44)
[*see* occidere].
(dum interficiuntur=ἐν τῷ σπᾶσαι, *cf* 23 ἐν τῷ ἀναιρεθῆναι
Eze xxvi 15, **45**
interfectione *h*
in euaginatione *w*.
(σφαγεῖν) Esai xiv 21, **71**, **77** (=*Habetdeus* 315).

interire (ἀπολωλέναι) Eze xxxvii 11, **36** (=*m*424)
periit *Cyp* 158.

interitus (ἀπώλεια) Eze xxvi 16, **45** (=*w*); xxxii 15, **45**
(perditio *h* Eze xxvi 16)
cf Mt vii 13 interitum *k Cyp*119, perditionem *rell*
[*see* exterminium, perditio].

intrare (εἰσέρχεσθαι) Ge xix 23, **85**
Hier xvii 25, **62**
Eze xx 38, **35**
Ro xi 25, **34**
[*see* introire].
(εἰσπορεύεσθαι) Hier xvii 20, 27, **62**
[*see* ingredi].

introire (εἰσέρχεσθαι) Ps cxlii 2, **20**
Esai xxiv 10, **47**
Mt vii 21, **69** (=*k Cyp*²/₂)
[*see* intrare].

inualere (ἐνισχύειν) Os xii 3, 4, **28**
[*see* ualere].

inuocare (ἐπικαλεῖν) Ps xc 15, **3**
elsewhere uocare *e.g.* Esai xliii 6, **9**.
(καλεῖν) Hier xxxii 29ᵇ, **54**.

inuocari (ὀνομάζεσθαι) Hier xxxii 29ᵃ, **54**.

inutilis—inutilia=τὰ ἀγενῆ [τοῦ κόσμου] 1 Co i 28, **20**
ignobilia *m*567 d_2 vg *Aug*.

ira (θυμὸς) Esai xiii 3, **50**
Eze xx 33, 34, **35**; xxxvi 6, **36**; xxxvi 18, **32**
[*see* animatio, indignatio].
(ὀργὴ) Esai xiii 9, 13, **51**
Hier xxv 37, **49**
Ro ii 5 *bis*, **84**; iv 15, **13**, **24**; Col iii 6, **83**.

iste (οὗτος) Ps xxiii 5, **29**
Zech xiv 15, **49**
Esai xxiv 3, **47**; xlix 6, **38** (*om* LXX)
Hier iii 12, **75**; xvii 20, **62**
Mt v 19, **69** (=*rell*); xxv 40, **68** (=*corb Hil*¹/₂)
Mc x 30, **59** (=*k*)

Lc xviii 30, **59** (=*e* *Cyp*^{3}/$_3$)
1 Ioh ii 3, **68**; iv 2, **68**.

(=*art.*)
in isto mundo=ἐν τῷ κόσμῳ 1 Ioh iv 3, **68**, *but* in hoc mundo 1 Ioh iv 1, **67**
iste qui uenit=ὁ ἐρχόμενος 2 Co xi 4, **5**
[*see* hic, ille].

ita (οὕτως) Esai xiv 20, **71**, **77** (=*Habetdeus* 315)
Mt xxiv 46, **11** (=*d e*)
Gal iv 29, **30** (=*rell*)
elsewh. sic.

ita ut (ὥστε) Hier xxxii 28, **54**.

itaque (οὖν) Col iii 5, **83** (=*Cyp*645 *Iren*)
so k Mt i 17, iii 8, v 48, *etc*
[*see* ergo].
(ὥστε) Gal iii 24, **18** (=*rell*).

itinera (ἄμφοδα) Hier xvii 27, **62**, **64**
cf ἐπὶ τοῦ ἀμφόδου Mc xi 4
in platea *a*
in transitu(m) *b* (*c*) *d ff i q*
in biuio *f* vg.

iucundari (εὐφραίνεσθαι) Esai xxiv 7, **47** (=Esai (xli 16;) liv 1; lxv 13 *Cyp*)
[*see* laetans].

iucunditas (εὐφροσύνη) Esai xxiv 8, 11, **47**
Eze xxxvi 5, **35**
cf Ac xiv 17 iucunditate *d h*
laetitia e_2 vg
[*see* laetitia].

iuratio (ὅρκος) Ge xxvi 3, **23**.

iussum (πρόσταγμα) Esai xxiv 5, **47**
[*see* imperium, praeceptum].

iuxta (ἐγγὺς) Hier xxxii 26, **53**
[*see* proxime].

laedere (ἀδικεῖν) Ap ix 10, **60** (*cf Prms* ad laedendi)
nocere vg
nocendi *h*.

laetans (εὐφραινόμενος) Ps cxxv 3, **67** (=Hier vii 34 *Cyp* 85)
but iucundatus *Aug on* Ps cxxv
[*see* iucundari].

laetitia (εὐφροσύνη) Eze xxxv 14, **73**
[*see* iucunditas].

lamenta (θρήνημα) Eze xxvii 32, **45**
'lamentas, fletus facere,' *Pacuv ap Non* 132.
θρήνημα does not occur again in the Greek Bible.

lamentatio (θρῆνος) Eze xxvi 17, **45** (=*h w*); xxvii 32, **45** (=Am viii 10 *Cyp* 91)
[*see* lamentum].

lamentum (θρῆνος) Eze xxviii 12, [77,] **80** (=*w*)
[*see* lamentatio].

laudabilis (ἐπαινετὸς) Eze xxvi 17, **45** (=*h w*).

laudatio (αἴνεσις) Hier xvii 26, **62**.

legatus (πρέσβυς) Esai xiii 8, **50**
[*see* senior].

lenire (παύειν, *so Lucian and* 62-147)
Esai xiii 3, **50**.
cod R *has* mitigare
cf Nu xxv 11 leniuit *Cyp* 785,
but mitigauit *Opt* 63.

liberare (ῥύεσθαι) Eze xxxvii 23, **34**
Mt vi 13, **17**
Ro xi 26, **34**.

liberari (σώζεσθαι) Ro ix 27, **27**
[*see* saluari].

longe (πόρρω) Esai xxix 13, **8**
Hier xxxii 26, **53**.
(μακρὰν) Eph ii 17, **18** (=*rell*)
(*never* a longe) *cf* de longinquo.

longinquus
de longinquo=ἐκ γῆς πόρρωθεν
Esai xiii 5, **50**
de terra longinqua=ἀπὸ γῆς πόρρωθεν
Esai xliii 6, **9**
(*Probably the O. Latin read* τῆς *for* γῆς *in* Esai xiii 5, *as* B *does in* Esai xliii 6)
cf Lc xvii 12 *e* (=ἐκ πόρρωθεν)
[*also* Mc xi 13, xiv 54, xv 40 *k*=ἀπὸ μακρόθεν].
longinquus fieri (μακρύνεσθαι)
Ps cxix 5, **10**.

lucere *followed by cognate acc.* (φαίνειν)
luna non lucebit lumen eius
=σελήνη οὐ μὴ φάνῃ τὸ φῶς αὐτοῦ Eze xxxii 7, **44**, **45**
omnia quae lucent lumen
=πάντα τὰ φαίνοντα φῶς Eze xxxii 8, **44**, **45**
cf luces cereum *Plaut Curc* I 9; lucebis...facem *Cas* I 30.
NB *This construction is variously avoided in* Ap viii 12.

lugere (πενθεῖν) Esai xxiv 7 *bis*, **47**
[*see* plangere].

lumen (φῶς) Sap v 6, **73**
Am viii 9, **74** [; Mi iii 6, **74**]
Esai x 17, **48**; xiii 10 *bis*, **51**; xlix 6, **38**; lix 9, **74**
Eze xxxii 7, 8, **44**
2 Co iv 6, **57**
[*see* lux].

Mi iii 6 dies luminis *for* dies (*so* V, *hiat* R), *probably only by confusion with* Am viii 9.
Esai xiii 10 lumen et *for* et lunae
[*see* permanere].

lux (φῶς) Esai xlii 16, **9**; liii 11, **2**
Lc xvi 8, **79** (=*Cyp* 793 *rell*)
1 Ioh ii 9, **68** (=*Cyp* 116, *not h*)
[*see* lumen].

magistratus (ἄρχοντες) Esai xiii 2, **50**
elsewhere princeps=ἄρχων.
cf k Mt x 18 magistratus=ἡγεμόνες (praesides *rell*)
d Lucif 269 Ac xvi 19 magistratus=ἄρχοντες (principes e_2 vg).

magnificare (δοξάζειν) Esai x 15, **79**
Ro i 21, **84** (=d_2 *Aug*$^1/_{16}$ *Ambst*)
clarificare *Faust ap Aug*
honorificare *Habetdeus* 315 *Aug*$^1/_{16}$
honorare *Zeno* *Aug*$^1/_{16}$
glorificare vg *Aug*$^{13}/_{16}$
[*see* glorificare].

maledictum (ὀνειδισμὸς) Esai xliii 28, **9**
cf Hier vi 10 *Cyp* 41
[*see* obprobrium].

malus (πονηρὸς) Mt vi 13, **17** (=*rell*); xii 35 *bis*, **84**
nequa(m) Mt xii 35 *bis k* *Cyp* 670
[*see* nequam].

mandatum (ἐντολὴ) Mt v 19, **69** (=*rell*)
Lc i 6, **13** (=*rell*, *exc e f*)
1 Ioh ii 4, **68** (=*Cyp* 546)
Ro vii 11, **15** (=*rell*)
[*see* praeceptum].

manducare (ἐσθίειν) 3 Regn ii 46^a, **65**
Esai x 17, **48**
[*see* edere].

(κατεσθίειν) Eze xxxvi 8, **36**.

manere (κοιτάζειν) Cant i 7, **73** (=*Ambr*).

manufacta, -orum (χειροποίητα) Esai xix 1, **43**.

mercator (ἔμπορος) Eze xxvii 36, **46**
[*see* negotiator].

mercatus (ἐμπορία) Nah iii 16, **42**
Eze xxviii 5, **77**, **79** (=*w*)
[*see* negotiatio].

(meretrix) *cf* Ap xvii 4, **82**
[*see* fornicaria].

metueri (φοβεῖσθαι) Esai xliii 5, **9**
cf e.g. Mt x 28 *k* *Cyp*$^4/_4$
Mt i 20 *k*
[*see* timere].

militare (ἐπιστρατεύειν) Zech xiv 12, **49**.
minorari (ἡττᾶσθαι) Esai xix 1, **43**
[*see* superari].
miseratio (ἔλεος) 2 Mach vii 29, **21** (=*Cyp rell*).
misericordia (ἔλεος) 2 Regn vii 15, **37**
Ps xvii 51, **5**
in misericordia et miseratio (R; *tr* V)=ἐν ἐλέει καὶ οἰκτειρμοῖς
Ps cii 4, **21**
[*for the change in order, see* nimbus].
[**mitigare**]=lenire *in cod* R Esai xiii 3, **50**
[*see* lenire].
mittere *(ἀποστέλλειν *passim*).
(ἐμβάλλειν) Ies Naue vii 11, **39**.
(ἐξαποστέλλειν) Hier xxv 38, **49**.
modo (ἄρτι) Mt xxvi 64, **4**, **45**
2 The ii 7, **52**, **74**
[*see* adhuc, nunc].
multiplicari (πλεονάζειν) Ro v 20, **13**, **18**
abundare *rell, which also appears in an allusion p* **15**.
mundare (καθαρίζειν) Eze xxxvi 25 *bis*, 33, **33**
[*see* emundare].
(σώζειν) Eze xxxvi 29, **33**
probably a mere piece of carelessness on the part of Tyconius.
mundus (κόσμος) Ioh i 9, **4**; xvii 5, **2**, **37**
1 Ioh iv 1, 3, **67**, **68**
Ro iv 13, **13**.
saeculum=κόσμος *does not occur.*
mysterium (μυστήριον) 2 The ii 7, **30**, **74**, **84** (=d_2 vg *Aug etc*)
arcanum *Tert Res Carn* 24
[*see* sacramentum].
(διακονία) 1 Co xii 5, **69** RV
(mysteriorum *for* ministeriorum): *same corruption* *Ambr*$^1/_3$ (*ap Sabat.*), *and on p* **30**[27] R *has* ministerium *for* mysterium.
[**narrare**]—narrabis (λέγων ἐρεῖς)
Eze xxviii 9, **80**
only in the repetition of the continuous quotation pp **77**, **78**.
(*cf* Ps xxi 23 narrabo (διηγήσομαι) nomen tuum fratribus meis)
[*see* dicturus].
nasci—quae nascuntur (τὰ γενήματα)
Eze xxxvi 30, **33**
cf nascentia Hab iii 17 *Cyp* 365
quae nata sunt Lc xii 18 *b ff i q* vg.
natio (ἔθνος) Sap vi 3, **72**
Esai x 13, **75**

Eze xxviii 19, **78**, **85**; xxxii 9, 10, 12, **44**; xxxvi 7, **36**; xxxvi 19, 20, 21, 22, 23[a], 30, **32**, **33**

elsewh. gens

e.g. Eze xxxvi 53[b], 24, 36, **33**, **34**.

In Cyprian's quotations from the Prophets

natio *occurs* Mi iv 3, Esai lv 4[a]

gens *occurs* 25 *times*

gentiles *only* Hier x 2 (*codd-opt*)

[*see* gentiles].

ne (=ut non) Esai v 6, **73**; xxiv 10, **47**
Eze xxxvii 23, **34**
1 Co i 17, **31**.

ne *prohibitive does not occur; but* noli *w. infin.*
Esai xliii 5, 6, **9**; xliv 21, **9**
Hier xvii 21 *bis*, **62**
Ioh v 28, **37**.

negotiatio (ἐμπορία) Esai xxiii 18 *bis*, **46**, **47**, **84**
Eze xxviii 16, **78**, **83** (=*w*); 18, **78**, **84**
[*see* mercatus].

(ἔμποροι) Eze xxxviii 13, **84**
negotiationes V, *perhaps for* negotiatores.
(πορισμὸς) 1 Tim vi 6, **84**
quaestus *r* d_2 *m*514 vg *Lucif Aug Amb Ambst*

negotiator (ἔμπορος) Mt xiii 45, **84** (=*c* vg)
negotianti *rell*, *incl* $Cyp^2/_2$.
(*On p* **84** *cod* R *is missing, so perhaps Tyconius wrote* negotianti.)

nepotes (τέκνα) Esai xiii 18, **52**.

nequam (πονηρὸς) Esai xiv 20, **71**, **77** (=*Habetdeus* 315)
(*cf* Mt xxiv 48, **11**)
[*see* malus].

nequitia (πονηρία) Eph vi 12, **30**, **54** (=*rell*).

nimbus (γνόφος) Esai xliv 22, **9**
also Ps cxvi 2, **73** (nimbus et nubes = νεφέλη καὶ γνόφος
(caligo *rell*: γνόφος *does not occur in any verse quoted by Cyp*).

nimis (σφόδρα) Ex i 7, **55** (σφόδρα σφόδρα LXX)
Zech xiv 14, **49**
Eze xxvii 25, **78** (=*k* Mt ii 10; Mc xvi 4).

non (μηδαμῶς) Eze xx 49, **40**
cf Ac x 14 *d*.

non *with verbs of knowing:*
non nouerunt (οὐκ ἔγνωσαν) Esai xlii 16[a], **9**
(οὐκ ᾔδεισαν) Esai xlii 16[b], **9**;
but Tyconius emphasises the distinction between
non cognouisti (οὐκ ἔγνως) Esai xlv 5[a], **8** *and*
nesciebas (οὐκ ᾔδεις) Esai xlv 5[b], **8**.

noua nupta (νύμφη) Esai xlix 18, **82**
cf Ap xxi 9 *Cyp* 85 *Prms*
elsewhere sponsa, *e.g.* Esai lxi 10, **3.**
nugari (ματαιοῦσθαι) Ro i 21, **84**
euanuerunt d_2 vg *Habetdeus* 315 *Faust ap Aug Aug*
cf euanuerunt 4 Regn xvii 15 *vind.*
nunc (ἄρτι) Ioh v 17, **61** (=*a Victn-Afer*)
modo *e rell*, adhuc *b*
[*see* adhuc, modo].
obprobrium (ὀνειδισμὸς) Eze xxxvi 6, **36**; xxxvi 30, **33**
cf Hier xxiv 9, *de Pasch Comp* 259
[*see* maledictum].
obscurare (συσκοτάζειν) Mi iii 6, **74** (*vb. neut.*)
tenebricare *Vig*
Eze xxxii 7, 8, **44, 45**
[*see* tenebricare].
obscurus—obscura nocte (ἐν ἀωρίᾳ)
Esai lix 9, **74**
cf intempesta nocte Ps cxviii 147 *Aug*
i.e. "*the dead of night,*" *when no one knows the time; cf Fest ap Lexx.*
obtinere (κατέχειν) 2 The ii 7, **52**
Tyconius quotes the verse for the sake of this word; on p **74** *he quotes it with* detinere
[*see* detinere].
(κρατεῖν) Ps cxxxvi 9, **52**
[*see* continere].
occidere (ἀποκτέννειν, ἀποκτείνειν)
Ex iv 23, **6**
Esai xiv 20, **71, 77** (*Habetdeus* 315)
Mt xvi 21, **61** (=MSS *exc e*)
2 Co iii 6, **21** (*Tert rell*)
[*see* interficere].
onerari
onerata es=ἐβαρύνθης Eze xxvii 26, **78**
(*suggested by Sabatier in loc.*
honorata es V [*hiat* R], *but* V* *actually has* honore *for* onere *p* **63**[23].
βαρύνειν *elsewhere is always represented by* [ad]grauare, *yet it is most improbable that* ἐδοξάσθης, *the reading of Aquila and Theodotion should have found its way into the text of Tyconius.*)
onerari (φορτίζεσθαι) Mt xi 28, **63** (=*rell*).
optimus (χρηστὸς) Eze xxviii 13, **78, 81** (=*w Tert*)
bonus=χρηστὸς Mt xi 30 *k* $Cyp^2/_2$
optimus=bonus Mc x 17, 18 *bis k*
[*cf* pessimus].
***orbis terrae** (ἡ οἰκουμένη) Esai xxiv 1, 4, **47** *etc.*

in 1 Par xvi 30, **75** orbem terrae *corresponds to* τὴν οἰκουμένην, *as in Lucian.*

*orbis terrarum ([ἡ] οἰκουμένη)
Esai lxii 4, **81** *etc.*

ornamentum (κόσμος) Esai xlix 18, **82**; lxi 10, **3**
[*see* ornatura].

ornatura (κόσμος)
omnis ornatura caeli Esai xiii 10, **51** *ex coni* = πᾶς ὁ κόσμος τοῦ οὐρανοῦ
omnis creatura... R
omnis ex ea rura... V
omne ornamentum *m*418
cf 1 Tim ii 9 *d* ornaturis capillorum = ἐνπλέγμασιν
[*see* ornamentum].

ostendere (δεικνύναι) Ps cx 16, **3**
Esai xlviii 9, **9**; liii 11, **2.**

ostensio—ostensio *est* duorum *populorum*, **28**
cf αὗται γάρ εἰσιν δύο διαθῆκαι Gal iv 24
and haec sunt enim duo testamenta, siue duae ostensiones, sicut inuenimus interpretatum *Tert adv Marc* v 4.

parabola (παραβολὴ) Eze xx 49, **40.**

participles:
present participles occur over a dozen times, but are often avoided by construction with qui
[*see* dum].
participle in **-urus**
desolaturus Eze xxxv 14, **73**
dicturus Eze xxviii 9, **77** (=*w*)
futurus Gal iii 23, **18**
for Eze xxviii 9 *see Introd p* l.

parturitio (ὠδὶν) Esai xiii 8, **50** (=*k* Mc xiii 8, *Cyp* Mt xxiv 8)
(dolor *rell*, *incl e*).

perditio (ἀπώλεια) Esai xiv 23, **52**
Eze xxvii 36, **46**; xxviii 7, **77, 80,** 19, **78, 85**
[*see* exterminium, interitus].
(προνομὴ) Esai xxxiii 23, **10**
[*see* uastatio].

peregrinari (παροικεῖν) Ps cxix 6, **10.**

peregrinatio (παροικία) Ps cxix 5, **10.**

perficere (καταρτίζειν) Ps lxxix 16, **6.**
(ἐπιτελεῖν) Zech iv 9, **81.**

perflare (διαπνεῖν) Cant iv 16, **74.**

perire (ἀπολλύναι) Esai xxiv 12, **47**; xliii 28, **9**
Eze xxviii 10, **77, 80**
[*see* interire].

permanere—et lunae non permanebit lumen eius = καὶ ἡ σελήνη οὐ δώσει τὸ φῶς αὐτῆς Esai xiii 10, (**51**).

*This is also the rendering in m*418.
Tyc **51** *has* lumen et *for* et lunae
[*see* lumen].

(μείνειν) 1 Ioh iii 14, **68** (=*h q*)
manere *rell*
[*see* perseuerare].

perseuerare (μείνειν) Esai xiv 24, **52**
[*see* permanere].

pessimus (πονηρὸς) Eze xxxvi 31, **33**
[*see* malus, nequam, *and cf* optimus].

pinna (πτέρυξ) Mal iv 2, **74** (=*de Pasch Comp* § 19)
but ala *Cyp* 293.

plangere (πενθεῖν) Esai xxiv 4 *bis*, **47**
cf Mt v 5 *k Cyp*, (lugere *rell*)
[*see* lugere].

plangere se (κόπτεσθαι) Mt xxiv 30, **4** (=*a c ff q*)
lamentari *e h Cyp* 336 [*exc* S]
lamentare se *Cyp cod* S
plangere *f* vg
concidere se *b*.

plebs (λαὸς) Esai xiv 20, **71, 77** (=*Habetdeus* 315); xliii 8, **9**
Ro x 21, **11** (=d_2); xi 2, **11** (=d_2 vg *Aug*)
elsewh. populus.

polluere (βεβηλοῦν) Eze xxxvi 20, 21, 22, 23 *bis*, **32, 33**
[*see* contaminare, profanare].

(μιαίνειν) Eze xxxvi 17, **32**
[*see* contaminare, inquinare].

portare (αἴρειν) Hier xvii 27, **62**
[*see* ferre, tollere].

(βαστάζειν) Ac xv 10, **12** (=e_2 vg *Iren etc*, baiulare *d*)
Gal v 10, **30** (=*rell*).

(φέρειν) Eze xxxvi 6, **36**
[*see* ferre].

potare (ποτίζειν, *used of human beings*)
Hier xxxii 15, 17, **53, 54**
so $k^3/_3$ $Cyp^2/_2$ $d^{\text{Mt (not Mc)}}$ [*hiat e*]
(potum dare *or* dare bibere *rell*)
[potionare Hier xxxii 15 *Ambr*=Mc xv 36 *n*; Esai xxix 10 *h* *m*68].

potentes (μεγιστᾶνες) Hier xxv 38, **49**; xxxii 19, **53.**

praebere aures (ἐνωτίζεσθαι) Sap vi 2, **72.**

praeceptum (ἐντολὴ) 1 Ioh ii 3, **68** (=*Cyp* 546)
NB 1 Ioh ii 3, 4 ἐντολὰς......ἐντολὰς
mandata......mandata *h* vg *Aug Lucif*
but praecepta......mandata *Cyp Tyc*
[*see* mandatum].

(πρόσταγμα) Eze xxxvii 24, **34**
[*see* imperium, iussum].

praeclarus (ἔνδοξος) Esai xlviii 9, **9**
cf Lc xiii 17 *latt*^{omn} *exc a* vg.

praeripium—et per praeripia fugient *corresponds to* καὶ οἱ βουνοὶ καὶ οἱ δρυμοὶ καὶ καταφάγεται ἀπὸ ψυχῆς ἕως σαρκῶν· καὶ ἔσται ὁ φεύγων
for praeripia *cod* V *has* precipitia, *but* praeripium (-rupium) *occurs in* *Tert adv Marc* iv 38, *and* per praeripium = κατὰ τοῦ κρημνοῦ Mc v 13 *e*; *see* Rönsch, *Collectanea* 275.

praesens est (ἐστὶν ἤδη) 1 Ioh iv 3, **68**
...est. Iam *q Aug*
[*cf* saluus].

praeualere (κατισχύειν, *vb. neut.*) Ex i 7, **55**
[*cf* uincere].

pressura (θλίψις) Col i 24, **6** (= *Tert Aug*)
Ap ii 10, **60**.
pressura *is* 'thoroughly African' (*k* lxxxi) *in most books, but it has disappeared from the Cyprianic text of the Apocalypse:*
tribulatio = θλίψις *Prms*$^5/_5$, *and wherever it occurs in h and Cyp, viz* Ap i 9, *h*; ii 22, *Cyp* 640; vii 14, *Cyp* 131, 343
but pressura Ap ii 22, *Tert de Pud* 19; vii 14, *Scorp* 12
[*see* tribulatio].

primitiuus (πρωτότοκος) Ex iv 22, 23, **6**.

princeps sacerdotum (ἀρχιερεὺς)
Mt xvi 21, **61** (= MSS *exc e, which has* sacerdotibus).

prodire (ἐξέρχεσθαι) 1 Ioh iv 1, **67** (= *q*)
exire *m*517 *Lucif* 261 *Iren Aug* vg
'processisse' *Tert adv Marc* v 16
[*see* egredi].

proeliari (παρατάσσειν) Zech xiv 14, **49**
praetendere *Tert adv Marc* iii 13.

proelium (πόλεμος) Eccl ix 11, **79**

profanare (βεβηλοῦν) Soph iii 4, **42**
contaminant *Lucif m*500
profanare *k* Mt xii 5 (βεβηλοῦν)
uiolare *rell*
[*see* contaminare, polluere].

profetare (*deponent imperative*)
Eze xx 46, **40**; xxi 2^a, **41**; xxxvi 6, **36**; xxxvii 12, **36** (= *m*424)
but profetabis *etc* *e.g.* Eze xxi 2^b, **41**.
so also Am vii 15, 16 *w*
Mc xiv 65 *k*.
(V *or* V*corr has* propheta$^3/_4$
so Eze xxxvii 12 *Cyp* 158.)

promiscuus (σύμμικτος) Hier xxxii 20, 24, **53**
[*see* commixtio].

promptuarium (ταμεῖον) Eze xxviii 16, **78** (=*w* *Arnob-jun*)
proma *Tert adv Marc* ii 10
cf cella proma *de Res Car* 27 (Esai xxvi 20)
promptuarium Mt xxiv 26, Lc xii 3 *e*
[*see* cubiculum].

prope (ἐγγὺς) Eze xxx 3, **43**
[*see* proximus, iuxta].

propter *etc*
propterea (διὰ τοῦτο)
Mi iii 6, **74**
Esai xxiv 6[a], **47**
Eze xxi 2, **41**; xxviii 6, **77, 79**; (7, **79**;) xxxvi 6, **36**; xxxvii 12, **36**
Ro iv 16, **24**.
propter hoc (ἀντὶ τούτου)
Eze xxviii 7, **77** (*not* **79**).
(διὰ τοῦτο)
Esai xiii 7, **50**; xxiv 6[b], **47**
[*for* propter quod *see* quod].

proxime (ἐγγὺς) Eph ii 17, **18**
iuxta d_2
prope *Cyp* 94 *Tert* *Hil* vg
[*see* iuxta, prope].

proximus (*adj.*) (ἐγγὺς) Esai xiii 6, **50**
Ioh xix 42, **59** (iuxta *rell*) (=*Cyp* 366 Esai xiii 6)
cf e Ioh ii 13
prope, in proximo *rell*
[*see* iuxta, prope].

prudentia (σύνεσις) Esai liii 11, **2**
[*see* intellectus].

purgare (καθαρίζειν) Esai liii 10, **2**
Hier xxxii 29, **54**
[*see* mundare].

purgatio (κάθαρσις) Hier xxxii 29, **54**.
quando (ὅτε) Ioh v 25, **37**.
quasi (ὡς, ὡσεὶ) Esai x 17, 18, **48**; xiii 8, 14, **51**; lix 10 *bis*, **74**
Gal iii 16 *bis*, **27** (=*Iren* vg)
[*see* sicut, tamquam, uelut, ut].

-que—abductosque (τοὺς ἐν ἐπαγωγῇ) Esai xiv 17, **70, 76**
eritque (καὶ ἔσται) Hier xvii 24, **62**; xxv 39, **50.**
***quia** *occurs about* 20 *times, but it is not nearly so common as* ***quoniam.**
This usage appears to be the same in all books of the Bible.
[quoad usque] (ἕως) 2 The ii 7, **74** (=*Ambst*)

but donec **8**, **52** (=d_2 vg *Tert Aug*).
quoad usque *occurs*
in the Prophets Cyp$^2/_2$ (Esai xxii 14; xlii 4) *in* $k^7/_{10}$;
but donec *occurs in the* NT *Cyp*$^3/_3$, *viz* Mt v 26, Lc xv 8; Ap vi 11
[*see* donec].

quod (*idioms*)
eo quod (ἀνθ' ὧν) Am i 3, **53**.
pro eo quod (ἀνθ' ὧν) Ge xxii 18, **23**; xxvi 5, **23**.
propter quod (ἀντὶ τοῦ) Eze xxxvi 6, **36**
(ἀνθ' ὧν ὅτι) Eze xxxvi 34, **34**
(διὰ τοῦ) Esai lxiii 9, **10**
(ἕνεκα τοῦ) Am i 11, **53**
(διὸ) 2 Co iv 13[a], **21**
but διὸ καὶ 2 Co iv 13[b] *is rendered by* ideoque et
[*cod* R *has* propter quod *here also with* vg].

quomodo (ὃν τρόπον) Esai xiv 20, **71** [, **77**] (=*Habetdeus* 315); xiv 24 *bis*, **52**
[*For the reading of* V *p* 77, *see Introd p* l].

quotquot (ὅσοι) Zech xiv 12, **49**
Gal iii 10, **14** (=d_2 *Ambst*)
quotquot annis (κατ' ἐνιαυτὸν)
Zech xiv 16, **49**
cf Lc ii 41 κατ' ἔτος
quodquod annis *e* (*so also Tyc* **49** *cod* V)
secundum tempus *d*
per omnes annos *a b c f ff q* vg.

recumbere (ἀνάκεισθαι) Mt xxii 11, **83** (=*Habetdeus* 314 *Iren*)
discumbens *rell*
but cf k Mt ix 10, Mc xiv 18.

redigere (διάγειν) Eze xx 37, **35**.

redimere (ἀπολυτροῦν) Soph iii 1, **42**.
(λυτροῦν) Esai xliv 22, **9**; lxiii 9, **10**.

remanere (καταλείπεσθαι) Esai x 19, **48**; xiii 12, **51**
elsewhere (*e.g.* Esai xiii 14, **51**) relinqui
[relinqui Ioh viii 9 *e ff*].

reminisci (μνησθῆναι) Eze xxxvi 31, **33**
[*see* commemorari].

replere (ἀνταναπιπλάναι) Col i 24, **6**.
(ἐμπιπλάναι) Esai xxiii 18, **46**, **47**
Eze xxviii 13, **78**, **81** (*but* inpl- *w*); xxxii 4, **44**
[*see* implere].
(πιμπλάναι) Ps cxxv 2, **67**
[*see* implere].

reprehensio (μῶμος) Cant iv 7, **10** (=*Habetdeus* 313, *Ambr*).

reprobari (ἀθετεῖν) Esai xlviii 8 *bis*, **9**
reprobauerunt Esai i 2 *Cyp* 40[codd opt] (spreuerunt *Cyp* 40[codd], 273, 430)

cf Lc vii 30 reprobauerunt *e*, spreuerunt *rell* vg
Ioh xii 48 reprobat *e*, spernit *rell* vg.

repromissio (ἐπαγγελία) Gal iii 18[b], **14**
elsewh. promissio.

requiescere facere (ἀναπαύειν) Mt xi 28, **63** (=*Cyp*48[vid], 183 [*k*] *f ger*[2])
[requiescere faciam *Cyp* 48 MBO_1O_3
requiescam *Cyp* 48 L
requiescere *k*]
but reficiam *sess*$^2/_2$ *a b rell* vg *Iren Hil Ambr Aug.*

resistere (ἀντιπίπτειν) Ac vii 51, **30** (=e_2 vg)
obstitistis *d*
contradixistis *h* (=αντ[ε]ιπατε *apparently*).

resoluere (ἐκλύειν) Esai xiii 7, **50.**

respectio (ἐπισκοπὴ) Esai xxiii 17, **46.**

respicere (ἐπιβλέπειν) Ps lxxix 15, **6**
Eze xx 46, **40**; xxi 2, **41**; xxxvi 9, **36.**

responsum (χρηματισμὸς) Ro xi 4, **28** R
V *adds* diuinum *with* d_2 *am*
[diuinum responsum vg[clem]].

restaurare (ἀνακεφαλαιοῦσθαι) Eph i 10, **18** (=d_2 *Ambst*)
recapitulare *Tert adv Marc* v 17 *Iren*$^3/_3$
ad caput reciprocare *Tert de Monog*
instaurare *Aug* vg.

reuerti (ἀποστρέφεσθαι) Ge xv 16, **61**
[*see* conuerti (*and* auertere)].
(ἐντρέπεσθαι) Eze xxxvi 32, **33.**
(ἐπιστρέφεσθαι) Lc xvii 31, **66** (=*a e*)
conuertatur *d*
redeat *b ff i c f q* vg
[*see* conuerti].

rigari (ποτίζεσθαι) Eze xxxii 6, **44**
so 1 Co iii 7, 8 *latt.*

riuus (φάραγξ) Eze xxxvi 6, **36**
so Esai xxxv 6 *Cyp*71; xl 4 *Cyp*69
[*see* uepres].

ruina (πτῶσις) Eze xxvi 15, 18, **45** (=*h w*); xxvii 27, **45**; xxxii 10 *bis*, **44, 45**
[*see* strages].

sacramentum (μυστήριον) Eph v 32, **7** (=*Tert Cyp* d_2 vg *Aug Ambr*)
mysterium *Iren Ambst*
[*see* mysterium].

saeculum (γενεὰ) Ex i 6, **55**
Ps civ 8, **60** (=*k* Mc xiii 30)
[*see* generatio].
(καιρὸς) Mc x 30, Lc xviii 30, **59** (=*k* Mc x 30)

(tempus *Cyp*$^4/_4$ *rell*).
(αἰὼν) Esai lxiii 9, **10**
in saeculum (εἰς τὸν αἰῶνα)
Eze xxxvii 25, 26, 28, **35**
[*see* aeternum].

sagitta (τόξευμα) Eze xxxix 3, **74**
[*see* sagittatio].

sagittatio (τόξευμα) Esai xiii 18, **52**
[*see* sagitta].

saluari (σώζεσθαι) Ro xi 26, **34**
[*see* liberari].

saluatus (σεσωσμένος)
Eph ii 8, **20**.

saluatio (σωτηρία) 2 Co vi 2, **60** (salus *rell*)
[*see* salus].

salus (σωτηρία) Esai xlix 6, **38**
[*see* saluatio].

salutare (τὸ σωτήριον) Ps cx 16, **3**.

saluus—reliquiae...saluae factae sunt = λίμμα...γέγονεν Ro xi 5, **28**
saluae] *Tyc Aug Ambst* vg^{clem} ; *om* d_2 *am*
[*cf* praesens].

sanctimonia (ἁγιασμὸς) 1 Co i 30, **20**
sanctificatio *r* d_2 vg *Hil Ambr Aug*.

sanctitas (ἁγιωσύνη) Ro i 4, **6**
for $\overline{\text{sc}}$itatis R, *we find* $\overline{\text{sc}}$ificationis V = *Iren Hil* d_2 *Vg*
but cf 1 The iii 13 d_2 vg.

sanctus, sancte (ἁγνὸς, ἁγνῶς) 2 Co xi 2, **5** (= *Habetdeus* 313)
Phil i 17, **69** (= d_2)
caste *r Aug*, sincere vg
but castus (ἁγνὸς)
Prov xx 9, **20**.

sanitas (ἴασις) Mal iv 2, **74**
but curatio *Cyp*293 *de Pasch Comp* 266.

sapientia (φρόνησις) Sap viii 21, **20**
Eze xxviii 4, **77**, **79**.
*(σοφία) *e.g.* Hier ix 23, **79**.
(ἐπιστήμη) Eze xxviii 3, **77**, **79**
[*see* doctrina].

satiare (ἐμπιπλάναι) Eze xxvii 25, **78** ; xxvii 33, **46** ; xxxii 5, **44**
[*see* implere, replere, saturare].

saturare (ἐμπιπλάναι) Eze xxxii 4, **44**
[*see* satiare].

scelestus (ἄνομος) Esai xiii 12, **51** (iniquus *m*418).
in Isaiah facinerosus = ἄνομος

Esai liii 12, lv 7 *Cyp*
lxvi 3 *Habetdeus*
but sceleratus Eze xviii 20 *Cyp* 645
Lc xxii 37 *b*
[*see* iniquus].

scientia (ἐπιστήμη) Eze xxviii 4[a], 5, **79**; xxviii 7, **80**; xxviii 17, **83**
substituted by Tyconius for doctrina *in repeating his continuous quotation of* Eze xxviii 2—19.
[*see* doctrina *and Introd p* xlvii].

sedes (θρόνος) Esai xiv 13, **70, 71, 72** (=*Cyp*)
Hier xvii 25, **62, 63**; xxv 38, **49**
Eze xxvi 16, **45** (=*h w*).
θρόνος = sedes Esai xiv 13 *Cyp* 669
= thronus Esai lxvi 1 *Cyp* 76, 117 (*perh. influenced by* Ac vii 49).
In the NT *and Psalms* thronus *is predominantly African, exc* Lc i 52.
[*see* thronus].

seducere (πλανᾶν) Mt xxiv 4, **5** (=MSS)
but fallere *Cyp* 365.

senior (πρέσβυς) Esai lxiii 9, **9** (=*Cyp* 72 *Iren*)
but legatus *Tert adv Marc* iv 22; *de Car Chr* 14
Hier[loc]
Vig$^2/_2$
nuntius *Priscillian* 31
[*see* legatus].

sermo (λόγος) Am i 1, **53**
Hier iii 12, **75**
Eze xx 45, **40**; xxi 1, **40**; xxviii 11, [**78**,] **80**; xxxvi 16, **32**
Ro ix 6, **27** (uerbum d_2 vg *Aug*)
[*see* uerbum].

si qui (οἵτινες) Esai xiii 15, **51**.

sicera (σίκερα) Esai xxiv 9, **47**.

sicut (ὃν τρόπον) Esai xiv 20, **77** (*cod* V)
[*see* quomodo].
(καθὰ) Ies Naue vii 25, **39**.
(καθάπερ) 1 Co xii 12, **6** (=*rell*)
2 Co iii 18, **21** (=*Hil Ambr*, tamquam *rell*).
(καθὼς) Hier xvii 22, **62**
1 Ioh ii 18, **5**
Ro xi 26, **34**.
(κατὰ τὸ γεγρ. = sicut scriptum est)
2 Co iv 13, **21** (=*rell*).
(ὥσπερ) Ioh v 26, **37** (=*Tert rell*, quomodo *e*)

Gal iv 29, **30** (= d_2, quomodo vg)
*(ὡς) *more than* 20 *times in all books*
[*see* quasi, tamquam, uelut, ut].

signaculum (ἀποσφράγισμα) Eze xxviii 12, **78, 80** (= *m*675)
consignatio *w Arnob-jun;*
both probably derived from
resignaculum *Tert adv Marc* ii 10
codd known to Hieron.
cf Hier xxii 24 signaculum *Iren*
significationem *h.*
(σφραγὶς) Ag ii 24, **81.**

simul
simul crescere (συναυξάνεσθαι) Mt xiii 30, **29** = *d chad.*

simulacrum (εἴδωλον) Eze xxxvi 25, **33**; xxxvii 23, **34**
1 Ioh v 21, **70** (idolum *q Tert*)
[*see* idolum].

sine (= ἀ- *privative*)
sine aqua (ἄνυδρος) Ioel ii 20, **73**
Soph ii 13, **42**
[inaquosus *Cyp* Esai (xli 19,) xliii 20, *k* Mt xii 43].
sine macula (ἄμωμος) Eze xxviii 15, **78, 83** (= *w*)
[inuituperabilis *Tert adv Marc* ii 10].
sine querella (ἄμεμπτος) Lc i 6, **13**; Phil iii 6, **12** [= *rell*].
but cf insanabilis (ἀνίατος)
(aurum) quod non tetegit ignem (τὸ ἄπυρον).

species (κάλλος) Esai lxii 3, **81** = *Cyp* 77 *sic* (Esai liii 2)
[*see* decor].

speciosus (καλὸς) Cant iv 7, **10**
καλὸς = decorus Cant i 5, **10** *bis.*

spiritu elatus (πνευματοφόρος) Soph iii 4, **42**
[spiritalis *Lucif*].

splendor (λαμπήνη *vid*) Esai lxvi 20, **63.**

stella (ἀστὴρ) Ge xxvi 4, **23**
Esai xiii 10, **51**; xiv 13, **70, 71, 72**
Ap ii 28, xxii 16, **71**
Abd 4, **72** (= ἄστρων, *but* א* *has* ἀστέρων)
[*see* astrum].

strages (πτῶσις) Zech xiv 12, 15 *bis*, **49**
[*see* ruina].

studia, -orum (ἐπιτηδεύματα) Os xii 2, **28**
[*see* cogitationes].

stupere (ἐξιστάναι) Eze xxvi 16, **45** (= *w*); xxvii 35, **46**; xxxii 10, **44.**

stupor—in stupore mentis (ἐκστάσει)
Eze xxvi 16, **45** (= *h w*)
[*cf* mentis alienatione].

sub *with acc.*
sub uirgam meam = ὑπὸ τὴν ῥάβδον μου
Eze xx 37, **35**
(sub uirga mea V).
subditus (ὑπόδικος) Ro iii 19, **12**.
(ὑποχείριος) Esai lviii 3, **76**
Baruch ii 4 *ger*
*but Cyp*108 *has* subiectos *in quoting* Esai lviii 3.
subiectus esse (ὑποτάσσεσθαι) Ro viii 7, **16**.
subintrare (παρεισέρχεσθαι) Ro v 20, **13**, *also* **18** *cod* V (=*rell*)
[*see* subintroire].
subintroire (παρεισέρχεσθαι) Ro v 20, **18**
subintrare *rell and p* **13**
introire *and its compounds are characteristically African*
[*see* subintrare].
subsolanus (ἀπηλιώτης) Hier xxxii 26, **53**
Eze xx 47, **40**; xxi 4, **41**.
substantia (τὰ ὑπάρχοντα) Mt xxv 14, **61**, **84** (=*d f Hil*)
cf facultates **82**[31]
and O. L. Bibl. Texts II 135, *where we may add to* Lc xii 15 res uestras *Cyp*$^2/_2$.
succendere (ἀνάπτειν) Hier xvii 27, **62**
[*see* incendere].
(ἐκκαύειν) Eze xx 48, **40**.
superari (ἡττᾶσθαι) Esai xiii 15, **52**
[*see* minorari].
superducere (ἐπάγειν) Gen xviii 19, **24**
Esai xlviii 9, **9**
Hier xxv 36, 37, **49**.
superinponere (περιτιθέναι) Esai xlix 18, **82**.
superlatives (*for positives*)
[*see* optimus, pessimus, proximus].
surgere (ἀνιστάναι) Hier xxxii 27, **54**.
suscitare (οἰκοδομεῖν, *but cf* Mc xiii 2, xiv 58 D)
Mt xxvii 40, **75**.
sustinere (μένειν *and* ὑπομένειν) Esai lix 9 *bis*, **74**.
tactus (ἁφή) 2 Regn vii 14, **37** (actibus *for* tactibus RV)
Eph iv 16, Col ii 19, **3**.
tamquam (ὡς) Eze xxviii 2, **77**, **79** (=*w*)
1 Pet ii 5, **83** (=*Aug Fulg Priscil*68 vg)
1 Co iv 7, **79** (*quasi Cyp*116 *rell*).

In Eze xxviii 6, *where there is the same phrase in the Greek as in ver* 2, *both w and Tyc have* sicut *for* ὡς.

[quasi 1 Pet ii 5 *Hil*]

[*see* quasi, sicut, uelut, ut].

tantum (-πλασίων) Ps lxvii 18, **60**
Mc x 30, **59** (=MSS *exc k*)
Lc xviii 30, **59** (=*Cyp rell*).

tenebrescere (σκοτάζειν) Esai xiii 10, **51**

[*see* obscurare].

tenebricare (συσκοτάζειν) Am viii 9, **74** (tenebricabit)=‘*Tert*’ *adv Iud* § 13
also { *Cyp* Mt xxiv 29 (σκοτίζειν)
k Mc xiii 24 (σκοτίζειν)
Vig Mi iii 6 (συσκοτίζειν).

In Am viii 9 R *has* tenebriscauit ; *other renderings are*
contenebrescet *w*
contenebrabit *Tert adv Marc* iv 41
tenebrescet ‘*Tert*’ *adv Iud* § 10
obtenebrabitur *Cyp* 91.

cf contenebricauit (συνεσκότασεν) 3 Regn xviii 45 *Lucif*

[*see* obscurare].

thronus (θρόνος) 2 Regn vii 13, 16, **37**

[*see* sedes].

timere (φοβεῖσθαι) Esai xiii 2, **50**
Eze xxvi 16, 18, **45** (=*h w*) ; xxvii 28, **45**
1 Ioh iv 18, **25** (=*Tert* $^2/_2$ *rell*)

[*see* metuere].

titulus (στήλη) Esai xix 19, **43**.

tollere (αἴρειν) Esai xiii 2, **50** ; xxxiii 23, **10**
Hier xvii 21, **62**
Lc xvii 31, **69** (=*rell*)

[*see* auferre, extollere, tollere].

totus (πᾶς) Eze xxxvi 10, **36**
so k Mt ii 3, iii 5 ; Mc xi 18 : *elsewh.* omnis *or* uniuersus.

transgressio (παράβασις) Ro iv 15, **24**
praeuaricatio d_2 vg *Aug*.

transire, *vb. neut.* (προκόπτειν) Ro xiii 12, **57** (=*Cyp* 425)
praecessere d_2 vg *Aug Ambr*.

transmigratio (παροικεσία) Eze xx 38, **35**
incolatus *m*455.

tribulatio (θλίψις) Ps xc 15, **3**

[*see* pressura].

triticum (σῖτος) Eze xxxvi 29, **33** (=Hier xxiii 28 *h Cyp* 715)
Mt xiii 25, 29, 30 MSS *incl e* (not *k*)
Lc xxii 31 *Cyp* 288, 499 *rell* ;
but frumentum
Ag i 11 *Cyp* 355
Hier xxiii 28 *Habetdeus* 314

Mt xiii 25, 29, 30 *k*
Lc iii 17 *e*.

tumultus (ταραχὴ) Eze xxx 4, **43**
[*cf* Mc xiii 8+et turbelae *q*].

uagulari (ῥεμβεύειν) Esai xxiii 16, **46**.
uagulari *is apparently* ἅπαξ λεγόμενον. ῥεμβεύειν *does not again occur in the Greek Bible.*

ualere (ἰσχύειν) Ex i 9, **55**.
(ἐνισχύειν) Esai xxxiii 23, **10**
[*see* inualere].

uastare (διασπείρειν) Esai xxiv 1, **47**.
(προνομεύειν) Esai x 13, **75** ; xxiv 3, **47**.

uastatio (ἐρήμωσις) Mt xxiv 15, **5** (=*e Cyp* 335)
'desolutionis' *k* Mc xiii 14
[*see* desolatio *and* abominatio].
(προνομὴ) Esai xxiv 3, **47**
Eze xxxvi 5, **36**
[*see* perditio].

uelut (ὡς) Ps cxiii 4 *bis*, **73** ; cxxv 1, **67**
Esai x 14 *bis*, **75** ; xiv 19, **70**, **76** ; xxiii 15, **46** ; xliv 22[a], **9**
[*see* quasi, sicut, tamquam, ut].

uepres (φάραγξ) Eze xxxii 6, **44**
[*see* riuus].

uerbum (λόγος) Esai i 10, **50**
Hier xvii 20, **62**
Eze xx 47, **40**
Ioh i 14, **7**, **68** ; v 24, **36** (sermonem *e*)
[*see* sermo].
(ῥῆμα) Esai xlii 16, **9**.

uestis (ἱματισμὸς) Zech xiv 14, **49**.

uestitus (ἔνδυμα) Mt xxii 11, **83**
uestem *or* uestimentum *rell.*
uestitus=ἔνδυμα *e.g.* Mt iii 4, vi 28, vii 15 *k* ; xxviii 3 *e*.

uexare (κακοῦν) Hier xxxii 29, **54**
cf Ps xciii 5, cv 32, cvi 39 lat$^{vt\text{-}vg}$ (*not*^{heb}).

uincere (κατισχύειν *with gen*)
Mt xvi 18, **63** (=*a e corb Cyp*$^{2}/_{2}$ *Opt Aug*$^{3}/_{3}$)
praeualere *rell*
[*cf* praeualere].
(νικᾷν) Ap ii 26, **71** (=*rell*).

uindicator (ἐκδικητὴς) Ps viii 3, **76**
(ἅπ. λεγ. *in* LXX)
'*nonnulli codices* defensorem *habent, sed uerius* uindicatorem' *Aug*^{loc}.

uires (ἰσχὺς) Zech xiv 14, **49**
cf k, xciii
[*see* fortitudo, uirtus].

uirtus * (δύναμις, *passim*).
(δυναστεία) Sap vi 3, **72**.
(ἰσχὺς) Eze xxxii 12 *bis*, **44**
[*see* fortitudo, uires].

ultra (ἔτι *in negative sentences*)
Eze xx 48, **40**; xxi 5, **41**; xxvii 36, **46**; xxxii 13, **45**; xxxvi 30, **33**; xxxvii 22 *bis*, **34**
[*see* iam, adhuc].

unguentum (ἄρωμα) Cant iv 16, **74**.

uocem dare (φωνεῖν, *used of a bird's cry*)
Soph ii 14, **42**
(cantare *is used of the cock-crow in all* MSS *of the Gospels*).

ut (ὡς) Soph iii 3 *bis*, **42**
Ro i 21, **84** (=*Habetdeus* 315)
[*see* quasi, sicut, tamquam, uelut].

On the whole I believe the list bears out the conclusions which seemed to be indicated by direct comparison with Cyprian. Characteristic 'African' words are found in all parts of the Bible, words which can hardly be paralleled among O. Latin authorities outside *k e* or Cyprian himself[1]. Moreover there are several instances of strange or irregular readings, which prove on reference to be no inaccuracies of Tyconius, but true peculiarities of the Cyprianic version[2]. Indeed the use of *pressura* in the Apocalypse for θλίψις (= *Tert*), of the deponent imperative in *profetare* (= *k*), and of *saeculum* for καιρὸς in Mc x 30 (= *k*) seems to be a survival of a yet earlier stage of the African Latin. On the other hand there are not a few renderings which mark a stage in the African text later than Cyprian[3].

[1] E.g. *animatio, decenter, deformatio, facinus admittere, ille* (=art.), *imber, indignatio* (θυμὸς), *parturitio, potare, proximus* (ἐγγὺς), *quotquot annis;* we may add to these the marked preference for *iste, quoniam*, and the avoidance of *adpropiare, epulari, furor, ibi, improperare* and *a longe*.

[2] See *adesse, arbor, animus, cauere, emittere, expirare, imperium, lux, mandatum-praeceptum, plebs*, and *requiescere facere*.

[3] E.g. *erat* (ἦν) for 'fuit,' *euangelizare* for 'adnuntiare,' *pinna* for 'ala,' *plangere se* for 'lamentari,' *princeps sacerdotum* for 'pontifex,' *sanitas* for 'curatio,' *seducere* for 'fallere,' *sine* (=ἀ- privative), *tantum* for '-plicia,' and the constant insertion of the copula where not expressed in the Greek.

The only point to which I here wish to draw attention is the differing usage in the various books. There are certain words, among which are several of the most marked 'African' expressions, which are only found in certain parts of the Bible. The following list contains the most noteworthy examples; it will be noticed that the distinction is most marked between Isaiah and Ezekiel.

adhuc (ἔτι) *Soph*$^1/_1$ *Eze*$^1/_8$	ultra *Eze*$^7/_8$
altus (ὑψηλὸς) *Esai*$^4/_4$	excelsus *Eze*$^2/_2$
claritas (δόξα) *Esai*$^2/_3$ *Ioh*$^1/_1$ (? 2 Cor$^1/_1$)	gloria *Esai*$^1/_3$ (? 2 *Cor*$^1/_1$)
magnificare (δοξάζειν) *Esai*$^1/_1$ *Ro*$^1/_1$	glorificare *Ps*$^1/_1$ (*Dan*$^1/_1$)
colligere (συνάγειν) *Zech*$^1/_1$ *Esai*$^6/_6$	congregare *Eze*$^2/_2$
facinus (ἀνομία) *Esai*$^2/_2$ 2 *Thes*$^1/_1$	iniquitas *Eze*$^3/_3$
scelestus (ἄνομος) *Esai*$^1/_1$	iniquus *Eze*$^1/_1$
felix (μακάριος) *Ps*$^1/_1$	beatus *Mt*$^1/_1$ *Ioh*$^1/_1$
fortitudo (ἰσχὺς) *Esai*$^2/_2$	uirtus *Eze*$^2/_2$, uires *Zech*$^1/_1$
iniuria (ὕβρις) *Esai*$^2/_2$	contumelia *Eze*$^1/_1$
inquinare (μιαίνειν) *Esai*$^1/_1$	{contaminare *Eze*$^1/_2$ {polluere *Eze*$^1/_2$
introire (εἰσέρχεσθαι) *Ps*$^1/_1$ *Esai*$^1/_1$ *Mt*$^1/_1$	intrare *Gen*$^1/_1$ *Hier*$^1/_1$ *Eze*$^1/_1$ *Ro*$^1/_1$
lumen (φῶς) *Sap*$^1/_1$ *Am*$^1/_1$ *Esai*$^5/_7$ *Eze*$^1/_1$ 2 *Cor*$^1/_1$	lux *Esai*$^2/_7$ *Lc*$^1/_1$ (=rell) 1 *Ioh*$^1/_1$ (=Cyp)
maledictum (ὀνειδισμὸς) *Esai*$^1/_1$	obprobrium *Eze*$^2/_2$
pressura (θλίψις) *Col*$^1/_1$ *Ap*$^1/_1$	tribulatio *Ps*$^1/_1$
purgare (καθαρίζειν) *Esai*$^1/_1$ *Hier*$^1/_1$	mundare *Eze*$^3/_3$
sagittatio (τόξευμα) *Esai*$^1/_1$	sagitta *Eze*$^1/_1$
species (κάλλος) *Esai* $^1/_1$	decor *Eze*$^5/_5$

Thus there are at least twelve marked differences between the vocabulary of Tyconius' text of Isaiah and that of Ezekiel. This can be explained in two ways: either the original translations were independent, or the books of the African Bible suffered independent revision. Unfortunately there is but little extant testimony to decide this most interesting question. The fragments of the Weingarten MS (*w*), which agree so strikingly with the text of Tyconius in Ezekiel, contain no verses from Isaiah, and the quotations from Ezekiel in Cyprian amount only to twenty-three verses. The single piece of direct evidence relates to the rendering of *ἀνομία*, which appears in Tyconius as 'facinus' in Isaiah but 'iniquitas' in Ezekiel. 'Facinus' is also the word used by Cyprian in Isaiah, while in his quotation of Eze ix 4 we find 'iniquitas' (*Cyp* 90, 367); on the other hand 'facinus' is used in the same verse by 'Tert' *adv Iud* § 11 (Oehler ii 732)[1]. S. Cyprian therefore agrees with Tyconius, but the compiler of *adv Iud* retains what seems to be the older rendering. If then we might generalise from this single instance, it would seem that the difference of usage in the text of Tyconius was the result of partial revision of the African Bible anterior to S. Cyprian.

IX. *Selected Readings.*

The quotations of Tyconius are mainly useful to the Biblical critic for the study of the Latin versions and their history, but there are parts of the Latin Old Testament where Tyconius is an important witness to the text of the LXX. His exegetical method led him often to quote passages untouched by other writers, while the isolation of his position as a Donatist, an African schismatic, helped to preserve the Biblical text he used from emendation from the Greek. It is most important to remember, before discussing readings offered by Tyconius, that there is always a very considerable probability that any reading attested by him was derived from a text which had not been influenced by the Greek since the middle of the second century. In dealing with Tyconius' text we are antecedent to the Hexapla, antecedent to the Decian Persecution. Such a line of transmission may preserve genuine readings independent of all our Greek MSS. In a word, the textual genealogy renders it not absolutely impossible that the Latin Version, and therefore sometimes Tyconius as representing the Latin Version, may be right where all other authorities have gone wrong.

The following ten passages have been selected to shew what help the Old Latin sometimes affords us in the criticism of the text of the LXX, with special reference to the evidence of Tyconius.

[1] See above p lxviii.

1. Examples of spurious additions to the LXX, found in most MSS, but rejected by a small group including B *Tyc.*

Esai xxiv 5

ἤλλαξαν τὰ προστάγματα διαθήκην αἰώνιον B al^{p} cop *Hieron* *Tyc*47

προσταγματα] + κ̅υ̅ A + *μου* 301
+ *διεσκεδασε* 62-147
+ *διεσκεδασαν* ℵ 198 22-36-48-51-90-93-144-233-308

διεσκεδασαν is added under ⁜ in Q, but the word is rendered without remark in *Syr-Hex.*

The MS 198 is the same as 33 of the Gospels. The group 22-...-308 includes *all* the MSS assigned by Dr Field to the Lucianic recension[1]. The MSS 62-147 contain Lucianic readings, but their singular element is often akin to the Old Latin.

Eze xxx 3

ἡμέρα πέρας ἐθνῶν ἔσται B cop sah *Tyc*43

ημερα] *om* 106
+ *νεφελης* MSS *Hieron*

In the Hexapla *νεφελης* is added under ⁜ by 87 *Syr-Hex*

Thus here our Hexaplar authorities assert that *νεφελης* is an addition, but B is alone among Greek MSS in omitting it. It is found even in S. Jerome, who in his translations from the LXX in the Prophets is generally very faithful to the Vatican text.

2. Examples of spurious additions to the LXX, found in B, but rejected by other authorities including Tyconius.

Esai xxix 13

ἐγγίζει μοι ὁ λαὸς οὗτος τοῖς χείλεσιν αὐτῶν τιμῶσίν με ℵA 26 49 *h* sah *Iust Tryph* *Tyc*8

τοις χειλεσιν] *pr και εν* 301
pr εν (or *e sil*) 87 91 97 198 306

(ℵ has *μου* for *μοι* and *τιμουσιν* for *τιμωσιν*)

[1] Field, *Hexapla* lxxxviii. Where all or most of these MSS agree I shall quote them under the sign ƛ.

ο λαος ουτος] + *εν τω στοματι αυτου και εν* B ƛ 62-147(*om εν bis*) cop(*om και*) *Orig*$^{3, 492}$ *Hieron*

The words ἐν τῷ στόματι αὐτοῦ are in the Hexapla under asterisk (※). The words used by Tyconius are: "*non cognouisti* autem illi dicitur qui...Deo *labiis adpropinquet, corde tamen longe separatus sit.*" It is evident that the text of Tyconius contained ἐγγίζει, but as that word is construed with τοῖς χείλεσιν the addition ἐν τῷ στόματι κτλ could not have been there. *Tyc* therefore supports ℵA *h Iust.* No punctuation is given to ℵA *h*, but in the Sahidic τοῖς χείλεσιν is joined with τιμῶσιν, which seems preferable to the division adopted by Tyconius.

Dr Hatch (*Essays in Biblical Greek* pp 177—179) tries to prove the existence of a still shorter form of the text in Isaiah, a form in fact identical with Mt xv 8 = Mk vii 6, in which ἐγγίζει μοι is wanting. But the theory rests on Patristic authority only, and in such cases it is often difficult to tell whether a Father is not quoting the Prophet through the medium of the Gospel. In the case of S. Cyprian this is certainly what has happened. He quotes the words in the same form three times (Hartel 712 736 and 801), the last place being the clearest and fullest. He there says: "Sicut per Esaiam prophetam clamat et dicit *Populus iste labiis honorificant me, cor uero eorum...doctrinas hominum docentes.* item Dominus in euangelio increpans similiter et obiurgans ponit et dicit *Reicitis mandatum Dei, ut traditionem uestram statuatis.*" The last line is Mk vii 9 as quoted elsewhere by S. Cyprian $^3/_3$, and seeing that the Gospel passage was in his mind it seems more reasonable to refer the whole quotation to S. Mark (with the text of which it agrees literally), than to postulate a direct reference to Isaiah. The fact that the prophet is distinctly mentioned does not militate against this view, since in the Gospel also Isaiah's name is prominently brought forward.

But if the passages in S. Cyprian are references to the Gospel, the evidence for an early African shorter recension of the verse breaks down, and we can put in its place the form found in the quotation from Tyconius, which supports the reading of ℵA sah and *h* (the fifth century Latin Palimpsest of the Prophets at Würzburg).

Esai xlix 18

Ζῶ ἐγώ, λέγει Κύριος, ὅτι πάντας αὐτοὺς ἐνδύσῃ ℵA 26 49 86 198 239 306 (106 *-σει*) cop *Tyc*82 '*Aug*' *de Vnit Eccl*

ενδυσῃ] *pr ως κοσμον* B al *Hieron*

\+ *ως στολην* λ 62-147 *Ambr*

\+ *ως κοσμον* 23

Here again B *Hieron* are convicted of false addition, the words being under asterisk in the Hexapla[1].

3. Examples of corrupt readings which are found in all extant Greek MSS of the LXX, but not in the Old Latin.

Eze xxviii 7

καὶ τρώσουσιν τὸ κάλλος σου εἰς ἀπώλειαν w *Tyc*77 cop sah[2]

τρωσουσιν] *στρωσουσιν* MSS *Hieron* (humiliabunt)

The Hebrew is וְחִלְּלוּ, which might be translated *καὶ βεβηλώσουσι* (as Theodotion and most other interpreters), or *τρώσουσι* (as Tyconius, who has *uulnerabunt*), but never *στρώσουσιν*. The Vulgate has *polluent* agreeing with Theodotion. The corruption of *τρώσουσιν* to *στρώσουσιν* was easy.

The expression "they shall wound thy beauty" is very harsh, but for that reason all the more certainly the genuine rendering of the LXX, since it is a literal translation of the Hebrew original. Nevertheless *τρώσουσιν* has disappeared from *all* our Greek MSS, a fact which tends to shew that in some books at least of the Bible they all have a common element later than the chief versions.

Eze xxxvi 8

ὁ λαός μου ὅτι ἐγγίζουσιν τοῦ ἐλθεῖν *Tyc*36 *m*660

εγγιζουσιν] *ελπιζουσιν* MSS cop

The Hebrew is כִּי קָרְבוּ לָבוֹא, so that it is evident that the

[1] In the latter half of the same verse *Tyc* reads *ὡς κόσμον νύμφης* with ℵA and almost all other authorities including *Hieron*, but B 23 have *ὡς κόσμον ὡς νύμφη*. I believe B to have a worse text in Isaiah than in the rest of the Prophets; the readings given above are comparable to the Western element in the Pauline Epistles (Hort, *Introd* § 204).

[2] The Sahidic is ⲛ̄ⲥⲉⲕⲱⲛⲥ; for the rendering compare Iob xxxiii 23, Prov vii 26 in the same version.

reading of the MSS ελπιζογςιν is a corruption of εγγιζογςιν, as in fact Schleusner conjectured in the last century[1]. Here two points are worthy of notice:—(i) Tyconius and the Speculum stand alone against all extant LXX authority in supporting the true reading ἐγγίζουσιν[2]; (ii) Tyconius and the Speculum do not agree literally in their Latinity. The renderings run as follow:

populus meus, qui adpropinquat uenire	*Tyc*36
populus meus, qui adpropriant uenire	*m*660

Possibly *qui* stands in the place of an original *quia* (Cod V* of Tyconius actually reads *quiapropinquat*), and the singular verb in *Tyc* looks like a correction caused by 'populus.' But *adpro-p(r)iare*[3] is a word not used in the earlier African text (*k Cyp*), and is therefore a correction in *m*. The circumstance is worth noting, as illustrating what has been said before, that the extensive variations from earlier African authorities found in *m* do not seem to have arisen through revision from the Greek.

Esai xiv 13, stellas Dei (*Cyp*669 *Tyc*70) as a rendering of τῶν ἀστέρων τοῦ οὐρανοῦ (Gk MSS cop *Ambr Aug Hieron*) has been noticed in the preceding section[4]. Here again the African Latin agrees with the undoubtedly genuine Hebrew text against the other LXX authorities.

4. In the preceding examples Tyconius has been the constant member in a small group which has preserved the true text of the LXX in places where the mass of authorities have transmitted a corruption. I shall now give some examples of readings where, owing to the defective state of the African Latin evidence, Tyconius stands almost or quite alone in witnessing to the true text.

Ps lxxix 16

καὶ κατάρτισαι αὐτὴν ἣν ἐφύτευσεν ἡ δεξιά σου,
καὶ ἐπὶ υἱὸν [ἀνθρώπου ὃν] ἐκραταίωσας σεαυτῷ.

[1] Schleusner, *Novus Thesaurus philologico-criticus*, quoted by Cornill, p. 412.

[2] The Sahidic (*Ciasca* 299) is unfortunately wanting. The Coptic (*Tattam* 190) has: "for they hope (ςεερϩελπις) to come to this place."

[3] For the spelling of *adpropiare* see Lc x 34 in Bp Wordsworth's *Vulgate*, Clem. *ad Cor* 25 (lat), etc.

[4] p lix.

The words in brackets are omitted by Tyconius 6.

It will be convenient to divide the discussion into two parts.

i. The original reading of Tyconius and the Old Latin.

ii. The original reading of the LXX.

i. The text of Tyconius on p 6 is

et perfice eam quam plantauit dextera tua
et in filium conroborasti tibi.

This is the reading of *cod* R. In *cod* V the last line is

et filium hominis quem confirmasti tibi.

The Monza Epitome (M) as usual abridges the quotation, reading

"uineam de egypto *et ct usque* filium hominis quem confirmasti tibi."

Now the reading of VM only differs from the reading of the ordinary Psalters by omitting 'super' before "filium hominis." The reading of R on the other hand is not that of any of the common texts, and it approves itself as African by the word 'conroborare' for the more usual 'confirmare.' 'Conroborare' has found a place elsewhere three times in the Psalms in various texts[1], but its true character is best seen from the readings in Lc i 80, ii 20, the only places where κραταιοῦσθαι occurs in the Gospels. Here *e* has 'corroborare' in each place, while other texts have 'confortare' or 'confirmare'[2].

But the reading of R as the genuine text of Tyconius, and therefore also of the African Latin, is supported by two pieces of negative evidence. The half verse *et* [*in*] *filium...tibi* is omitted by the S. Germain Psalter (the text printed by Sabatier as his chief authority), and a quotation of Ps lxxix 9—16 in *m* 642, 643 breaks off at *quam plantauit dextera tua.* Thus we have (1) the common text of ver. 16^{b}, a smooth inoffensive reading; (2) two authorities for omission, one in a continuous text, the other a judicious 'non-quotation'; (3) the reading of *cod* R, which is harsh. Does it not seem likely that (3) is the original form of the version?

[1] Ps cii 11 (vg), Ps civ 4 (codd. known to *Aug*); Ps cxli 7 (*Aug Prosp*).

[2] 'Corroborare' also occurs Eph iii 16 vg, but no African evidence is here extant.

ii. When we apply the reading *et in filium conroborasti tibi* to the criticism of the LXX text, the first point to notice is that the construction which made a possible sense in Latin is impossible in the Greek. The sense cannot be "...the Vine which thy right hand planted and made strong for thyself into a son," for the Greek is *ἐπὶ υἱὸν* not *εἰς υἱὸν*. In other words the Greek which underlies the quotation of Tyconius was almost impossible to construe, and consequently invited emendation. It is not till we refer back to the Hebrew that we get any light. It runs thus:

וכנה אשר נטעה ימינך
ועל בן אמצתה לך

Whatever the true interpretation of this very difficult passage may be, there can be little doubt that here our present Hebrew text is the parent of the LXX. When we find that the best text of the Old Latin agrees verbally in an unintelligent word-for-word rendering of the Hebrew, it is difficult to avoid believing that the *ἀνθρώπου ὃν* of the common text is an interpolation from the similar words in ver. 18, inserted to make some kind of sense. How close and how unintelligent this translation was may be best seen by comparing the Hebrew and the Latin word for word. Nothing but the influence of the original Hebrew, as expressed through two faithful unintelligent translations, explains the omission of the relative before 'conroborasti.' We can scarcely suppose Tyconius would or could have emended his Latin Psalter from the Hebrew directly; his text therefore must have come through the Greek LXX in a purer form than survives to-day in our MSS.

If this view of the passage be accepted, it is important to notice that the bizarre spectacle of the reading of a single 9th century Latin patristic MS preferred to all other LXX authorities is quite justifiable from a genealogical point of view. *Cod* R is the best MS of Tyconius, our other authorities for his text having been corrupted in this passage from the Vulgate; Tyconius is in this place the only representative of the African version, our other authorities being absent, or omitting the half verse; the African version is our oldest direct authority for the LXX, and it has been several times proved to be right when the best Greek MSS have gone wrong.

Esai xiii 3

The MSS of the LXX vary so much in this verse that it will be convenient to quote at once the Hebrew as it stands in the Massoretic text as a sort of standard.

אני צויתי למקדשי גם קראתי
גבורי לאפי עליזי גאותי

The MSS of the LXX fall into two groups

a includes ƛ and 62-147
β includes B* cop sah *Hieron* and ℵAB^mg.

It will be convenient to take the half verses separately, the division being after קראתי, as in all LXX texts, not after למקדשי as in the Massoretic punctuation.

The readings after *ἐγὼ συντάσσω,* which begins the verse in all authorities except 62-147 (which have *ἐγὼ συντελέσω*) are:—

a. *ἡγιασμένοι εἰσίν· καὶ ἐγὼ ἄγω αὐτούς·* ƛ 62-147
β. *καὶ ἐγὼ ἄγω αὐτούς·* B* cop sah *Hieron*
και εγω] *om εγω* sah[1]
β₂. *καὶ ἐγὼ ἄγω αὐτούς· ἡγιασμένοι εἰσίν· καὶ ἐγὼ ἄγω αὐτούς* ℵAB^mg *Syr Hex* al.

A comparison of *a*, *β* and β_2 with the Hebrew will I think shew the general superiority of *a*. It has equivalents, though they are unintelligent, for each Hebrew word in its proper order: at the same time if this equivalence had been reached by emendation from the Hebrew we should have expected *αὐτούς* to disappear; and, further, *ἐγὼ ἄγω* is scarcely a translation to קראתי, "I have called."

β differs from *a* by dropping the awkward clause *ἡγιασμένοι εἰσίν,* which hangs in the air; while the most natural explanation of β_2 is that it is an unsuccessful attempt to emend *β* by *a*. *a* in fact has been added to *β*. It is of course conceivable that *β* has been derived from β_2 by homoeoteleuton, but in that case it is very difficult to explain how β_2 ever came into existence. It

[1] The Bodleian MS of the Sahidic (D) gives the reading β_2, but as Ciasca remarks (*Introd* vol 2, xxxiv) the readings of this MS are of no value for the original form of the version.

does not commend itself as an original, or as a translation, and it does not appear in any text earlier than the Hexapla.

The reading of *Tyc* 50 is

quia ecce ego praecipio · sanctificati sunt et uoco eos.

"Quia ecce" is prefixed by no other authority and must be a Latin insertion, either due to the translator, or to Tyconius himself, or more probably to a copyist[1]. Similarly *cod* R here prefixes *qui* to *sanctificati sunt.* This is rightly omitted by *cod* V, which has however the corruption *uocē* for *uoco eos.* In passages like this, which in any case make no intelligible sense in the Latin, those readings which are more in literal agreement with some Greek text are to be preferred.

If then we reject "quia ecce," we get as the Greek text underlying Tyconius

ἐγὼ συντάσσω· ἡγιασμένοι εἰσίν· καὶ καλῶ αὐτούς

that is *a*, but with the better reading καλῶ for ἐγὼ ἄγω. Unless therefore we fall back once more on the inconceivable hypothesis that Tyconius has emended directly from the Hebrew, the Old Latin has again preserved the true rendering of קראתי where our Greek MSS have a corruption[2].

The αὐτούς of LXX probably comes from a mistaken reading of קראתי as קראתי' (*i.e.* קְרָאתִים) 'I have called them.' So also the next word גִּבּוֹרַי is read גִּבּוֹרִים in the LXX. How למקדשי appears in the LXX as ἡγιασμένοι εἰσίν is difficult to say; there is no trace of a reading ΗΓΙΑΣΜΕΝΟΙΣ, though if we may conjecture that as the original rendering of the LXX the common text might easily have arisen from it by reading the C as \\, a contraction for εἰσι (see Maunde Thompson's Palaeography *p* 96, *note*).

Thus by taking the text of Tyconius, and reading ΗΓΙΑΣΜΕΝΟΙΣ for the disconnected ΗΓΙΑΣΜΕΝΟΙΕΙΣΙ, we bring the LXX into line

[1] Compare *quia* added before Os xii 3 by *Tyc* 28, and *quae* added after *columba* Zeph iii 1, 2 by *Tyc* 42.

[2] Parsons MS 301 has εγω συντασσω και εγω καλω αυτους· ηγιασμενοι εισιν. This may be a reminiscence of the text preserved in Tyconius, but the position of the clause και εγω...αυτους shews the text of this MS is the result of some complicated process.

with the Hebrew. It is to be noticed that this text is quite independent of the renderings of Aquila, Symmachus and Theodotion, fragments of whose versions are given in Field.

In the second half of Esai xiii 3 the attestation falls into the same two groups. For גבורי לאפי we find

a. γίγαντες ἔρχονται τὸν θυμόν μου παῦσαι λ 62-147 *Tyc*50
...πανσαι τον θ. μου 106

β. γίγαντες ἔρχονται πληρῶσαι τὸν θυμόν μου ℵAB cop sah.

To render παῦσαι in Tyconius we find *linire* (*i.e.* lenire) in *cod* V, but *mitigare* in *cod* R. I have accepted *lenire*, mainly because παύειν is rendered by *lenire* in *Cyp* 785, but by *mitigare* in *Opt* 63. Thus *lenire* appears in the earlier African text, *mitigare* in the later; as both readings are found in the MSS of Tyconius, it is more likely that *mitigare* is the correction and *lenire* the original than *vice versa.* In any case they represent the same Greek text.

It is very suggestive to find a pair of rival readings such as these in the LXX text, both pre-Hexaplar, and neither agreeing with the Hebrew as we have it. This is not the place to discuss the origin of the LXX paraphrase; I am only here concerned to point out that the addition of Tyconius,—that is the Old Latin,—to the witnesses for παῦσαι is another proof of the existence of an extremely ancient element in the mixed 'Lucianic' text. That text contains many Hexaplar additions and other such changes, but we also find in it readings demonstrably ancient and yet independent of other known texts.

To sum up. What do we learn from the Old Latin Version of the Prophets, of which version Tyconius is so often the only representative? The answer may be divided into five heads.

1. The Old Latin brings us the best independent proof we have that the Hexaplar signs introduced by Origen can be relied on for the reconstruction of the LXX. Passages in Hexaplar MSS to which is prefixed the asterisk (⁎) profess to be no part of the original LXX, but to have been added from other sources. *No such passage is found in any genuine form of the African Latin.* The only apparent exceptions to this statement, and they are

surprisingly few, are cases where we have reason to suppose that the asterisks themselves are misplaced.

2. The Old Latin together with the Hexaplar text (omitting of course the passages under asterisk) often agree as to omission with the text of B. The greater number of the passages under asterisk are not found at all in B, nor throughout Isaiah in A, though in many cases the words in question are inserted without any qualifying mark into the text of all or nearly all other MSS.

3. Yet the same authorities (the Old Latin and the Hexaplar text) convict B here and there of interpolation, especially in Isaiah. It sometimes happens in the course of a few verses that B will in one place be almost the only MS which does not witness to an interpolation, while in another B supports an interpolation, either almost alone, or in company with a considerable following of other Greek MSS.

4. When we turn from questions of insertion and omission to questions of rendering of the Hebrew and the substitution of one Greek word for another, we find that the Old Latin in the Prophets sometimes supports 'Lucianic' readings. This fact proves that among the constituents of the eclectic text most used by the Antiochene Fathers of the fourth century there was an ancient element akin to the Old Latin, but quite independent of our leading MSS codd. AℵB. Of the numerous conflations and interpolations found in 'Lucianic' MSS there is naturally no trace in Tyconius.

5. There are renderings found in the Old Latin representing Greek readings which have disappeared from every known Greek MS, but which, by comparison with the Hebrew, are shewn to preserve the genuine text of the LXX, from which the readings of our present Greek MSS are corruptions. In these passages the Old Latin is sometimes, but not always, supported by one or both Egyptian versions. Such readings as those of the Old Latin in Eze xxviii 7 and xxxvi 8 prove that our Greek MSS, so imposing by their number and apparent independence, have common corrupt elements, and that the agreement of these MSS does not of necessity imply the general voice of antiquity.

To those who assent to these five conclusions the study of the ancient versions of the Greek Bible cannot fail to be regarded as of more importance than is generally recognised. If the three or four dozen known Greek codices of the Prophets be not really independent, but coincide here and there in palaeographical error, then those versions in which these errors are not found have a great independent value. We ought not to regard them as merely secondary authorities to be used as supports to one side or another when the Greek MSS are divided, but rather as primary authorities whose variants are worthy always of careful attention and sometimes of adoption, even when the Greek MSS are unanimous on the other side.

Finally, may it not be asked whether what has just been said has not a bearing on our view of the authorities for the text of the New Testament? If the Greek codices of the Prophets, in spite of their variations, be not wholly independent in text, and coincide in errors from which some of the early versions are free, is it impossible that the same may be the case here and there in the New Testament? If here and there B falls from its habitually high standard of purity of text and admits interpolations, may not that be the case elsewhere than in Isaiah? The general character of the 'Neutral' text so often represented by B alone stands on a sure basis, but B may here and there desert that text by an interpolation or by a substitution which may not necessarily be self-betraying.

These however are but secondary considerations compared with the general result, that in the Old Testament as in the New the text of our oldest MSS as a whole is proved by the evidence of the versions to be immensely superior to the later eclectic texts commonly used in the Greek-speaking churches from the middle of the fourth century. These later revisions sometimes preserve valuable fragments of older texts which would otherwise have been lost altogether, but it is for such fragments alone that these recensions are valuable, and not for their continuous text.

Additional Note on the "Altercatio Simonis et Theophili."

THE *Altercatio Simonis Judaei et Theophili Christiani*, a work of the 5th cent., has been shewn by Harnack (*Texte und U.* I, pt 3) to be a recasting of a much earlier document, probably the lost Dialogue of Jason and Papiscus. Moreover the earlier form of the *Altercatio* exercised a very important influence upon African writers in their choice of Messianic proof-texts from the Old Testament. As this is especially the case in S. Cyprian's *Testimonia* and in the tract *adversus Iudaeos* commonly ascribed to Tertullian, it becomes important to consider what influence the lost Dialogue, so far as we can recover it from the *Altercatio*, may have had upon the Biblical text in those works. If the text of the *Testimonia* were dependent upon the original of the *Altercatio*, it would cease to be our primary authority for the oldest 'African' Version.

Fortunately the Biblical text of the *Testimonia* appears in the vast majority of cases to be entirely uninfluenced by any extraneous source. Whatever circumstances may have guided S. Cyprian in his choice of passages, he seems to have verified them most accurately from his Bible, and variations in the *Testimonia* from the ordinary printed texts of the LXX have generally MS support. Moreover several of the favourite 2nd cent. proof-texts which rest on a corrupt reading are significantly absent from S. Cyprian's compilation; Harnack (p. 107) notices for instance that the well-known "Dominus regnauit *a ligno*" (Ps cxv 10) is not found in it.

We may therefore assume with confidence that the text of the *Testimonia* is also the text of S. Cyprian's Bible. Nevertheless the influence of the lost Dialogue remains a very probable explanation of the rare lapses into inaccuracy which occur now and then in the *Testimonia*. The texts in the *Altercatio* are not unfrequently quoted quite loosely; it is not greatly surprising to find there Deut. xxviii 44 (οὗτος ἔσται εἰς κεφαλήν, σὺ δὲ ἔσῃ εἰς οὐράν) in the form: *Eritis gentes in caput, incredulus autem populus in cauda.* But the same strange paraphrase is found in *Test* I 21[1]. Similarly the

[1] This striking resemblance is not noticed by Harnack, though it seems one of the strongest arguments for the dependence of the *Testimonia* upon some form of the *Altercatio*. This paraphrase also occurs in Commodian, possibly not directly quoted from the *Testimonia*.

inaccuracies in the quotation of Esai xxix 11, 12 (*Test* I 4) may be partly due to the Dialogue which lies behind the *Altercatio*.

Much the same results seem to come from the comparison of the tract *adv Iudaeos* with the *Altercatio*, though the quotations in the *Testimonia* reach a higher standard of accuracy than those in *adv Iudaeos*. The question of the authorship of this curious compilation would need a detailed study. As is well known, about half the work consists of extracts from the third book of Tertullian against Marcion; the remainder has been shewn to be dependent upon an early form of the *Altercatio* by Harnack, who however accepts the ascription of the whole to Tertullian[1]. But to the Biblical critic the authorship is chiefly of importance as determining the date, and from the character of the independent Biblical quotations alone this must be placed at least as early as S. Cyprian[2], and probably earlier still. Whether therefore the tract be compiled by Tertullian or not is a comparatively secondary consideration, as in either case it belongs to the earlier stages of the African Church.

The quotations of Tyconius appear to be quite independent of any form of the *Altercatio*.

1 Dr Noeldechen's study on this Treatise (*Texte und U.* XII, pt 2) has only come into my hands as these sheets are passing through the Press. He not only accepts the traditional authorship, but places the date in the earlier part of Tertullian's literary activity. On this hypothesis Tertullian used his book against the Jews as material for his larger work against Marcion.

2 See above, p lxviii.

LIBER REGVLARVM TYCONII.

R cod. Remensis 364, *saec.* ix.

V cod. Vaticanus Reginensis 590, *saec.* x.

M cod. Modoetianus, *saec.* ix—x.

D the excerpt from Rule v in the commentary of John the Deacon.

Eug the quotations from the Rules made by S. Augustine in *de Doctrina Christiana* III 30 ff. As there is no critical text of this work yet published, I have cited S. Augustine by the excerpts of Eugippius (from Knoell's edition, Vienna 1885). The preface of Tyconius is quoted by S. Augustine, but not included in Eugippius' extracts.

All readings of R and V are given, but I have not recorded all the singular readings and omissions of M.

The numeration in the margin gives the pages of the *Maxima Bibliotheca Veterum Patrum* tom vi, the edition used by Sabatier.

LIBER REGVLARVM TYCONII.

49 NECESSARIVM duxi ante omnia quae mihi uidentur libellum RV regularem scribere, et secretorum legis ueluti claues et [*Aug*] (M) luminaria fabricare. sunt enim quaedam regulae mysticae quae uniuersae legis recessus obtinent et ueritatis thesauros aliquibus inuisibiles faciunt; quarum si ratio regularum sine inuidia ut communicamus accepta fuerit, clausa quaeque patefient et obscura dilucidabuntur, ut quis prophetiae inmensam siluam perambulans his regulis quodam modo lucis ¶ *Aug* tramitibus deductus ab errore defendatur.¶

Sunt autem regulae istae:

I. De Domino et corpore eius.
II. De Domini corpore bipertito.
III. De promissis et lege.
IV. De specie et genere.
V. De temporibus.
VI. De recapitulatione.
VII. De diabolo et eius corpore.

I. DE DOMINO ET CORPORE EIVS.

Dominum eiusne corpus, id est Ecclesiam, Scriptura loquatur, sola ratio discernit, dum quid cui conueniat persuadet

Titulus. INCIPIT LIBER REGVLA|RVM TYCONII R *rubro*; IN NOMINE DNI INCIPIT | THICONI (THICONII V[a]) REGVLA LIB . I . | DE DNI CORPORE BIPERTITO. V f. 91

1—9 Necessarium ...... defendatur] *ap Aug de Doct Christ* III 30; *lectiones excerpsi e cod Vat Pal* 188 *saec ix* 2 regularem] RV*M; regulare *Aug* (MS); regularum V*corr*, *Aug* (*edd*) legis] M *Aug*; leges V; *om* R 11—17 I II etc] *om* V* 13 promisis R 14 speciae V* *et sic aliquando* 18 *titulum non habent huic regulae* RV 19 eiusne] eiusque V loquitur V*corr* 20 cui] cuique V

RV (M)

uel quia tanta est uis ueritatis extorquet. alias una persona conuenitur quam duplicem esse diuersa duorum officia edocent.

Esai liii 4, 5, 6 Sic per Esaiam: *Hic* inquit *peccata nostra feret et pro nobis dolet, ipse uulneratus est propter facinora nostra, et Deus tradidit eum pro peccatis nostris,* et cetera quae in Dominum conuenire omnis Ecclesiae ore celebratur. *Ib* 10, 11 sequitur autem et dicit de eodem: *Et Deus uult purgare illum a plaga et uult Deus a dolore auferre animam eius, ostendere illi lucem et formare illum prudentia.* numquid ei quem *tradidit pro peccatis nostris uult ostendere lucem,* et eum *formare prudentia,* cum ipse sit lux et sapientia Dei, et non corpori eius? qua re manifestum est sola ratione uideri posse quando a capite ad corpus transitum facit.

cf Dan ii 34, 35 Danihel quoque *lapidem de monte praecisum* et *inpegisse* in corpus regnorum mundi et *in puluerem commoluisse* Dominum dicit, *montem* uero *effectum et impleuisse uniuersam* 50 *terram* corpus eius. non enim—sicut quidam dicunt in contumeliam regni Dei inuictaeque hereditatis Christi, quod non sine dolore dico—Dominus totum mundum potestate et non sui corporis plenitudine occupauit. dicunt enim eo monte mundum impletum, quod liceat Christiano in omni loco, quod antea non nisi in Sion licebat offerre. quod si ita est, non opus erat dicere ex lapide montem effectum et incrementis mundum cepisse. Dominus enim noster Christus cf Ioh xvii 5, 24 *ante mundi constitutionem hanc habuit claritatem,* et cum homo in illo Dei filius fieret non paulatim ut lapis sed uno tempore accepit omnem potestatem in caelo et in terra. Dan ii 35 lapis autem incrementis *factus est mons magnus* et crescendo terram omnem texit. quod si potestate implesset uniuersam

2 diuersa] *om* R 3 edocet V* 4 sic] *pr* IN ISAIA (*sic*) R *rubro* 5 ipse] *pr* et VM 6 eum] illum V 7 dominum] d̄m R omni V ęcclesiae R, *et sic aliquando* 8, 9 illum purgare V 9 aufe^{r}re R (*sic*) 13 corpori× R* 14 faciat V 15 danihel] *pr* IN DANIELO R *rubro*; daniel R *hoc loco* praecisum] precissum R et] *om* V 16 puluere R commoluisse] comminuisse V 23 antea] ante ea R 25 coepisse R 27 in illo] ille V 29 magnus] *om* V 30 implesset] implesse R

RV [Eug] (M) terram non corpore, lapidi non compararetur. potestas res est inpalpabilis, lapis uero corpus palpabile. nec sola ratione manifestatur corpus non caput crescere, sed etiam apostolica auctoritate firmatur: *Crescimus* inquit *per omnia in eum qui* Eph iv 15, 16 *est caput, Christus, ex quo omne corpus constructum et conexum per omnem tactum subministrationis in mensuram unius cuiusque partis incrementum corporis facit in aedificationem sui.* et iterum: *Non tenens caput, ex quo omne corpus per tactus et* Col ii 19 *coniunctiones constructum et subministratum crescit in incrementum Dei.* non ergo caput, quod ex origine idem est, sed corpus crescit ex capite.

Ad propositum redeamus. scriptum est de Domino et eius corpore—quid cui conueniat ratione discernendum—: *Angelis suis mandauit de te ut custodiant te in omnibus* Ps xc 11–16 *uiis tuis, in manibus ferant te ne offendas ad lapidem pedem tuum. super aspidem et basiliscum ambulabis, et conculcabis leonem et draconem. quoniam in me sperauit eripiam eum, protegam illum quoniam cognouit nomen meum. inuocabit me et exaudiam eum, cum ipso sum in tribulatione, eripiam et glorificabo eum. longitudinem dierum adimplebo eum et ostendam illi salutare meum.* numquid de cuius obsequio *mandauit angelis suis* Deus eidem ostendit salutare suum, et non corpori eius?

§ Eug 866 Iterum: §*Sicut sponso imposuit mihi mitram et sicut* Esai lxi 10 ¶ Eug *sponsam ornauit me ornamento.*¶ unum corpus dixit utriusque sexus sponsi et sponsae, sed quid in Dominum quid in Ecclesiam conueniat ratione cognoscitur. et idem Dominus dicit in Apocalypsi: *Ego sum sponsus et sponsa.* et Ap xxii 16, 17 iterum: *Exierunt obuiam sponso et sponsae.* Mt xxv 1

Et iterum quid capitis quid corporis ratione discernendum sit per Esaiam declaratur: *Sic dicit Dominus Christo* Esai xlv 1

1 potestas] + enim V; *pr* quia M 3 manifestatur] monstratur V 8 per tactus] peractu× V*; per tactum V*corr* M 14 te 2°] *om* V* 17 eum] illum V 18 inuocauit RV, *uide Sabat. ad loc*; ἐπικαλέσεται LXX 19 exaudiam] *pr* ego V ipso] eo V eripiam] + eum V 20 longitudinem] longitudine× V*; longitudine RV*corr*; μακρότητα LXX (*codd*) 21 obsequiu× V* 22 salutarē suum V* *vid* 25 ornamentum V* *vid* unum] unus R* *vid* 27 in ecc̄la V*M 28 sponsus] *uide p* 71[27] 30 quid corporis] & corpori V 31 isaiam V

RV (M)

meo Domino cuius ego tenui dexteram ut exaudiant eum gentes—sequitur et dicit quod non nisi corpori conueniat—*et dabo tibi thesauros absconditos, inuisibiles aperiam tibi, ut scias quoniam ego sum Dominus qui uoco nomen tuum Deus Israhel, propter Iacob puerum meum et Israhel electum meum.* propter testamenta enim quae disposuit patribus ad cognoscendum se Deus aperit corpori Christi thesauros 1 Co ii 9, 10 inuisibiles, *quod oculus non uidit nec auris audiuit nec in cor hominis ascendit,* sed obdurati hominis qui non est in corpore Christi; Ecclesiae *autem reuelauit Deus per Spiritum suum.* ista quidem, quamuis hoc quoque Dei gratia sit, adhibita tamen ratione aliquando facilius uidentur.

Sunt alia in quibus huiusmodi ratio minus claret, eo quod siue in Dominum siue in corpus eius recte conueniat dictum; quam ob rem sola et maiore Dei gratia uideri possunt. sic Mt xxvi 64 in Euangelio: *A modo* inquit *uidebitis filium hominis sedentem ad dexteram uirtutis et uenientem in nubibus caeli.* alio loco dicit non uisuros uenientem in nubibus caeli nisi in Mt xxiv 30 nouissimo tantum die: *Plangent se omnes tribus terrae, et tunc uidebunt filium hominis uenientem in nubibus caeli.* utrumque autem fieri necesse est, sed primo corporis est aduentus, id est Ecclesiae, iugiter uenientis in eadem claritate inuisibili, deinde capitis, id est Domini, in manifesta claritate. si enim diceret Modo uidebitis uenientem, solius corporis intellegendus esset aduentus; si autem Videbitis, capitis aduentus. nunc uero *A modo* inquit *uidebitis uenientem,* quoniam corpore suo iugiter uenit natiuitate et similium passionum claritate. si enim renati Christi membra efficiuntur et membra corpus efficiunt, Christus est qui uenit, quoniam natiuitas aduentus Ioh i 9 est sicut scriptum est: *Inluminat omnem hominem uenientem* Eccl i 4 *in hunc mundum.* et iterum: *Generatio uadit et generatio*

1 meo domino] dn̄o meo V 5 electum] dilectum R 6 testamenta] testa V* 9 obdurati homines V* 10 ecclesiae] eccl̄a V* reuelabit V* *vid* 11 gratiae dī V 12 aliquanto R 14 in dn̄o...in corpore V 16 a modo] ammodo R; modo V 19 plangent se] plangentes V 24, 25 intelligendus V*M 25 capiti V 26 corpore] corpori R 27 similium] + ea V passionem V* *mox corr* claritatem V*M 28 corpus] *pr* quae V

RV (M) *uenit.* et iterum: *Sicut audistis quia antichristus uenit.* 1 Ioh ii 18 iterum de eodem corpore: *Si enim iste qui uenit alium* 2 Co xi 4 *Iesum praedicat.* unde Dominus cum de signo aduentus sui interrogaretur, de illo aduentu suo coepit disputare qui ab inimico corpore signis et prodigiis imitari potest. *Cauete* Mt xxiv 4 inquit *ne quis uos seducat; multi enim uenient in nomine meo,* id est in nomine corporis mei. nouissimo autem aduentu Domini, id est consummationis et manifestationis totius aduentus eius, nemo ut aliqui putant mentietur. sed quo plenius ista dicantur ordini suo relinquimus.

Nec illud erit absurdum quod ex uno totum corpus uolumus intellegi, ut filium hominis Ecclesiam; quoniam Ecclesia, id est filii Dei redacti in unum corpus, dicti sunt filius Dei, dicti unus homo, dicti etiam Deus sicut per apostolum: *Super* 2 The ii 4 *omne qui dicitur Deus aut quod colitur,—qui dicitur Deus* Ecclesia est, *quod* autem *colitur* Deus summus est,—*ut in templum Dei sedeat ostendens se quod ipse est Deus,* id est quod ipse sit Ecclesia. quale si diceret: *in templum Dei sedeat ostendens se* quod ipse sit Dei templum. aut: in Deum sedeat *ostendens se quod ipse* sit *Deus.* sed hunc intellectum synonymis uoluit obscurare.

Danihel de rege nouissimo *in Deum* inquit *locus eius* cfDan xi 36,38 *glorificabitur,* id est clarificabitur; ueluti Ecclesiam in loco Ecclesiae, *in loco sancto, abominationem uastationis* in cf Dan xi 31; Mt xxiv 15 Deum, id est in Ecclesiam, subornabit. et Dominus totum populum *sponsam* dicit et *sororem*; et apostolus Cant v 1 *uirginem sanctam,* et aduersum corpus *hominem peccati.* 2 Co xi 2 2 The ii 3 et Dauid totam Ecclesiam Christum dicit: *Faciens miseri-* Ps xvii 51 *cordias Christo suo Dauid et semini eius in aeternum.* et

3 iesum] ihm RM; xpm V 5 imitare R 7 id est] idē V* 9 mentietur] metietur V* *mox corr* 10 quo] quod R dicentur V* ordine V* 11 absordum R (*cf p* 26^{14}) 15 qui dicitur 1°] R*corr* (? *a p m*); quod dicitur R**vid* V 17 templum] RV*; templo V^bM sedeat] redeat R* (sedeat R^a) ipse est] ipse sit VM 18 templo VM 19 ostendit V 21 synonymis] *scripsi, suadente W R Smith:* si non nimis R (*ex* sinonimis); non nimis nouimus V obscurare.] *sic punctum habet* R 22, 23 danihel...clarificabitur] *supra ras in* R 22 rege] regno R 23, 24 in loco ecclesiae] *om* V*; *add* V*corr* 24 abominationem] abominatione RV 25 subornauit RV 28 christum] *om* V*; *habet in marg* misericordiam V* *vid* 29 in aeternum] usque in saeculum V

apostolus Paulus corpus Christi Christum appellat dicens: RV (M)
1 Co xii 12 *Sicut enim corpus unum est, membra autem habet multa,*
omnia autem membra ex uno corpore cum sint multa unum
corpus est, sic et Christus, id est Christi corpus quod est
Col i 24 Ecclesia. iterum: *Gaudeo in passionibus pro uobis et repleo*
quae desunt pressurarum Christi, id est Ecclesiae. nihil enim
cf Mt x 25 defuit Christi passionibus, quoniam *sufficit discipulo ut sit*
cf 1 The ii 19 *sicut magister.* sic ergo *aduentum Christi* pro locis accipiemus. item in Exodo omnes filios Dei unum filium et
omnes primogenitos Aegypti unum primogenitum esse sic
Ex iv 22, 23 Deo dicente cognoscimus. *Dices* inquit *Pharaoni: Haec*
dicit Dominus, Filius meus primitiuus Israhel. dixi autem,
Dimitte populum ut seruiat mihi; tu autem noluisti dimittere
eum. uide ergo, ecce ego occido filium tuum primitiuum. et
Ps lxxix 15, 16 Dauid uineam Domini unum filium sic ait: *Deus uirtutum*
conuertere, respice de caelo et uide, uisita uineam tuam. et
perfice eam quam plantauit dextera tua et in filium conroborasti tibi.

Et apostolus filium Dei dicit qui filio Dei mixtus est:
Ro i 1–4 *Paulus seruus Iesu Christi, uocatus apostolus, segregatus in*
euangelium Dei quod ante promiserat per prophetas suos in
scripturis sanctis de filio suo, qui factus est ei ex semine
Dauid secundum carnem, qui praedestinatus est filius Dei in
uirtute secundum Spiritum sanctitatis ex resurrectione mortuorum Iesu Christi Domini nostri. si diceret *de filio suo*
ex resurrectione mortuorum, unum filium ostenderat; nunc
autem *de filio* inquit *suo ex resurrectione mortuorum Iesu*
Christi Domini nostri. sed *qui factus est filius Dei ex re-*

1 dicens] *om* V(M) 2 unum corpus V 6 presurarum R; praessuram V* ecclesiae] ecclesia V* 8 magister] + eius VM 10 aegypti unum] aegyptiorum V 11 dicit inquit R; dicis inquit V* (dices V[b]) 12 primitiuus meus V 13 dimitte] demitte R; dimittere V* populum] populum meum V demittere R 14 eum] eam R 16 uisita] *pr* et V tuam] istam V 17 in filium] filium hominis quem VM; *uide Introd p* cxi conroborasti] confirmasti VM 19 filio dō V 20 uocatus apostolus] *om* RM 21 euangelio V* 23 praedistinatus V* *semp* 24 uirtutem RV sanctitatis] sanctificationis V 24—*p* 7, *l* 6 mortuorum...generaui te] R *supr ras, litteris minorib. sed ab antiqua manu* 25 suo] + ut V 28 sed qui] sed quis V**vid* M est] sit VM ex resurrectionem V*

RV *surrectione Christi* apertius ostendit dicens *de filio qui factus*
(M) *est ei ex semine Dauid secundum carnem, qui praedestinatus*
est filius Dei. Dominus autem noster non est Dei filius
praedestinatus (quia Deus est et coaequalis est Patri) qui ex
quo natus est hoc est, sed ille cui secundum Lucan dicit in
baptismo: *Filius meus es tu, ego hodie generaui te. Qui ex* Lc iii 22
semine Dauid, mixtus est *principali Spiritui* et *factus est* Ps l 14
51 ipse *filius Dei ex resurrectione Domini nostri Iesu Christi,* id
est dum resurgit in Christo semen Dauid; non ille de quo
ait ipse Dauid: *Sic dicit Dominus Domino meo.* itaque facti Ps cix 1 cf Esai xlv 1
sunt duo una caro. *Verbum caro factum est* et caro Deus, Ioh i 14, 13
quia *non ex sanguine sed ex Deo nati* sumus. apostolus
dicit: *Erunt duo in carne una. sacramentum hoc magnum* Eph v 31, 32
est, ego autem dico in Christum et in Ecclesiam. unum nam-
que semen promisit Deus Abrahae, ut quanticumque Christo
miscerentur unus esset in Christo, sicut Apostolus dicit:
Omnes uos unus estis in Christo Iesu. si autem uos unus Gal iii 28, 29
estis in Christo Iesu, ergo Abrahae semen estis et secundum
promissionem heredes. distat autem inter *unum estis* et *unus*
estis. quotienscumque alter alteri uoluntate miscetur *unum*
sunt, sicut Dominus dicit: *Ego et pater unum sumus.* quo- Ioh x 30
tiens autem et corporaliter miscentur et in unam carnem
duo solidantur *unus* sunt.

Corpus itaque in capite suo filius est Dei, et Deus in cor-
pore suo filius est hominis, qui cotidie nascendo uenit et *crescit* cf Eph ii 21
in templum sanctum Dei. templum enim bipertitum est, cuius
pars altera quamuis lapidibus magnis extruatur destruitur,

1 dicens] *om* V filio] + suo VM 2 praedistinatus RV* *et infr* 3 autem] etenim V; enim M noster] V *supr lin* non est] R *supr lin* d̄i filius praedistinatus R; praedistinatus d̄i filius V(M) 4 quia...patri] V *in mg*; *om* M 5 natus] creatus V lucan] R; lucam VM (secundū V *supr lin*) 10 ait | sic dicit × × × × d̄ns V*; *post* ait *add in mg* ipse dauid V*corr* 11 est] *in* V *supr lin* 12 sumus] sunt V* *mox corr* M 14 christum...ecclesiam] x̄po...ecclesia VM 15 x̄pi V 17 unus] unum RVM *utroque loco* 20 quotiescumque R unum] *pr* uni V 21, 22 quotiens] quoties R; quotienscumque V 22 miscentur] R*corr* V; misc×××× R* 23 unus] unum V sunt. corpus] *sic diuidit* RM 24 capite suo corpore R 27 destruitur] V[b]M; destruatur R; distruitur V*

cf Mt xxiv 2 neque in eo *lapis super lapidem relinquitur.* istius nobis RV (M) cf 2 The ii 7 iugis aduentus cauendus est, *donec de medio* eius discedat Ecclesia.

II. De Domini corpore bipertito.

Regula bipertiti corporis Domini multo necessarior et a nobis tanto diligentius perspicienda et per omnes Scripturas ante oculos habenda est. sicut enim ut supradictum est a capite ad corpus ratione sola uidetur, ita a parte corporis ad partem, a dextera ad sinistram uel a sinistra ad dexteram, transitus reditusque ut in supradicto capite claret.

Esai xlv 3 ff Dum enim dicit uni corpori: *Thesauros inuisibiles aperiam tibi, ut scias quoniam ego sum Dominus, et assumam te,* et adiecit: *Tu autem me non cognouisti quoniam ego sum Deus et non est absque me Deus, et nesciebas me;* numquid licet unum corpus adloquatur in unam mentem conuenit *thesauros inuisibiles aperiam tibi, ut cognoscas quia ego sum Deus propter puerum meum Iacob,* et *tu autem me non cognouisti?* in eandem et non accepit Iacob quod Deus promisit? aut in unam mentem conuenit *tu autem me non cognouisti* et *nesciebas me?* *nesciebas* enim non dicitur nisi ei qui iam scit, *non cognouisti* autem illi dicitur qui, licet ad hoc uocatus sit ut cognosceret, et eiusdem corporis sit uisibiliter, et Deo cf Esai xxix 13 *labiis adpropinquet, corde tamen longe separatus* sit. huic dicit *tu autem me non cognouisti.*

1 relinquetur VM 2 ca×endus V* eius] *cf p* 74[24]

3 Ecclesia] *add* DE DNO ET CORPORE EIVS REGVLA | DE DNI CORPORE BIPERTITO R *rubro*; EXPLICIT LIBER PRIMVS . ‖ INCIPIT LIB . II . | DE CORPORE DNI BIPERTITO V; FINIT M

5 multa R 9 dextera] R *sic semper*; dextra V *et sic saepius* 10 transitus reditusque ut] reditus V 11, 12 aperiam tibi inuisibiles V 12 dns R, *sine uirga*; ds V adsumam V* 16 quia] quoniam V 18 eandem] eadem V accipit R 20 enim] autem R 21 illi autem V dicitur] dr R*corr*; dic R* *vid* 23 labiis] + quidem V huic] hic V*

RV § Eug 867 (M) — Esai xlii 16 17 — Iterum: §*Ducam caecos in uiam quam non nouerunt, et semitas quas non nouerunt calcabunt, et faciam illis tenebras in lucem et praua in directum. haec uerba faciam et non* ¶ Eug *derelinquam eos. ipsi autem conuersi sunt retro.*¶ numquid quos dixit *non derelinquam* idem conuersi sunt retro, et non pars eorum?

Esai xliii 5—8 — Iterum dicit Dominus ad Iacob: *Noli metuere quia tecum sum. ab Oriente adducam semen tuum et ab Occidente colligam te. dicam Aquiloni adduc, et Africo noli uetare; adduc filios meos de terra longinqua et filias meas a summo terrae, omnes in quibus uocatum est nomen meum. in gloria enim mea paraui illum et finxi et feci illum, et produxi plebem caecam, et oculi eorum sunt similiter caeci et surdas aures habent.* numquid quos in gloriam suam parauit idem sunt caeci et surdi?

Esai xliii 27—xliv 1 — Iterum: *Patres tui primo et principes eorum facinus admiserunt in me et inquinauerunt principes tui sancta mea, et dedi perire Iacob, et Israhel in maledictum. nunc audi me puer meus Iacob, et Israhel quem elegi.* ostendit illum Iacob dedisse perire et Israhel maledictum quem non elegerat.

Esai xliv 21, 22 — Iterum: *Finxi te puerum meum, meus es tu Israhel, noli obliuisci mei. ecce enim deleui uelut nubem facinora tua et sicut nimbum peccata tua. conuertere ad me et redimam te.* numquid cuius peccata deleuit, cui dicit *meus es tu* et ne sui obliuiscatur commemorat, eidem dicit *conuertere ad me?* aut alicuius antequam conuertatur peccata delentur?

Esai xlviii 8, 9 — Iterum: *Scio quoniam reprobatus reprobaberis; propter nomen meum ostendam tibi dignitatem meam, et praeclara mea superducam tibi.* numquid reprobato ostendit dignitatem suam et praeclara inducit ei?

Esai lxiii 9, 10 — Iterum: *Non senior non angelus, sed ipse conseruauit eos,*

4 eos] V *supr ras* 4, 5 numquid...retro] V *ad calc pag* 8 ab occidentem V* *vid* 9 africum V* *vid* 11 gloriam...meam RM (= *Vg*); 12 paraui R[1] *supr ras* (ap×××R*) et feci] *om* V 16, 17 ammiserunt R 20 maledictum] *pr* in V 24 cuius] *om* V*; alicuius V[b] 25 eidem] + et V 27 scio] *om* R reprobaueris R 30 suam *add* V[a] *super lin* praeclara] + sua V 31 conseruauit] conseruabit R; considerauit V eos] illis V

RV [Eug] (M) *propter quod diligeret eos et parceret illis; ipse redemit eos et assumsit illos et exaltauit illos omnes dies saeculi. ipsi autem contumaces fuerunt et exacerbauerunt Spiritum Sanctum.* quos omnes dies saeculi exaltauit quo tempore contumaces fuerunt aut exacerbantes Spiritum Sanctum?

Iterum aperte Deus uni corpori firmitatem et interitum (Esai xxxiii 20) promittit dicens: *Hierusalem ciuitas diues, tabernacula quae non commouebuntur, neque agitabuntur pali tabernaculi tui in aeternum tempus, neque funes eius rumpentur.* et adiecit: (Esai xxxiii 23) *Rupti sunt funes tui quia non ualuit arbor nauis tuae, inclinauerunt uela tua et non tollet signum donec tradatur in perditionem.*

Iterum breuiter bipertitum ostenditur Christi corpus: (Cant i 5) *Fusca sum et decora.* absit enim ut Ecclesia (Eph v 27) *quae non habet maculam aut rugam*, quam Dominus suo sanguine sibi mundauit, aliqua ex parte fusca sit nisi in parte sinistra per (Ro ii 24) quam *nomen Dei blasphematur in gentibus.* alias tota speciosa (Cant iv 7) est, sicut dicit: *Tota speciosa es proxima mea et reprehensio non est in te.* etenim dicit qua de causa sit fusca et speciosa: (Cant i 5) §*Vt tabernaculum Cedar ut pellis Salomonis.*¶ duo taber- [§¶ Eug 866] nacula ostendit, regium et seruile: utrumque tamen semen Abrahae; Cedar enim filius est Ismahel. alio denique loco cum isto Cedar, id est cum seruo ex Abraham, diutur- (Ps cxix 5—7) nam mansionem, sic ingemescit Ecclesia dicens: *Heu me quoniam peregrinatio mea longinqua facta est, habitaui cum tabernaculis Cedar, multum peregrinata est anima mea. cum odientibus pacem eram pacificus, cum loquebar illis debellabant me.* non possumus autem dicere tabernaculum Cedar praeter Ecclesiam esse. ipse autem dicit tabernaculum *Cedar et Salomonis* unde *fusca sum* inquit *et decora;* non

1 eos] illos V *utroque loco* parceret] parcet R 2 assumṗsit R (*sic*); adsumpsit V* 3 exaceruauerunt V* 4, 5 fuerunt contumaces V 5 exacerbantes] exaceruauerunt V* 8 agitabunt RV 11 non tollet] noll& R 13 ostendit breuiter bipertitum V 15 sibi] *om* V 17 alias] alia V* 18 est...speciosa] *om* V*; *add* V[a] *supr lin* 19 non] nulla V 20 ut 1°] & V*; fusca sum et speciosa ut *Eug* tabernacula *Eug* caedar V *semp* pelles *Eug cod opt* 21 tamen] *om* V*; *add* V[b] *in mg* 22 ismahel V (*plene*); ismaḥel R (*sic*) 24 ingemescit] ingemit V 27 loquebar] loquerer V 28 me] + gratis VM possum V dicere autem V

RV (M) enim Ecclesia in his qui foris sunt fusca est. hoc mysterio Dominus in Apocalypsi septem angelos dicit, id est Ecclesiam septiformem, nunc sanctos et praeceptorum custodes, nunc eosdem multorum criminum reos et paenitentia dignos ostendit. et in Euangelio unum praepositorum corpus diuersi meriti manifestat dicens: *Beatus ille seruus quem* Mt xxiv 46 *adueniens dominus illius inuenerit ita facientem,* et de eodem: *Si autem nequam ille seruus,* quem *Dominus diuidit in duas* cf *Ib* 48, 51 *partes.* dico numquid omnem diuidet aut findet? denique non totum sed *partem eius cum hypocritis ponet,* in uno enim corpus ostendit.

Hoc itaque mysterio accipiendum est per omnes Scripturas sicubi Deus dicit ad merita Israhel periturum aut hereditatem suam execrabilem. apostolus enim copiose ita disputat, maxime ad Romanos, in parte accipiendum quicquid de toto corpore dictum est. *Ad Israhel* inquit *quid* Ro x 21 *dicit? Tota die expandi manus meas ad plebem contradicentem.* et ut ostenderet de parte dictum, *Dico,* inquit, *Numquid* Ro xi 1, 2 *reppulit Deus hereditatem suam? absit. nam et ego Israhelita sum ex semine Abraham tribu Beniamin. non reppulit Deus plebem suam quam praesciuit.* et post quam docuit quem ad modum haec locutio intellegenda esset, eodem genere locutionis ostendit unum corpus et bonum esse et malum dicens: *Secundum Euangelium quidem inimici propter uos, se-* Ro xi 28 *cundum electionem autem dilecti propter patres.* numquid idem dilecti qui inimici, aut potest in Caifan utrumque conuenire? ita Dominus in omnibus Scripturis unum corpus seminis Abrahae in omnibus crescere et florere atque perire testatur.

1 qui] quae V* *vid*; q̧ M 2 apocalypsim V dicit] *om* V*; *add* V *corr supr lin* 4 eosdem] + et V 9 numquid *in* V *supr ras* 9,10 diuidit...findit...ponit V 10 non totum] *pr* totum V partem... ponet] *cf Eug* 867 11 corpus ost.] *ras in* V 12 mysterio] corpus V 13 ad merita] merito V*; ob meritum V *corr*; ob merita M 16 quid] *om* V 19 hereditatem] plebem V 20 abrahae V 21 presciit V 22 loquutio R *semp* intelligenda V*M esset] esse V* 25 patres] pares V* 26 in caifan] M; in cain· R (*sic*); in causa V 27 in omnibus] omnibus gentibus VM

28 testatur] *add* EXPLICIT DE BIPERTITO DNI CORPORE | INCIPIT PROMISSIS (*sic*) ET LEGE REGVLA R *rubro;* EXPLICIT . LIBER . SECVNDVS . | INCIPIT LIBER . III . DE PROMISSIS ET LEGE V; DE CORPORE DNI BIPERTITO EXPLC. | INCIPIT DE PROMISSIS ET LEGE M

III. De promissis et lege. 52

Auctoritas est diuina neminem aliquando ex operibus RV
legis iustificari potuisse. eadem auctoritate firmissimum est (M)
numquam defuisse qui legem facerent et iustificarentur.
Ro iii 19, 20 Scriptum est: *Quaecumque lex loquitur his qui in lege*
sunt dicit, ut omne os obstruatur et subditus fiat omnis mundus
Deo, quia non iustificabitur ex lege omnis caro in conspectu
Ro vi 14 *eius. per legem enim cognitio peccati.* iterum: *Peccatum*
Gal ii 16 *uestri non dominabitur, non enim estis sub lege.* iterum: *Et*
nos in Christum credimus ut iustificemur ex fide et non ex
operibus legis, quia non iustificabitur omnis caro ex operibus
Gal iii 21, 22 *legis.* iterum: *Si enim data esset lex quae posset uiuificare,*
omni modo ex lege esset iustitia. sed conclusit Scriptura
omnia sub peccato ut promissio ex fide Iesu Christi daretur
credentibus. sed dicet quis: A Christo et infra non iustificat
lex, suo tamen tempore iustificauit. huic occurrit auctoritas
apostoli Petri, qui cum gentes a fratribus sub iugo legis
Ac xv 10 cogerentur sic ait: *Quid temptatis Dominum inponere uolentes*
iugum super collum discentium quod neque patres nostri
Ro vii 5 *neque nos potuimus portare.* et apostolus Paulus: *Cum*
essemus inquit *in carne passiones peccatorum quae per legem*
sunt operabantur in membris nostris ut fructum afferrent
Phil iii 6 *morti.* et contra idem apostolus dicit: *Iustitia quae ex lege*
est conuersatus sine querella. quodsi tanti apostoli auctoritas
deesset, quid dici potuit contra testimonium Domini dicentis:
Ioh i 47 *Ecce uere Israhelita in quo dolus non est.* quod etsi Dominus
hoc testimonium non dignaretur perhibere, quis tam
sacrilegus, quis tam tumore stuporis elatus diceret Mosen et

3 iustificare R 4 numquam] non V 5 scriptum est] *om* V*; *add* V*corr supr lin* 5, 6 dicit qui in lege sunt V 6 subditus] subiectus V 7 iustificatur V 8 cognitio] agnitio V peccatum] peccat× R* *mox corr* 10 in $\overline{\text{xpo}}$ V* et] *om* V* 11 quia] $\overset{a}{\text{qui}}$ R (a *ab antiqua manu*) 12 possit uiuificari V* 13 esset] esse V* 18 uolentes] *om* V*; *add* V[a] *supr lin* 22 adferent V* 23 morti] mortui R 25 dicentis] dicens V* 26 et] *om* R 27 testimonio V* 28 stupore R mosen] R (*sic*); moysen V

RV (M) prophetas uel omnes sanctos legem non fecisse aut justificatos non esse? cum et Scriptura dicat de Zacharia et uxore eius: *Erant iusti ambo in conspectu Dei ambulantes* Luc i 6 *in omnibus mandatis et iustificationibus sine querella;* et Dominus non uenerit *uocare iustos sed peccatores.* Mt ix 13

Lex autem quomodo iustificare potuit a peccato, quae ad hoc data est ut peccatum multiplicaretur? sicut scriptum est: *Lex autem subintrauit ut multiplicaretur peccatum.* illud Ro v 20 autem scire debemus et tenere: numquam omnino interceptum esse semen Abrahae ab Isaac usque in hodiernum diem. semen autem Abrahae non carnale sed spiritale, quod non ex lege sed ex promissione est. alterum enim semen carnale est, quod est ex lege *a monte Sina quod est Agar in seruitutem* Gal iv 24 *generans. ille quidem qui de ancilla carnaliter natus est,* Ib 23 *qui autem ex libera ex promissione.* non esse autem semen Abrahae nisi quod ex fide est apostolus dicit: *Cognoscitis ergo* Gal iii 7 *quoniam qui ex fide sunt hi sunt filii Abrahae?* et iterum: *Vos autem fratres secundum Isaac promissionis filii estis.* Gal iv 28

Semen ergo Abrahae non ex lege sed ex promissione est, quod ex Isaac iugiter mansit. si autem constat semen Abrahae ante legem fuisse, et illud esse semen Abrahae quod ex fide est, constat et quia numquam fuit ex lege. non enim potuit et ex lege esse et ex fide. lex enim et fides diuersa res est, quia lex non est fidei sed operum sicut scriptum est: *Lex non est ex fide, sed Qui fecerit ea uiuet in* Gal iii 12 *eis.* Abraham ergo fide filios semper habuit, lege numquam. *Non enim per legem promissio est Abrahae aut semini eius* Ro iv 13—15 *ut heres esset mundi, sed per iustitiam fidei. si enim qui per legem ipsi sunt heredes, euacuata est fides, abolita est promissio; lex enim iram operatur.* si ergo nec fides nec promissio Abrahae destrui ullo modo potest, ab ortu suo

2 et] *om* V zaccharia V 4 iustificationibus] + $\overline{di}$ V querela R*; quaerella V* 10 isaac] R*; issac R^a: *fortasse scribendum* Isac in hodiernum diem] ad hodiernum V 11 non carnale] *add* V*corr supr lin* 13 sina] sinai R seruitute V 14 de] ex V 18 autem] *om* V* 20 isaac] issac R^a 21 semen abrae V 22 et] *om* V 23 et 1°] *om* V 25 est ex] et ex R* *mox corr* 26 semper filios V 27 per legem] ex lege V 29 euacuata] uacua V abolita] et uacua V 31 ullo modo] *om* V

iugiter mansit. nec data lege inpedita est quo minus RV
Abrahae filii secundum promissionem fide generarentur. (M)
cf Gal iii 17 dicit enim apostolus *post CCCC et XXX annos* datam legem
Ib 18 non obfuisse nec destruxisse promissionem. *Si enim ex lege, non iam ex promissione; Abrahae autem per repromissionem*
Ib 21 *donauit Deus.* et alio loco: *Lex ergo aduersus promissa? absit.* videmus legem ad promissionem non pertinere nec aliquando alteram in alteram inpegisse sed utramque ordinem suum tenuisse. quia sicut lex numquam fidei obfuit, ita nec
Ro iii 31 fides legem destruxit, sicut scriptum est: *Legem ergo destruimus per fidem? absit, sed legem statuimus,* id est firmamus, inuicem namque firmant.

Ergo filii Abrahae non ex lege sunt, sed ex fide per repromissionem. quaerendum autem quem ad modum hi qui ex operibus legis negantur potuisse iustificari, in lege positi et legem operantes iustificati fuerint. quaerendum praeterea cur post promissionem fidei, quae nullo modo destrui potest, data est lex quae non est ex fide, ex cuius
Gal iii 10 operibus nemo iustificaretur quia *quotquot ex operibus legis sunt sub maledicto sunt. scriptum est enim: Maledictus qui non permanserit in omnibus quae scripta sunt in libro legis ut faciat ea.*

Apostolus denique huic quaestioni prospiciens, cum assereret omni modo filios Abrahae dono Dei semper fuisse per fidem non per legem factorum, ex alterius persona
Gal iii 19 respondit sibi dicens: *Quid ergo lex factorum?* id est, si ex fide filii cur data est lex factorum, cum sufficeret promissio
Gal iii 11 generandis filiis Abrahae et fide nutriendis, *quia Iustus ex fide uiuit?* ante quam enim se interrogasset *Quid ergo lex*

1 impedita R 2 fide] fidem V*; fidei V *corr* 3 quadringentos et triginta V 4 distruxisse V* 5 iam non V repromissionem] promissionem V* *mox corr* 6 promissa] + d̄i V 7 uidimus V promissionem] promissā V 8 impegisse R utraq. RV 9 numquam fidei] fide″ numquam R (*cf p* 35^{28}) 10 distr- V *semp* 14 promissionem V quemammodum R (*vid Appx* II) hii R 15 lege] legem V* 16 legem] *pr* in V* 17 quae] quem V 21 permanserit] manserit V 23 questioni RV *corr* 24 adserer& V* 25 personam V* 26, 27 id est...factorum] V *supr lin* 28 nutriendis] nutriendi V

RV (M) *factorum,* iam dixerat ut uiuerent qui ex lege iustificari non possent hoc modo: *Quoniam autem ex lege nemo iustificatur* Gal iii 11 *apud Deum, iustus autem ex fide uiuit.* ostendit propterea dictum esse per prophetam *ex fide uiuit,* ut manifestum fieret quem ad modum uiuerent qui legem facere non potuissent.

Sed minus liquet quid sit *Iustus ex fide uiuit.* non enim potuit quisquam iustus in lege positus uiuere nisi opera legis fecisset et omnia opera; sin minus maledictus esset. dedit Deus legem: dixit *Non concupisces.* statim Ro vii 7, 8 *occasione accepta peccatum per mandatum operatum est omnem concupiscentiam.* necesse est enim *passiones pecca-* cf *Ib* 5 *torum quae per legem* sunt operari *in membris* eius qui in lege est. propterea enim data est *ut abundaret peccatum,* Ro v 20 quia *uirtus peccati lex.* *uenundatus* autem *sub peccato iam* 1 Co xv 56 cf Ro vii 14 23 *non quod uult operatur bonum, sed quod non uult malum, consentit enim legi secundum interiorem hominem.* expugnatur autem *altera lege* membrorum trahiturque *captiuus* neque aliquando liberari potuit nisi sola gratia per fidem. est autem crimen magnum perfidiae non adtendisse genus armorum quibus uiolentia peccati expugnaretur: contra magnificae fidei est inquisisse et uidisse. est ergo sacrilega mens et male de Deo sentiens quae, cum legem nullo modo humanitus posse fieri et ad ulciscendum paratam uideret, non intellexit esse aliquod remedium uitae, nec fieri potuisse ut bonus Deus qui sciebat legem non potuisse fieri alterum uitae aditum non reliquisset, et aduersum homines quos ad uitam fecerat undique uersum uitae uias clusisset.

2 possint V* autem] ait R 3 deum] R* *vid*; dnm R[a] autem] *om* V* 3, 4 ostendit...uiuit] *add* V *ad calc pag* 5 quemammodum R potuissent] possint V*; possent V[a] 7 liquet] lic& V uiuet V *corr* (uiuit V*) 10 dixit] *pr* et V 11 occasionem acceptam V* peccatum] *om* V* 14 abund& R; habundar& V* 16 non quod] quod non V* non 2°] *in* V *supr lin* 18 altera lege] alteram legem R; aliter lege V 19 sola gratiam V* *vid* 20 attendisse V[a] 21 contra] & e contra V[a]; e contra M 22 magnifice RV 23 legem] lege R 24 ad ulciscendum] adulescendum R; ad ulciscendo V* *mox corr* 25 esse] *om* R*; *add* R[a] *supr lin* remedio V* *fortasse recte* 27 alteram R aduersus V* *vid* 28 clausisset V (*et infr* clausisse)

hoc fides non tulit, non admisit, sed cum infirmitate carnis RV
et uirtute peccati urgueretur dedit Deo claritatem. sciens (M)
Dominum bonum et iustum et uiscera miserationis suae
contra opera manuum suarum non clusisse, intellexit esse
iter ad uitam et faciendae legis remedium uidit. Deus
enim cum diceret *Non concupisces* non nudauit quem ad
modum id prouenire posset, sed seuere atque decise dixit
Non concupisces: quoniam id fide repperiendum reliquit.
si enim mandaret a se prouentum postulari, et legem de-
struxerat et fidem. ut quid enim legem daret, si legem in
omnibus facturum polliceretur? aut quid fidei relinqueret,
si fidem auxilium pollicendo praeueniret? nunc autem bono
cf Ro vii 13 fidei dedit legem ministram mortis, ut amatores uitae fide
uitam uiderent, et iusti fide uiuerent qui opus legis non ex 53
sua uirtute sed ex Dei dono fieri posse crederent. lex enim
a carne fieri non potest; quaecumque facta non fuerit
punit.

Quae ergo spes homini faciendae legis et fugiendae mortis
Ro viii 7—9 nisi opis et misericordiae Dei, quam fides inuenit? *Caro
legi Dei subiecta non est, neque enim potest. qui autem in
carne sunt Deo placere non possunt. uos autem non
estis in carne sed in spiritu, si quidem Spiritus Dei in
uobis est. si quis autem Spiritum Christi non habet, hic
non est eius.* ostendit Spiritum Dei et Christi idem
esse. ostendit praeterea qui Spiritum Dei habuerit in
carne non esse. si ergo unus est Spiritus Dei et Christi,
prophetae et sancti qui Spiritum Dei habuerunt Spiritum
Christi habuerunt. si Spiritum Dei habuerunt, in carne
non fuerunt; si in carne non fuerunt, legem fecerunt: quia
caro est inimica in Deum et *legi* eius *subiecta non est*;

1 adm- R *hoc loco* (*vid Appx* II)   1, 2 carnis et uirtute] *om* R   2 urgueretur] R*V*; argueretur R*corr*; urg×er&ur V *nunc*   4 non] *add* V* *supr lin*   6 denudauit V *nunc*; -abit V* *vid*   6, 7 quemammodum R   7 possit V*   dicise V*   8 concupiscis V*   relinquit V*   9, 10 distruxerat V*   10 si]+se M   11 facturum] factorum VM   relinqueretur V   13 fide] fidem R   15 dono] donum V*   16 quaecumque] quicumque V*; quae cum V*corr*   18 hominis V* *vid*   19 opis] V*; opes R V*corr*   27 qui] q̅u̅o̅ V (=quoniam)   29 si in carne non fuerunt] *om* V   fecerunt] *pr* non R

RV qui ergo ad Deum confugit accepit Spiritum Dei, quo accepto mortificata est caro; qua mortificata potuit facere legem spiritalis, liberatus a lege: *quia iusto non est lex posita;* et 1 Tim i 9 iterum: *Si Spiritu* Dei *agimini non estis sub lege.* Gal v 18

Qua re manifestum est quia patres nostri qui Spiritum Dei habuerunt non fuerunt sub lege. quamdiu enim quis in carne est, id est Spiritum Dei non habet, dominatur eius lex. si autem tradiderit se gratiae, moritur legi et facit in illo legem Spiritus, mortua carne quae legi Dei subiecta esse non potest. quod enim gerebatur id etiam nunc geritur. non enim quia sub lege non sumus cessauit interdictio illa concupiscentiae et non magis aucta est; sed nos in reuelatam gratiam concurrimus per fidem, edocti a Domino opus legis de eius misericordia postulare et dicere: *Fiat uoluntas tua,* Mt vi 10, 13 et *Libera nos a malo;* illi autem in non reuelatam per eandem fidem coacti metu mortis, quam ministra lege parato gladio intentari uidebant.

Lex data est *donec ueniret semen cui promissum est* et Gal iii 19 euangelizaret fidem. antea uero lex cogebat in fidem, quia sine lege non possit exprimi fides ad exquirendam Dei gratiam, eo quod peccatum uirtutem non haberet. data uero lege *passiones quae per legem sunt operabantur in membris* Ro vii 5 *nostris* urguentes in peccatum, ut uel necessitate urgueremur in fidem quae imploraret gratiam Dei in auxilium tolerantiae. custodiam carceris passi sumus, legem minantem mortem et undique uersum insuperabili muro ambientem, cuius ambitus sola una ianua fuit gratia. huic ianuae custos fides praesidebat, ut nemo illum carcerem effugeret, nisi cui fides aperuisset; qui hanc ianuam non pulsaret intra septum legis moreretur. legem paedagogum passi sumus, qui nos cogeret

2 qua] qui× V* 3 lex] *om* V 4 spiritu] s͞p͞m V 5 est] *om* V 11 cessauit] + enim V* *mox eras* 19 euangelizare V in fide V 20 sine] siue R ad exquirendam] adquirendam R 21 uirtutum R 23 urguentes] V*; urgentes V[a]; urgentem R urgeremur RV[a] 24 in fide V inploraret V in auxilio V 26 insuperabile V 27 custus V 27, 28 praesidebat] presidebat[r] R (*sic*); *cf p* 20[10] *ubi* 'ur' *irrepsit ante* 'ut' 29 qui] *pr* et V septum] sepultum V*

[RV (M)] studere fidei, qui nos cogeret in Christum. dicit enim apostolus propterea datam legem, ut nos custodia sui concluderet [cf Ro x 4] in fidem, quam futurum erat reuelari in Christum qui est *finis legis*, quo uixerunt omnes qui fide gratiam Dei ex- [Gal iii 23, 24] quisierunt. *Prius* inquit *quam ueniret fides, sub lege custodiebamur conclusi in eam fidem quam futurum erat reuelari. lex itaque paedagogus noster fuit in Christo, ut ex fide iustificaremur.*

Lex inquam fidei erat demonstratrix. sed dicit quis: Si in utilitate fidei data est lex, cur non ab origine seminis Abrahae, si quidem iuge fuit? re uera iuge fuit: iugis et fides ut genitrix filiorum Abrahae, iugis et lex per dinoscentiam boni et mali. sed post promissionem filiorum Abrahae, multiplicatis eis secundum carnem, multiplicandum erat et semen Abrahae quod non est nisi ex fide. quae multiplicatio euenire non posset sine adiutorio legis multiplicatae, ut multitudo in fidem necdum reuelatam ut iam dictum est uel necessitate deduceretur. prouidentia itaque Dei factum est augendo gubernandoque semini Abrahae, ut seueritate et metu legis multi compellerentur in fidem, et semen fulciretur [Ro v 20] usque ad fidei reuelationem. *Lex autem subintroiuit ut multiplicaretur peccatum. ubi* inquit *muliplicatum est peccatum superabundauit gratia.* non dixit *data est* sed *superabundauit.* ab initio enim data est per Christum fugientibus legis molestias atque dominium. abundauit autem multiplicata lege, superabundauit uero in omnem carnem reuelata in [cf Eph i 10, Eph ii 17] Christum, qui ueniens *restaurare quae in caelo et quae in terra euangelizauit* fidem *his qui proxime et qui longe*, id est peccatoribus Israhel et gentibus. iusti enim Israhel ex fide in eandem fidem uocati sunt. idem namque Spiritus, eadem

1 xpo V   2 nos] non V   concludere V*   3 xpo V   4 uixerunt] fixerunt R   fide gratiam] fidem gratiae V   5 inquit] inquid V* *et sic plerumque*   7, 8 iustificaremur] iustificar&ur R   10 ab originix V*   15 nisi] *om* V   16 posset] posse R; possit V   adiutorium V*   ut] et V   17 ut iam] sicut iam V   18 factum est] scm ē V (= sanctum est)   20 fulceretur V*   21 subintroiuit] subintrauit VM   22 inquid V*   23 gratiam V   data est] nata ē V   23, 24 superhabundauit V*   26 lege] legem V   reuelatam R   30 eandem] eadem V

RV (M) fides, eadem gratia per Christum semper data est, quorum plenitudinem ueniens remoto legis uelamine omni genti largitus est, quae modo non genere a futuris differebant. aliter enim numquam fuit semen Abrahae.

Quod si quisquam praeter haec iustificatus est, filius Abrahae non fuit. quoniam filius Abrahae dici non potest, si ex lege et non sicut Abraham ex fide iustificatus est. ab eadem namque imagine gratiae et spiritus in eandem transisse Ecclesiam docet apostolus dicens: *Nos autem omnes reuelata facie* [2 Co iii 18] *gloriam Dei speculantes in eandem imaginem commutamur a claritate in claritatem.* dicit et ante passionem Domini gloriam fuisse et negat ex lege excludi, id est exprimi, produci, effici, potuisse. unde manifestum est ex fide fuisse. *Vbi ergo* [Ro iii 27] inquit *gloriatio? exclusa est. per quam legem? numquid operum? non: sed per legem fidei. Quid enim Scriptura* [Ro iv 3] *dicit? credidit Abraham Deo et deputatum est ei ad iustitiam. in gloriam ex* eadem *gloria* transiuimus quae non fuit ex [cf 2 Co iii 18] lege. *si enim ex operibus*, fuit gloria, *sed non ad Deum.* [cf Ro iv 2]

Etenim impossibile est sine gratia Dei habere aliquem gloriam. una est enim gloria et uno genere semper fuit. nemo enim uicit nisi cui Deus uicerit, quod non est in lege sed qui fecerit; in fide autem infirmum facit Deus aduersarium nostrum, propterea *ut qui gloriatur in Domino glorietur.* [1 Co i 31] si enim quod uincimus nostrum non est, non est ex operibus sed ex fide, et nihil est quod ex nobis gloriemur. nihil enim habemus quod non accepimus. si sumus, ex Deo sumus, ut magnitudo uirtutis sit Dei et non ex nobis. omne opus nostrum fides est, quae quanta fuerit tantum Deus operatur nobiscum. in hoc gloriatur Salomon, scisse se non ex homine sed ex Dei dono esse continentiam. *Cum sciui* inquit [Sap viii 21]

2 gente R 8 imaginem R spiritus] spūi V* *vid*; spu V *nunc* eadem V* 9 dicens] dic××× R* reuelatam faciem V 10 eadem V* 14 inquid V* gloriatio] + tua R numquid] *pr* et V 16 deputatum] reputatum V est] *om* V ad] in V 17 in gloriam] *om* in V 18 gloria] gloriam V*; habet gloriam V*corr* deum] dnm R 19 aliquem] aliquam V 20 gloria] gloriam V* 22 deus infirmum facit V 23 ut] *om* V 25 et nihil] nihil V 26 accipimus R 29 nobiscum] *scripsi*; in nobis. cum RV se] *om* V 30 continentiam] *pr* omne× V; hominis continentiam V*corr*

quoniam aliter non possum esse continens nisi Deus dederit, et hoc RV
ipsum autem erat sapientiae, scire cuius esset hoc donum, adii
Dominum et deprecatus sum. iudicio Salomonis credendum
est non ex operibus sed gratia Dei omnes iustificatos, qui
scierunt opus legis a Deo impetrandum quo possent gloriari.
1 Co i 29 dicit autem apostolus quem ad modum *omnis caro non glo-*
rietur in conspectu Dei: mali omni modo quod Deum non
1 Co i 28—31 cognouerint, iusti quod non suum sed opus Dei sint. *Inu-*
tilia inquit *et abiecta elegit Deus, quae non sunt ut quae sunt*
euacuaret, ut non gloriatur omnis caro in conspectu Dei. ex
ipso autem uos estis in Christo Iesu, qui factus est nobis
sapientia a Deo et iustitia et sanctimonia et redemptio, ut se-
cundum quod scriptum est: qui gloriatur in Domino glorietur.
Eph ii 8—10 et iterum: *Gratia estis saluati per fidem. et hoc non ex*
uobis, Dei donum est; non ex operibus ne forte quis glorietur.
ipsius enim sumus figmentum creati in Christo.

Sic nulla caro aliquando ex lege, id est ex operibus, iusti-
ficari potest, ut omnis iustus ex Deo gloriam haberet. est
aliud quo nemo glorietur in conspectu Dei. Deus enim sic
Iob xiv 4, 5 suis operatur ut sit quod et dimittat, *nemo est enim mundus*
Ps cxlii 2 *a sorde nec si unius diei sit uita eius.* et Dauid dicit: *Non*
introeas in iudicio cum seruo tuo, quoniam non iustificabitur
coram te omnis uiuens. et Salomon in prece dedicationis
3 Regn viii 46 Ps l 6 templi: *Non est* inquit *homo qui non peccauit.* iterum: *Tibi*
Prov xx 9 *soli deliqui*, et: *Quis enim gloriabitur castum se habere cor,*
aut quis gloriabitur mundum se esse a peccato? parum fuit
de casto corde, id est a cogitationibus, nisi et a peccato mun-
dum se nemo gloriaretur. omnis uictoria non ex operibus sed
Ps cii 4 Dei miseratione conceditur, sicut scriptum est: *Qui coronat* 54

1 quoniam] quia V 2 autem] *om* V hoc donum esset V 3 depraecatus R 5 impetrandum] implendum V possint V 6 quemammodum R 8 opus dei] $\overline{di}$ opus V sint] R^a; sunt R* 10 euacuaret ut] *conieci*; euacuar&urut R*; euacuarentur ut Rcorr V; euacuet *Sp* 567 *not* =καταργήσῃ: *cf p* 17[28] in conspectu $\overline{di}$ omnis caro V 11 nobis] uobis V 13 glorietur] glorisetur V (*sic*) 19 quo] quod V 20 demittat R 23 coram te] in conspectu tuo V prece dedicationis] praedicationis V 25 deliqui] delinqui V (*sic*); peccaui R et: quis] *om* et V 27 corde casto V a 2°] *om* V 28 se] *om* V ex] *om* V 29 qui te coronat V

RV *te in misericordia et miseratione.* et mater martyrum filio
(M) suo sic dicit: *Vt in illa miseratione cum fratribus te recipiam.* 2 Mach vii 29
iusti autem perfecerunt uoluntatem Dei uoto atque conatu
quo nituntur et concupiscunt Deo seruire.

Non est bene et melius in lege, quae si iustificasset omnes
iusti unius essent meriti, quia parem de omnibus exigit ob-
seruationem; sin minus operaretur maledictio. sin autem
disparis erant meriti—quis quantum credidit sibi dari tantum
gratiae Dei miserantis accepit,—ergo transformati *a gloria in* 2 Co iii 18
gloriam sicut a Domini Spiritu, id est ex eodem in eundem.
tale est enim quia post Christum fides data est quale quia et
Spiritus Sanctus, cum semper omnes prophetae et iusti eodem
Spiritu uixerint. non enim aliter uiuere potuerunt quam
Spiritu fidei. quotquot enim sub lege fuerunt occisi sunt,
quia *littera occidit Spiritus autem uiuificat.* et tamen dicit 2 Co iii 6
Dominus de eodem Spiritu: *Nisi ego abiero ille non ueniet,* Ioh xvi 7
cum et apostolis iam dedisset eundem Spiritum. apostolus
autem sic dicit eundem Spiritum apud antiquos fuisse: *Ha-* 2 Co iv 13
bentes autem eundem Spiritum fidei, sicut scriptum est: credidi
propter quod locutus sum. eundem Spiritum fidei dixit habu-
isse eundem qui dixit: *credidi propter quod locutus sum,* et
id confirmat dicens: *Et nos credimus ideoque et loquimur.* 2 Co iv 13
dicendo *et nos* ostendit et illos eodem Spiritu fidei credidisse.
unde manifestum est quia haec iusti non ex lege sed Spiritu
fidei semper habuerunt.

Et quicquid per Dominum uenit plenitudo est, cuius pars fuit per eundem, sicut paruulus qui, cum nihil minus habeat a uiro, tamen uir non est, et per incrementa non nouorum sed eorundem membrorum in eum uenit plenitudo corporis, ut

1 miseratione et misericordia V 2 in illa] illa V fratribus] + tuis V 5 bene] *om* V iustificassent R*, *sed* n *exp* Rcorr 7 sin autem] si autem V 8 dispares erant R; disparis erat V 9 ergo] *om* V a] *om* V 10 domini] d̄i V 11 et] *om* V 17 apostolis] apostolos R; ap̄l:s V *nunc* 18 sic dicit] ××dicit V* aput V* 19 sicut] sicr V* *mox corr in scribendo* 20 loquutus R 20, 21 eundem spiritum...locutus sum] *om* R 20 fidei] V *supr lin* 22 ideoque] propter quod R; *cf Nov de Trin p* 630 24 spiritu] sp̄x R*; sp̄u R *nunc* 26 dominum] donū R 29 eorundem] eorum R

[cf Ioh vii 39] [RV (M)] sit perfectus idem tamen qui fuerat paruulus. re uera *non erat Spiritus Sanctus* ante passionem Domini, sed in illis qui per ipsum praesentem credebant, ut in ipso uictore et cuncta [cf Eph i 13] perficiente *signati* perficerentur. nam iusti quos hic inuenit habuerunt Spiritum Sanctum, ut Symeon et Nathanael et Zacharias et Helisabeth et Anna uidua filia Fanuhel.

Promissio ergo a lege separata est, neque cum sit diuersum misceri potest, nam conditio infirmat promissionem. cogimur autem nos loqui ea quae sine igne doloris audire non possumus. dicunt enim quidam, qui promissionum firmitatem et quae ex lege est transgressionem nesciunt, promisisse quidem Deum Abrahae omnes gentes, sed saluo libero arbitrio, si legem custodissent. et si pericula imperitiae quorundam in eorum salutem patefacere prodest, sed cum de Deo omnipotente sermo est moderari dicenda debemus, ne silenda refutando memoremus, et ex ore nostro aliena licet audiantur. quare cum tremore loquentes sua cuique pericula consideranda relinquimus.

Manifestum est praescisse Deum futuros de libero arbitrio quos Abrahae promisit aut non futuros. alterum est duorum: si futuros finita quaestio est, si non futuros fidelis Deus non promitteret. aut si hoc est statutum apud Deum tunc promissos dare si promissi uelint, profecto diceret, ne seruus [Ro iv 21] eius *credens quia quod promisit* Deus *potens est et facere* ludificaretur Abraham. promissio autem illa est quae nihil conditionis incurrit, sin minus nec promissio est firma nec fides integra. quid enim stabile remanebit in Dei promissione aut in Abrahae fide, si id quod promissum et creditum est in eorum qui promissi sunt penderet arbitrio? ergo et Deus alienum promisit et Abraham incaute credidit. ut quid

1 non erat]+in eo V 3 in ipso] ipso V 5 simeon V nathanael] Rcorr; nathanithel R* *vid*; natanahel V 6 helisabeth] R*; helizabeth Rcorr; elisab&h V 8 nam] non V 9 cogemur R 11 transgressione V* 14 in eorum] iustorum V salute V 16 refutando] reputando V 17, 18 consideranda] *om* R 19 prae×scisse V* 21 fidelis] fideles V 22 statutum] statum R* *mox corr* 23 uelint] uellent V 24 deus] *om* V et] *om* V 27, 28 quid... aut] R *supr ras*; (Q×××××× ... R*) 29 penderet] pend& R

RV (M) etiam ipsa promissio debitum post modum facta est dicente Deo: *Benedicentur in te omnes gentes terrae, pro eo quod* Gen xxii 18, 16 *audisti uocem meam et non pepercisti filio tuo dilecto propter me?* quia autem ex his quibusdam facile est et aduersum Abrahae meritum liberi arbitrii calumnia strepere, etiam post mortem ipsius Abrahae debitorem se eius confirmat Deus, et propter eum se statuturum quod eius filio promittebat dicens: *Ero tecum et benedicam te: tibi enim et semini tuo* Gen xxvi 3–5 *dabo terram hanc; et statuam iurationem meam quam iuraui Abrahae patri tuo, et multiplicabo semen tuum sicut stellas caeli, et dabo tibi et semini tuo omnes gentes terrae, pro eo quod audiuit Abraham pater tuus uocem meam.* ecce firmatum est debitum Abrahae, non enim potuit per liberum arbitrium post mortem amittere quod uiuus meruerat.

Noluerunt autem gentes credere. quid faciet Abraham cui debetur? quomodo accipiet fidei et temptationis suae debitum, cuius debitore Deo securus fuit? cui si dictum esset Dabo quod promisi et reddam quod iuraui si uoluerint gentes, non crederet sed expectaret fortuitum. si conditione opus est cum operario esse potest non cum mercede. operarius enim potest uelle accipere aut nolle, non merces reddi aut non reddi. omnes enim gentes in mercedem fidei datae sunt Abrahae sicut Deus dicit: *Merces tua multa est.* non enim Gen xv 1 si futuri essent et non quia futuri erant promisit. quia non propter fidem Abrahae placuit Deo saluas fore omnes gentes, quas non ante fidem Abrahae sed ante mundi constitutionem possedit. sed quaesiuit fidelem cui id donaret ex quo esset quod futurum statuerat. Abraham ergo non id meruit ut essent sed ut per ipsum essent qui futuri erant quos Deus elegerat, et *conformes imaginis filii sui* futuros esse praeuiderat. Ro viii 29 in Genesi namque de praescientia Dei omnes gentes

1 ipsa] in ipsa R 1, 2 dicente deo] dicendo V (*sic*) 4, 5 quia autem...abrahae] R *supr ras* (Q×××× ... R*) 4 quia] ne qui V quibusdam] quibus V 5 meriti V 6 eius] ipsius V 7 statuturum] staturum R 14 uiuus] iuuus R* 16 debetur] debitur R *post ras* 17 debitore] debere V 19 expectare V* *mox corr* 21 merces] mercis V *ut infra* 23 mercis R*V 27 id] *om* R*M 28 quod] cui id V 29 sed ut per ipsum essent] *om* R

Gen xviii 18, 19 Abrahae promissas Scriptura testatur dicens: *Abraham autem fiens fiet et erit in gentem magnam et multam, et benedicentur in eo omnes gentes terrae. sciebat enim quia disponebat Abraham filiis suis et domui suae post se, et custodient uias Domini facere iustitiam et iudicium, ut superducat Deus in Abraham quaecumque locutus est ad eum.* RV (M)

cf Esai i 19 Inuenimus autem et conditiones ut: *Si me audieritis et uolueritis.* ubi praescientia Dei, ubi firmitas promissionis in huiusmodi conditionibus? dicit etiam apostolus propterea ex fide et non ex lege datam esse promissionem ut firma esset Ro iv 15, 16 promissio. *Lex* inquit *iram operatur; ubi enim non est lex neque transgressio est. propterea ex fide ut secundum gratiam firma esset promissio omni semini.* recte *ut firma esset promissio,* adiecta enim conditione non est firma. satis enim stultum est et proteruum credere in totum corpus conuenire quod bipertito corpori dicitur. absit ut his dicat Deus *si me audieritis* quos sciebat audituros, et quos antequam faceret nouerat in imagine Dei perseueraturos, quos et promisit. non est data conditio, id est lex, nisi impiis et peccatoribus, ut aut ad gratiam confugiant aut iustius puniantur si irritam fecerint. 1 Tim i 9 ut quid lex ad iustos quibus *lex posita non est;* qui propitio Deo legem sine lege faciunt, qui liberi Deo seruiunt, qui ad imaginem et similitudinem Dei et Christi uiunt? uolentes boni sunt. qui enim sub lege est metu mortis non est apertus homicida; non est talis misericors, non est imago Dei. displicet illi lex sed metuet ultricem, nec perficere potest, quod non uoto sed necessitate faciendum putat. tradatur necesse est propriae uoluntati, ut uoluntatis profecto praemium recipiat qui animam non miscuit uoluntati Dei. dis-

4 domui suae] domus suae V 4, 5 et custodient...facere] ut custodiens...faceret R (*sed cf* LXX) 7 et 1°] *om* R; ut R^b *supr lin* 9 etiam] enim V 11 inquid V* 14 adiecta] aiecta V* condicione V (*uid Appx* II) 15 et proteruum] & p̄peum V (= et propter eum); V^b *exp has litteras corruptas* 17 et] *om* V 18 in] *om* V 19 data data V* (*corr a* V^a) 20 irritam] irritum V 20, 21 fecerint ut] fecerunt R*, -rint R^a 21 non est posita V 22 qui liberi deo seruiunt] *om* RM 24, 25 non est apertus homicida] *om* V 26 metuet] timet V 27 tradatur] traditur R 28 ut uoluntatis] V*; *om* R; ut uoluntas V*corr* profecto] pro facto V 29 dei] *om* R

RV (M) plicet illi quod Deus uoluit. etenim uoluntate malus est qui necessitate bonus est. lex operi inpedimento est non uoluntati. non est coniunctus Deo qui si mali poena non esset malum sequeretur; nec uoluntatem Dei facit qui gemit quod non suam faciat. et non est misericors qui timet esse crudelis: sub lege est, seruus est. non furtum odit sed poenam metuit. furetur autem necesse est persuasus et uictus, quia carnalis est sub uirtute peccati, Spiritum Dei non habens. qui autem amat bonum imago Dei est et fide dominica uiuit, ut heres iam non sit ancillae filius qui accipit legem in cf Gal iv 30 timorem, sed liberae secundum Isaac qui *non* accepit *spiritum* Ro viii 15 *seruitutis in timorem sed adoptionis filiorum clamantem Abba pater.* qui diligit Deum non timet seruiliter. scriptum est: *Timor non est in dilectione, sed consummata dilectio foras* 1 Ioh iv 18 *mittit timorem. quoniam timor poenam habet, qui autem timet non est consummatus in dilectione.* timor enim seruilis cum odio est disciplinae, filii autem cum honore patris.

Aliud est timere ex lege, aliud honorare pro ueneratione tremendae Dei maiestatis. eiusmodi similes sunt patri suo qui in caelis est, commemorati et edocti amant bonum oderunt malum. non metu fugiunt malum, non necessitate faciunt bonum; sine lege sunt, liberi sunt, ipsi promissi sunt.
55 non ipsis dicitur Si me audieritis. cui dicitur Si me audieritis potest et non audire; numquid conuenit in eum quem Deus ante mundum praeuidit auditurum? et iusti quidem *quos* Ro viii 29 Deus *praesciuit* sunt in ista lege. dicitur et ipsis Si me audieritis, sed alia causa, non quia possunt non audire, sed ut semper solliciti sint suae salutis, incerti exitus sui. non enim securus est unusquisque ex numero se esse praescitorum, apostolo dicente: *Ne ipse reprobus fiam.* non est ergo 1 Co ix 27 illis irae operatrix ista lex sed fidei exercitium, quo iugiter

2 impedimento R 5 suam] sua R et] *om* V 7 quia] qui V 9 et] *om* V 10 ut...sit] et...est V accipit] accepit V 11 timorem] timore V 12 in timore V adoptionem V 16 dilectione] dilectu V 18 honorare] *om* V 21, 22 faciunt] faciant V* 23 cui dicitur si me audieritis] *om* V 24 et non] etenim V conueniet V 25 ante] *om* V 26 praesciuit] praesciit V 27 alia] ad alia R 28 incerti] et certi V 29, 30 praescitorum] praesciturum V* 31 operatrix|rix V* (*sic*) *mox corr* quo] quod R

Dei gratiam quaerant laborantes ut perficiatur quod in illis RV Deus praeuidit, et de libero arbitrio fuerint ad uitam destinati. alias inpossibile est non audire eum quem Deus auditurum praeuidit, promisit, iurauit.

In quam uero partem lex proprie conueniat, licet uni detur corpori, Dominus in Euangelio declarat dicens apostolis: Ioh xiii 17, 18 *Si haec scitis beati estis si feceritis ea. non de omnibus uobis dico; ego scio quos elegi.* magna breuitas ostendentis unum corpus et separantis! si enim diceret: Non de uobis dico, aut: Non de omnibus dico, non ostenderet unum corpus. nunc autem *non de omnibus uobis dico* ostendit quia et si non de omnibus de illis tamen dixit, sicut quis dicat Non de toto te dixi. duo autem corpora mixta sunt uelut unum, et in commune unum corpus laudatur aut increpatur. sicut in Exodo, cum quidam contra uetitum sabbati exissent manna Ex xvi 28 colligere, ait Deus Moysi: *Quousque non uultis audire legem meam*, cum Moses semper audierit?

Quid de illa lege dicemus quae aperte promissioni uidetur cf Esai xlviii 18, 19 aduersa? sicut scriptum est in Esaia: *Si me audisses Israhel, esset sicut harena maris numerus tuus.* ecce increpatur Israhel quod uitio suo non fuerit factus sicut harena. superest intellegere quia si semper non audierit semper exiguus erit. et ubi firmitas promissionum? sed hoc fit quia prius uolumus intellegere quam credere et fidem rationi subicere. si autem credamus omni modo ita fieri ut Deus iurauit, dabit rationem fides quam perfidum est rationem quaerere, et intellegemus firmitatem magis esse promissionum quam putamus infirmitatem. hoc enim dictum *si me audisses Israhel* commemoratio est iustitiae Dei et conformatio promissionum,

1 gratia V* 2 libero] libĕro R (*sic*) fuerint] fuerunt R ad uitam] in uitam V 5, 6 uni detur] uidetur R 7 scitis] V^b *supr ras* 10 aut non de omnibus dico] *om* R ostendere V* 13 autem] enim V uelut] uɫ R (=uel); uelat V 14 commune] commone R (*cf p* 5^{11}); commate V 15 sabbati] sabbatis V exissent] exisse ut V*; exisset ut V *corr* 16 colligeret V 17 moses] moÿses V 18 dicimus V 19 sicut] *om* V esaia] isaia V^b 20 arena V 20, 21 maris...sicut harena] *om* R 21 harena] arena maris V 24 subicere] RV; subiecere R^a 26 rationem] rationes V 26, 27 intellegimus V

RV ne quis putaret non libero arbitrio sed dispositione Dei quosdam factos ad mortem quosdam uero ad uitam. propterea praesentibus dixit *si me audissetis*, ut manifestum fieret post promisit, ut harenam futuros quia praeuidit audituros. ante Dominum enim Christum, cum de hoc dictum est, numquam fuit semen Abrahae sicut harena maris. quod probare facile est. primum quia in Christo promisit hanc multitudinem: *Non in seminibus quasi in multis sed quasi in uno, et semini* Gal iii 16 *tuo quod est Christus.* deinde quia omnes gentes promisit, quod ante Christum fieri non potuit. et si fuit ante Dominum numerus filiorum Israhel sicut harena maris, sed cum falsis fratribus qui non sunt filii Abrahae. non enim quia omnes ex Abraham omnes filii Abrahae aut quia ex Israhel ii Israhel. sicut apostolus, cum se *anathema optaret* pro cf Ro ix 3 ff Israhel *quorum* esset *filiorum adoptio* et *testamenta*, ostendit non esse huiusmodi filios Abrahae, sed de affectu carnalis necessitudinis doleret quod ex ipso numero non essent, non quod promissio Dei excidisset, dicens: *Non tamen excidit* Ro ix 6–8 *sermo Dei, non enim omnes qui sunt ex Israhel hi sunt Israhel neque quia sunt semen Abrahae omnes filii, sed in Isaac uocabitur tibi semen; id est non qui sunt filii carnis hi sunt filii Dei, sed filii promissionis deputantur in semen.*

Ergo in antiqua multitudine non fuit Abrahae semen, nisi illi qui secundum Isaac fidei et promissionis filii erant. etiam hoc exemplum inducit: *Si fuerit numerus filiorum Israhel* Ro ix 27 *sicut harena maris, reliquiae liberabuntur*, id est exiguum. et: *Nisi Dominus Sabaoth reliquisset nobis semen sicut Sodoma* *Ib* 29 *essemus.* ipsae reliquiae fuerunt semen Abrahae, ne omnis Iudaea ut Sodoma esset. iterum cum assereret numquam Deum hereditatem suam reliquisse sed sicut in aduentu Domini pars Israhel salua facta est ita semper fuisse. *Quid* Ro xi 4, 5

1 ne quis...sed] *om* V 2 ad] aut V* uero] ××××ero V* 3 post] quia quos V 4 harenam R *semp*; V *hic, et infr* futuros] + ideo promisit V 5 de hoc] hoc V 7 hanc] hunc V* 13 ex israhel] *om* ex V 14 ii Israhel] *conieci*: uel ir⁊ R; omnes israhel V optaret] + esse V 18 excedit R 21 hi] hii RV 24 etiam] &|iam V*; &i|am *uoluit* V *corr* 28 ipsae] ipse V (e *pro* ae *saepe occurrit in* V *et uice uersa*)

RV (M)

inquit *dicit responsum? reliqui mihi septem milia uirorum qui non curuauerunt genua Bahal. sic nunc reliqiuae secundum electionem gratiae saluae factae sunt.* dicendo *sic nunc in hoc tempore* ostendit et ante sic factum in Israhel ut reliquiae, id est modicum, saluum fieret.

Si autem nec fides nec ratio persuadet, sed ei qui pro- [cf Esai xlviii 18, 19] missus fuerat dictum est: *Si me audisses Israhel, esset sicut harena maris numerus tuus.* et Iacob qui ante quam nasceretur electus est, idem de libero arbitrio post modum repro- [Os xii 2—4] batus est, sicut Osee dicit: *Iudicium Domini ad Iudam ut uindicet in Iacob secundum uias eius,* et *secundum studia eius retribuet ei.* quia *In utero supplantauit fratrem suum et in laboribus suis inualuit ad Deum, et inualuit cum angelo et potens factus est.* si autem constat in Iacob dilectum consummasse, non est idem qui *in laboribus inualuit ad Deum* et [cf Gen xxv 23] *supplantator,* sed duo in uno corpore. figura est enim duplicis seminis Abrahae, id est duorum populorum in uno utero matris Ecclesiae luctantium. unus est secundum electionem de praescientia dilectus, alter electione suae uoluntatis iniquus. Iacob autem et Esau in uno sunt corpore ex uno [cf Gal iv 24] semine. sed quod perspicue duo procreati sunt *ostensio* est *duorum* populorum.

Et ne quis putaret ita perspicue fore separatos duos populos, ostensum est ambos in uno corpore futuros in Iacob, qui [cf Deut xxxii 15] et *dilectus* uocatus est et *fratris supplantator* expressus. itaque in duobus quantitas expressa est non qualitas separationis. ceterum ambo qui separati sunt in uno futuri ante [Gen xxvii 35] quam diuiduntur ostensi sunt. et Isaac *Venit* inquit *frater tuus cum dolo et accepit benedictionem.* nisi ista locutio mystica sit breuiter ostendentis duo in uno corpore, nonne contra rationem est ut benedictionem in proximum dolosus acce-

1 inquid V responsum]+diuinum V 2 genua] genu V 3 gratiae] *om* V dicendo] dicente R 9 electus] relictus V* *mox corr* idem de] id est de R; idem V; *saepe in MSS* idem (idē) *uix differt ab* id est (id ē) 10 osee] osse R (*cf* issac *p* 13[10] *not*) 12 supplantabit V* 19 alter] aliter V* electionem V* 21 ostensio] ostentio R: *ad Gal iv* 24 *cf Tert adv Marc V* ii 284 23 perspicue] V*corr*; ×××spicu×× V* 28 diuidantur V 29 dolo et accepit] dilectaccepit V* loquutio R 31 dolosus] dolos V*; dolose V[a]

RV (M) perit, Scriptura dicente: *Qui non iurauit proximo suo in dolo, iste accipiet benedictionem a Domino?* (Ps xxiii 4) numquam autem Iacob, id est Ecclesia, uenit ad benedictionem non comitante dolo, id est falsis fratribus. sed non quia innocentia et dolus simul ueniunt ad benedictionem simul benedicentur, quia *qui potest capere* capit, (cf Mt xix) et unum semen pro qualitate terrae prouenit.

Non est autem contrarium quod malum fratrem uidetur supplantasse, quia non dixit *in utero supplantauit Esau* sed *fratrem suum.* Esau autem ubique signum est et nomen malorum, Iacob autem utrorumque, illa ratione quod pars mala simulet se Iacob et sint duo sub uno nomine. pars autem bona non potest se simulare Esau: inde est hoc nomen malorum tantum, illud uero bipertitum. ceterum de libero arbitrio nec Iacob omne semen bonum nec Esau omne malum, sed ex utroque utrumque. ex Abraham ita bipertitum semen ostensum est. natum est unum ex ancilla in figura, ut ostenderetur et seruos futuros ex Abraham, et recessit cum sua matre. post quam uero recessit inuentum est in alterius semine, quod est ex libera, quod est ex Israhel qui accepit legem *in monte Sina, quod est Agar in seruitutem generans.* (Gal iv 24) illic in eodem populo secundum Isaac ex libera *promissionis filii,* id est sancti et fideles, multi procreati sunt. separatis itaque a credentibus figuris Ismahel et Esau, in uno populo totum post modum prouenit. illic ab origine utrumque Testamentum Agar et Isaac, sed pro tempore alterum sub alterius nomine, delituit et delitescit, quia neque reuelato nouo quiescit uetus generando. non enim dixit *Agar quae in senectute generauit,* sed *Quae est Agar in seruitutem generans.*

Oportet autem *ambos simul crescere usque ad messem.* (Mt xiii 30) sicut ergo tunc sub professione ueteris Testamenti latuit

1 scriptura] scriptum · ē R suo] *om* V 5 benedicuntur V 6 capit] capiat V 9 et] *om* R 10, 11 utrorumque...pars mala] R *supr ras* 10 quod] quo R 11 sint duo sub] sine dubio V 12 inde] *om* V, *spatio relicto* 16 natum] natunc V* unum] unam V* 17 et seruos] etiam seruos V 20 in seruitute R 21 secundum] secundi V 21, 22 ex libera...fideles] R *supr ras* 23 ismahel et] *conieci*: ir-l (=israhel) R; israhel et V 25 isaac] R*V; issac R[a] 26 dilituit et dilitescit R; delituit et delitiscit V 27, 28 in senectute ...est agar] *om* V 29 ambos] ambo V

nouum, id est gratia quae secundum Isaac promissionis filios RV
generaret ex libera, quod in Christo reuelatum est; ita et
nunc optinente nouo non desunt seruitutis filii generante
Agar, quod Christo iudicante reuelabitur. confirmat apostolus
id nunc quoque inter fratres geri quod tunc inter illos gere-
Gal iv 28–29 batur dicens: *Vos autem fratres secundum Isaac promissionis
filii estis. sed sicut tunc qui secundum carnem natus est per-
sequebatur spiritalem, ita et nunc.* et necessario addidit:
Ib 30 *Quid dicit Scriptura? expelle ancillam et filium eius, non
enim coheres erit filius ancillae cum filio liberae.* quod autem
dixit *sicut tunc persequebatur ita et nunc,* non est inane.
apostolus enim interpretatus est *persequebatur.* nam Scrip-
cf Gen xxi 9 tura dicit: *Ludebat* Ismahel *cum Isaac.* numquid fratres
qui circumcisionem Galatis praedicabant aperte illos et non
per lusum, id est sine indicio persecutionis, insequabantur?
sicut ergo Ismahel genere ludendi persecutorem dixit, ita et 56
istos, qui filios Dei uelut per communem utilitatem, id est
disciplinam legis, a Christo separare et matris suae Agar filios
facere militant.

cf Gal ii 4 Alia enim non est causa qua filii diaboli inrepant *ad ex-
plorandum libertatem nostram,* et simulent se fratres et in
Paradiso nostro uelut Dei filios ludere, quam ut de subacta
cf Gal v 10 libertate filiorum Dei glorientur; *qui portabant iudicium
qualescumque illi fuerint,* qui omnem sanctum persecuti sunt,
cf Ac vii 51 qui prophetas occiderunt, qui *semper Spiritui Sancto restite-
Phil iii 18 runt; inimici crucis Christi, negantes Christum in carne* dum
I Ioh iv 3
cf 2 The ii 3, 7, 9 eius membra oderunt, corpus *peccati, filius exterminii* in *mys-
terium facinoris,* qui ueniunt *secundum operationem Satanae
Eph vi 12 in omni uirtute signis et prodigiis falsitatis, spiritalia nequi-*

1 gratia quod V 3 nouo non desunt] nouandę sunt V filii] fili V 7 filii] fili V qui] quae R* *mox corr* natus] na×tus V* 9 quid] sed quid V 10 cum] *om* V 12 interpraetatus R, *et sic aliquando* 14 circumcisionem] circumcisionis V*; -ones V*corr* 15 insequabatur V 16 ismahel]+de V dixit] ××xit R* 17 communem] commonē R (*cf supra p* 26[14]) 18 matris] matri V 20 *inter* Alia *et* enim *rasura in* R inrepant] increpant V 21 simulant R 22 paradẏso V ut] *om* V 23 portabant] RV*; portabunt V[a] 26 in carnem V 27 filius exterminii] V* *vid,* filii exterminii V *nunc*; filius •ē• extermini R 27, 28 mysterium] V; ministerium R 29 signi R

RV (M) *tiae in caelestibus*, quos *Dominus* Christus quem in carne per- 2 The ii 8 secuntur *interficiet spiritu oris sui et destruet manifestatione aduentus sui.* tempus est enim quo haec non in mysteriis sed aperte dicantur, inminente *discessione* quod est reuelatio cf 2 The ii 3 *hominis peccati*, discedente Loth a Sodomis.

IV. De specie et genere.

De specie et genere loquimur, non secundum artem rhetoricam humanae sapientiae, quam qui magis omnibus potuit locutus non est, *ne crucem Christi* fecisset *inanem* si cf 1 Co i 17 auxilio atque ornamento sermonis ut falsitas indiguisset. sed loquimur secundum mysteria caelestis sapientiae magisterio Spiritus Sancti, qui cum ueritatis pretium fidem constituerit mysteriis narrauit in speciem genus abscondens, ut in ueterem Hierusalem totam quae nunc est per orbem, aut in unum membrum totum corpus ut in Salomone. sed hoc tam occultum est quam cetera quae non solum specie breuiante sed etiam multiformi narratione occultantur. quam ob rem Dei gratia in auxilium postulata elaborandum nobis est, et *Spiritus* cf Sap vii 22, 23 *multiplicis ingressus* legendi eloquiumque *subtile*, quo, dum ad cf Sir i 7 inpedimentum intellectus speciei genus aut generi speciem inserit, genus speciesne sit facile uideri possit. dum enim speciem narrat ita in genus transit ut transitus non statim liquido appareat, sed talia transiens ponit uerba quae in

1, 2 persecuntur] R (*sic*) ; ꝑ sequantur V (*sic*) 3 quo] quod V in mysteriis] *om* in V

5 Sodomis] *add* EXPLICIT REGVLA ET PROMISSIS ET LEGE | INCP DE SPECIE ET GENERE R *rubro*; EXPL· DE PROM· ET LEGE || INCIP· DE SPECIE ET GENERE·| LIBER ·IIII· V ; *nulla diuisio sectionum in* M

7 artem] uirtutem V; *om* M 8 r&horicam RV 12 cum] quo V 13 mysteriis] mysterii V 15 tam] non V; non tam M 16 speciae R *sic aliquando* breuiante] uerbiante V 17 multiformis V 19 multiplici V eloquiumque...ad] *om* R eloquium . quę V *nunc* suptile V quo dum] *scripsi* : quod V 20 generi speciem] R *nunc*; generis speciem R**vid* V 21 sit] si V possit uideri V 22 non] R *supr lin*

RV [*Eug*] (M)

utrumque conueniant, donec paulatim speciei modum excedat et transitus dilucidetur, cum quae ab specie coeperant non nisi in genus conuenerint. et eodem modo genus relinquit in speciem rediens.

Aliquando autem ab specie in genus non supradicto modo sed euidenter transit et supradicto more reuertitur. aliquando supradicto modo transit et euidenter reuertitur simili ordinis uarietate, aut ab specie in genere aut a genere in specie finit narrationem. aliquando redit ex hoc in illud non semel, et omnis narratio nec speciem excedit nec genus praeterit in utrumque conueniens. haec uarietas translationis et ordinis exigit fidem quae gratiam Dei quaerat.

Sic Deus per Ezechielem loquitur et regressui eorum qui ab Hierusalem capti et disparsi fuerunt gentium iungit aduentum, et in terra quam patres nostri possiderant exprimit mundum. septem enim gentes Abrahae promissae figura est omnium gentium. *Factus est* inquit *ad me sermo Domini dicens: fili hominis, §domus Israhel habitauit in terra et polluerunt illam in uia sua et in idolis suis et peccatis suis; secundum inmunditiam menstruatae facta est uia eorum ante faciem meam. et effudi iram meam super eos, et disparsi illos inter nationes et uentilaui eos in regiones, secundum uias eorum et secundum peccata eorum iudicaui eos.¶ et ingressi sunt inter nationes quas ingressi sunt illic, et polluerunt nomen meum sanctum, dum dicunt ipsi Populus Domini hic, et de terra sui egressi sunt. et peperci illis propter nomen meum sanctum quod polluerunt domus Israhel in nationibus*

Eze xxxvi 16–36 — § *Eu* 869 — ¶ *Eug*

2 cum quae] cumq· RV 6 more] modo VM reuertitur] reuert&ur R 8, 9 in speciem V 12 quae] quę R*; qui R*corr* 13 sic deus] sed ds R; sic dicit dns V*; ds M ×××zechielem R*; hiezechielum R[b]; ezechielum V regressui] regibus V 14, 21 disparsi V*; dispersi R V*corr* fuerant VM 15 in terram RM possiderunt V*M; possederunt V*corr* 17 inquid V* 18 fili] filii R, *uid Appx* II habitabit V* 19, 20 (pol)luerunt...secundum] *supr ras in* R 19 illam] illum V et peccatis] et in peccatis R* *vid, mox corr* 19, 20 peccatis suis] *om* suis V 22—24 et uentilaui...inter nationes] *om* V 22, 23 secundum uias eorum et] *om* R*; *add* R[a] 24 illic et pollerunt R; et polluerunt illic V 25 hic] hi V; *cf auct ad Nouat* § 10 26 sui] sua V

RV *in quas ingressi sunt illic. propter hoc dic domui Israhel: haec* [Eug] (M) *dicit Dominus, non uobis ego facio domus Israhel, sed propter nomen meum sanctum quod polluistis in nationibus in medio* § Eug 869 *in quas ingressi sunt illic.* incipit iungere genus: §*Et sanctificabo nomen meum sanctum illud magnum quod pollutum est inter nationes quod polluistis in medio earum, et scient gentes quoniam ego sum Dominus, dum sanctificor in uobis ante oculos eorum, et accipiam uos de gentibus et congregabo uos ex omnibus terris et inducam uos in terram uestram.* aperte excedit speciem: *Et aspergam uos aquam mundam et mundabimini ab omnibus simulacris uestris, et mundabo uos et dabo uobis cor nouum, et spiritum nouum dabo in uobis, et auferam cor lapideum de carne uestra et dabo uobis cor carneum, et spiritum meum dabo in uos, et faciam ut in iustitiis meis ambuletis et iudicia mea custodiatis et faciatis. et habitabitis in terra quam dedi patribus uestris, et eritis mihi in populum et ego ero uobis in Deum, et mundabo* ¶ Eug *uos ex omnibus inmunditiis uestris.*¶ adtingit speciem non tamen relinquens genus: *Et uocabo triticum et multiplicabo illud et non dabo in uos famem, et multiplicabo fructum ligni et quae nascuntur in agro, ut non accipiatis ultra obprobrium famis in nationibus. et reminiscemini uias uestras pessimas et cogitationes uestras non bonas, et odio habebitis eas ante faciem eorum in iniquitatibus uestris et in abominationibus eorum. non propter uos ego facio, dicit Dominus; notum est uobis, confundimini et reuertimini de uiis uestris, domus Israhel. haec dicit Adonai Dominus: in die qua mundabo uos ab omnibus iniquitatibus uestris et inhabitari faciam ciuitates,*—in figura terrae Iudae quae bellis uastata fuerat promittit innouari mundum qui a Deo recesserat,—*et reaedi-*

1 in] *om* R*; *add* R^b 4 iungere] ungere R 5 meum sanctum] *tr* R illud] illum V 6 eorum R 7 dum] qui V 10 aspergam] adspergam *Eug* 10, 11 aquam mundam] V (*sic*); aqua munda R *Eug*; aquam munda *Eug* (*cod*): *cf* Lev v 9; Nu viii 7 *Cod Lugd* 11 simulachris V *Eug* (*cod opt*) 13 uobis] uos V 14 uos] uobis R* 18 immunditiis *Eug* attingit V 22 reminiscimini R 23 odio habebitis] odietis V 24 abhominationibus R*corr* 27 adonai dominus] d̄n̄s adoneae d̄n̄s R 28 faciam R*; faciem R^b 29 figura] figurā R

ficabuntur deserta et terra quae exterminata fuerit coletur, RV (M) *propter quod fuit exterminata sub oculis omnis praetereuntis. et dicent: Terra illa quae fuerat exterminata facta est sicut hortus deliciarum, et ciuitates desertae et demolitae munitae consederunt. et scient gentes quaecumque derelictae fuerint in circuitu uestro quia ego sum Dominus. aedificaui demolitas et plantaui exterminatas, quia ego Dominus locutus sum et feci.*

Apostolus quoque in ingressu Iacob promissum esse
Ro xi 25, 26 introitum gentium sic interpretatur dicens: *Donec plenitudo gentium intret, et sic omnis Israhel saluabitur. sicut scriptum est: Veniet a Sion qui liberet et auferet impietates ab Iacob,*
Ib 28 et eodem genere locutionis redit in speciem dicens: *Secundum Euangelium quidem inimici propter uos.*

Item in Ezechiele incipit ab specie quae conueniat et in genus, et finit in solo genere ostendens terram patrum mundi
Eze xxxvii 21—28 esse possessionem. *Haec dicit Dominus, Ecce ego accipiam omnem domum Israhel de medio gentium in quas ingressi sunt illic, et congregabo eos ab omnibus qui sunt in circuitu eorum et inducam eos in terram Israhel. et dabo eos in gentem in terra mea et in montibus Israhel, et princeps unus erit eorum. et non erunt ultra in duas gentes nec diuidentur ultra in duo regna, ne contaminentur adhuc in simulacris suis. et liberabo eos ab omnibus iniquitatibus eorum quibus peccauerunt in eis, et emundabo eos, et erunt mihi in populum et ego Dominus ero illis in Deum.* aperte transit in genus: *Et seruus meus Dauid princeps in medio eorum erit, pastor unus omnium qui in praeceptis meis ambulabunt et iudicia mea custodient et facient ea. et inhabitabunt in terra sua quam ego dedi seruo meo Iacob ubi habitauerint patres eorum, et inhabitabunt in ea*

1 fuerit] fuerat V 2 fuit] *om* R 4 hortus] ortus V 5 considerunt R 9 in ingressu] ingressu R 12 liberet et auferet] eripiat et auertat R (=*Vg*) 13 loquutionis R 15 ezechiele] hiezechielo R[a] *supr ras*; ezechielo V* *vid*; ezechiel V *nunc* 20 inducam] ducam R terram] terra R 20, 21 terra mea] trã meã V 21 montibus] omnibus R 22 duos V* *mox corr* 23 ne] nec R simulachris V (*sic*) 24, 25 et emundabo] *om* et V 26 aperte] V*; a parte V[b] 28 ambulant V 30 habitauerunt V inhabitabunt] habitabunt V

RV *ipsi, et Dauid seruus meus princeps eorum in saecula. et disponam illis testamentum pacis et testamentum aeternum erit cum illis, et ponam sancta mea in medio eorum in saecula et erit habitatio mea in eis, et ero illis Deus et ipsi erunt mihi populus. et scient gentes quia ego sum Dominus qui sanctifico eos, dum sunt sancti in medio eorum in saecula, dicit Dominus.*

Item illic regressui dispersionis Israhel gentium inserit aduentum, et Aegypti heremum figuram populi deserti in quo Ecclesia nunc esse manifestatur, et quod idem mali, quamuis una cum populo Dei ex gentibus reuocentur in terram Israhel, tamen in terra Israhel non sint. *Viuo ego* Eze xx 31–38 *dicit Dominus si respondero uobis, et si ascenderit in spiritum uestrum hoc. et non erit quem ad modum dicitis uos: Erimus sicut gentes et sicut tribus terrae ut seruiamus lignis et lapidibus. uiuo ego, dicit Dominus, nisi in manu forti et brachio excelso et in ira effusa regnabo super uos, et educam uos de populis et recipiam uos de regionibus in quibus dispersi estis in manu forti et brachio excelso* <*et*> *in ira effusa, et*
57 *adducam uos in desertum populorum, et disputabo illic ad uos facie ad faciem, quem ad modum disputaui ad patres uestros in deserto terrae Aegypti sic iudicabo uos, dicit Dominus. et redigam uos sub uirgam meam et inducam uos in numero, et eligam impios de uobis et desertores, quoniam ex transmigratione eorum educam eos et in terram Israhel non intrabunt, et cognoscetis quia ego sum Dominus.*

Item illic captiuitati montium Israhel promittit Deus ubertatem et multiplicationem populorum usque in finem. *Quoniam dederunt* inquit *terram tuam sibi in possessionem* Eze xxxvi 5–10 *cum iucunditate inhonorantes animas, ut exterminarent in*

2 test. pacis et] *om* R 3 et ponam] ponam et R 4 eis] illis V 6 sancti] sancta V; τὰ ἅγιά μου LXX 7 regressui] regressio R dispersiones V* 8 aegypti] ęegýptum V (*sic*), ‘a’ *exp* Va (*sic fere semp*) figuram] + fuisse V 9 esse] est V; *exp* Va 11 terram] V*corr*; terra RV* 17 uos] *om* R *utroque loco* 18 et in ira] et *om* RV 19 in deserto V illic] illis V* *corr in scribendo* 21 sic] sicut V* *mox corr* 22 sub uirga mea V, *cf Roensch* 412 23 impios] im *supr ras in* R 24 eos] uos R in terra R 25 cognoscitis R 26 captiuati V* 28 dederunt inquit] *tr* R *mox corr* inquid V* 29 iocunditate V ut] atque V

RV (M) *uastationem; propterea profetare super terram Israhel et dic montibus et collibus et riuis et nemoribus: haec dicit Dominus, Ecce ego in zelo meo et in ira mea locutus sum, propter quod obprobrium gentium portastis. ecce ego leuabo manum meam super nationes quae sunt in circuitu uestro, hi iniuriam suam accipient; uestri autem montes Israhel uuam et fructum uestrum manducabit populus meus qui adpropinquat uenire. quia ecce ego super uos et respiciam super uos et colemini et semina<bi>mini, et multiplicabo super uos totam domum Israhel usque in finem, et habitabuntur ciuitates, et quae desolatae erant aedificabuntur.*

Item illic uelut in nouissima resurrectione prima significatur. (Eze xxxvii 11—14) *Locutus est* inquit *ad me Dominus dicens: fili hominis ossa haec omnis domus Israhel est. ipsi dicunt: arida facta sunt ossa nostra, interiit spes nostra, expirauimus. propterea profetare et dic: haec dicit Dominus, Ecce ego aperiam monumenta uestra et educam uos de monumentis uestris et inducam uos in terram Israhel, et scietis quia ego Dominus cum aperiam sepulchra uestra et educam de monumentis populum meum, et dabo Spiritum meum in uos et uiuetis, et ponam uos super terram uestram et scietis quia ego sum Dominus.* numquid cum perspicue surrexerimus tunc sciemus Dominum, et non nunc cum per baptisma resurgimus? aut mortui poterunt dicere: *Arida facta sunt ossa nostra*, aut merito mortuis id promissum esse credamus? quod est enim sacramenti ne in ambiguum ueniret aperuit Deus. nam de nouissima carnis resurrectione neminem Christianum credimus dubitare. et Dominus per Iohannem has resurrectiones manifestat dicens: (Ioh v 24—29) *Amen dico uobis quia qui uerbum meum audit et credit ei qui me misit habet uitam aeternam, et in iudicium non uenit sed*

1 profetare] prophetare RV*; propheta V^a, *uide p* 40^{18} *et Appx* II 3 meo] mea R^a 4 portastis] portatis V leuabo] zelabo R 5 hi] *om* R 6 accipiunt R 7 manducauit V* apropinquat V*; appr- V*corr* 8 et respiciam super uos] *om* V 9 seminamini RV 16 prophetare R; propheta V 20 uiuitis R 22 cum perspicue] perspicue V*; perspicue cum V*corr* surrexerimus] M; surreximus R *nunc*, surre *supr ras*; resurrexerimus V 23 potuerunt R 24 aut] ut R 26 ambigum V* 28 per] secundum VM 30 et *supr ras in* V uenit] ueniet V

RV (M) *transit de morte ad uitam. amen dico uobis quoniam uenit hora et nunc est quando mortui audient uocem filii Dei et qui audierint uiuent. sicut enim Pater habet uitam in se, sic dedit Filio uitam habere in se. et potestatem dedit ei et iudicium facere quia filius hominis est.* iungit nouissimam resurrectionem: *Nolite mirari hoc, quia ueniet hora in qua omnes qui in monumentis sunt audient uocem filii Dei, et exient qui bona fecerunt in resurrectionem uitae, qui male fecerunt in resurrectionem iudicii.* primo dixit *Mortui qui audierint uiuent,* secundo *Omnes qui in monumentis sunt exient.*

Item quod in uno homine totum corpus significetur, in Regnorum promittit Deus Dauid Salomonem dicens: *Suscitabo semen tuum post te qui erit ex utero tuo et parabo regnum eius. ipse aedificabit mihi domum.* (2 Regn vii 12—16) ista et in speciem et in genus conueniunt. excedit speciem dicens: *Et dirigam thronum eius usque in aeternum.* iterum in utrumque: *Ego ero ei in patrem et ipse erit mihi in filium. et si uenerit iniustitia eius arguam eum in uirga hominum et in tactibus filiorum hominum; misericordiam autem meam non auferam ab eo sicut abstuli a quibus abstuli e conspectu meo, et fidelis fiet domus eius.* iterum excedit speciem: *Et regnum eius usque in aeternum in conspectu meo, et thronus eius erit confirmatus usque in aeternum.* quod autem uidetur in excessu speciei thronum Christi promittere in aeternum, thronum filii hominis promittit, ita corporis Christi, id est Ecclesiae. non enim propter Dauid promisit Deus regnaturum Christum, qui *ante constitutionem mundi habuit hanc claritatem.* (cf Ioh xvii 5, 24) et per Esaiam sic dicit Deus Christo: *Magnum tibi erit* (Esai xlix 6)

1 transit] transiet V*corr* de] a V 2 quando] quo R* *vid* audient] audiunt R 3 habet uitam] *tr* V 4 se] semetipso V 6 mirare R 7 filii] fili V, *uid Appx* II 8 qui] + uero R (= *Vg*); + autem V male] mala V 8—16 male fecerunt...in aeternum] R *supr ras in char minore* 10 secundo...exient] R *ad calc pag* 11 uno hominem V (*sic*) 14 aedificauit V* 14, 15 ista...genus] *om* V 15 excedit] *pr* et R*corr* (*supr lin*) V 16 iterum] item V 17 patre ...filio V 18 tactibus] *scripsi*; actibus RV: ἀφαῖς LXX 20 e conspectu meo] conspectumeo V*; conspectũ meũ V*corr* 21 iterum] item R 22 usque] *om* V meo] eius R 24 specie V 25 fili V* promittit ita] *conieci*; promitti R; promi & ita V*; promisit & ita V*corr* 27 habuit] promisit V 28 esaiam] R*V*; isaiam R*corr* V*corr* *inter* deus *et* christo *ras in* R

istud, ut uoceris puer meus et statuas tribus Iacob et Israhel RV (M) *dispersionem conuertas; ecce posui te in testamentum generis in lumen gentium, ut sis in salutem usque in nouissimum terrae.* quid maius filio Dei uocari puerum eius et Israhel dispersionem conuertere, aut per eum factum esse ipsum Israhel et caelum et terram et quae in eis sunt uisibilia et inuisibilia? sed ei dicit magnum esse qui filio Dei mixtus est ex semine Dauid. omnis enim promissio Abrahae et Dauid ipsa est, ut semen eorum misceretur ei cuius sunt omnia, et esset coheres in aeternum, non ut propter ipsos regnaret Christus qui est omnium rex a Patre constitutus.

Quid dicemus de Salomone? cum Deo est, an post idolatriam reprobatus est? si cum Deo dixerimus, impunitatem spondebimus idolorum cultoribus. non enim dicit Scriptura paenitentiam egisse Salomonem, aut recepisse sapientiam. si autem reprobatum dixerimus, occurrit uox Dei quae dicit ne terrae quidem regnum Salomoni auferre propter Dauid, 3 Regn xi 11 —13 sicut scriptum est in Regnorum: *Disrumpens disrumpam regnum tuum de manu tua et dabo eum seruo tuo. uerum in diebus tuis non faciam haec propter Dauid patrem tuum; de manu filii tui accipiam eum. uerum omne regnum non accipiam, sceptrum unum dabo filio tuo propter Dauid seruum meum, et propter Hierusalem ciuitatem quam elegi.* quid enim prodest Dauid, si propter eum filius eius regnum terrae consequeretur caeleste perditurus? quo manifestum est cum Deo esse Salomonem, cui ne regnum quidem terrae 2 Regn vii 14, 15; cf Ps lxxxviii 33 ablatum est propter Dauid, quod et dixerat: *Arguam in uirga hominum delicta eius, misericordiam autem meam non auferam ab eo.* quod si neque reprobatus est neque idolorum cultores regnum Dei possident, manifestum est figuram fuisse cf 3 Regn iv 25 Ecclesiae bipertitae Salomonem, cuius *latitudo cordis* et

2 conuertas] R*corr*; conuerta× R* 3 ut sis] et sis V in salute R 4 puerum eius] puer meus V 10 coheredes V* non ut] ut non R 12 dicimus V salamone R 12, 13 idolatriam] RV (*sic semper*); *uid Appx* II 13 inpunitatem V 15 salamonem R aut] R*corr*; a×× R* 16 si autem...uox dei] R *supr ras* occurr& R 17 salomoni auferre] salamoni auferre R; aufert salomone V*; auferret salomone V*corr* 21 omnem regnum V* 25 caelesti V* *vid* 26 salamonem R ne] *om* V 27 arguam]+eum V 28 delicta] peccata V misericordia...mea V 31 salamonem R altitudo cor R

RV (M) *sapientia sicut harena maris* et idolatria horribilis. *Disrumpens* [3 Regn xi 11 12] inquit *disrumpam regnum tuum de manu tua, uerumtamen in diebus tuis non faciam; de manu filii tui accipiam illud.* sufficeret *disrumpam*, quid *disrumpens disrumpam?* aut quomodo *de manu Salomonis*, si dicit *Non faciam in diebus tuis* sed *de manu filii tui accipiam illud?* iugis operationis est *disrumpens disrumpam*, sicut *Benedicens benedicam* [Ge xxii 17] *et multiplicans multiplicabo semen tuum.* ostendit enim semper futurum Salomonem in filio, id est in posteris, cuius postumis Salomonis temporibus non auferet Deus regnum sub promissa patrum, sed corrigit illud usque in aeternum et aufert iugiter, secundum idolatriam Salomonis in suo peccato perseuerantis. alias quomodo de manu Salomonis disrumpens disrumpit aut non disrumpit, si non nunc est Salomon in filiis bonus aut malus? quod autem dicit: *Verum non* [3 Regn xi 13] *omne regnum accipio* in speciem redit, incipiens aliam figuram in filio Salomonis et seruo.

In Hiesu Naue quoque sic Dominus manifeste in uno homine futurum corpus ostendit, sed hoc loco malum tantummodo. *Peccauit* inquit *populus et transgressus est testamentum* [Ies Naue vii 11] *quod disposui ad illos, furati sunt de anathemate, miserunt in uasa sua,* cum solus Achar de tribu Iuda id fecisset. quod corpus semper futurum intellegens Hiesus sic ait, cum eum occideret: *Exterminet te Deus sicut et hodie.* [*Ib* 25]

Illud etiam multo necessarium est scire, omnes omnino ciuitates Israhel et gentium uel prouincias, quas Scriptura alloquitur aut in quibus aliquid gestum refert, figuram esse Ecclesiae: aliquas quidem partis malae, aliquas bonae, aliquas uero utriusque. ergo si sunt aliqua quae etiam in gentes

2 inquid V* 2, 3 uerumtamen] uerum V 4—6 sufficeret...accipiam illud] *om* V 5 *et* 10 salamonis R 9 salomonem R* *sic*; salamonem R[a] 9, 10 postumi R 10 auferet] aufert V sub] secundum V 11, 12 ut aufert V 12 idolatria V salamoni R 13 alias] alios V* salomonis R *et sic infra* 14 aut non disrumpit] *om* R 18 hiesu] R; IHu V sic] +dicit V manifeste] RV* *vid*; manifestans V*corr* 19 ostendi V 20 inquid V* 21 denathemate V* 22 achar] achan M; a×××× V*; acham V*corr* tribu iuda] tribuloda R* 23 hiesus] $\overline{\text{ihs}}$ RV 28 partis] partes V malae] +tantum V 29 ergo si sunt] et si sint V

quae foris sunt uideantur conuenire, in parte tamen quae RV
intus est conuenitur omne corpus aduersum, sicut in Israhel captiuo promittitur gentibus ad Dominum reditus. inpossibile est enim legem loqui ei qui in lege non est; de eo loqui potest, non tamen ad ipsum. et si alicubi sine ista occasione nominis Israhel specialiter alienigenas alloquitur, intus omni modo credendi sunt, quoniam, et si eueniebat specialiter quod profetatum est, Ecclesia tamen est. proprietas denique non omnibus speciebus euenit. nam et Damascus et Tyrus —quae et Sor—et aliae multae usque nunc extant, quas Dominus penitus tolli nec restaurari dixerat.

In alienigenis autem ciuitatibus Ecclesiam conueniri apertum est in Ezechiele, cui cum Deus diceret praedicere interitum in Theman, quae est Esau, et in Dagon, quod est idolum Allophylorum, intellexit parabolam esse aduersus
Eze xx 45–xxi 5 Hierusalem et templum. *Factus est* inquit *sermo Domini ad me dicens: fili hominis confirma faciem tuam super Theman, respice in Dagon, profetare in siluam summam* 58
Nageb, et dices saltui Nageb: audi uerbum Domini; haec dicit Dominus, Ecce ego incendo in te ignem, et comedet in te omne lignum uiride et omne lignum aridum. non extinguetur flamma incensa, et conburetur in ea omnis facies in ea a Subsolano usque ad Aquilonem, et cognoscet omnis caro quia ego Dominus succendi illud, non extinguetur ultra. et dixi: non, Domine. ipsi dicunt ad me: nonne parabola est haec quae dicitur? et factus est sermo Domini ad me dicens: prop-

1 partem R* *mox corr* 2 conuenitur] conuiuitur V* 3 promittit R dominum] $\overline{\text{dm}}$ V 5 ad ipsum tamen non V si alicubi] si alicui R; sine alicubi V 6 alienigena R 8 prophetatum RV ecclesia] ec$\overline{\text{c}}$l V (*sic aliquando, sine terminatione*) 9, 10 tyrus quae] tyrusque R; tirus quae V 10 sor] soor V aliae] aliquae V 11 dominus] $\overline{\text{ds}}$ V 13 hiezechielo R; ezechielo V cui cum] quidim V* *vid* 15 allofilorum V: *uid Appx* II aduersum V 16 factus] factum RV inquid V* 18 profetare] V; proph&are R 19 et dices saltui nageb] *om* V 20 incendo] R*; incendio R*corr*; incendam V commed& R 22 flamma] *pr* in ea R incensa] incensio R $\overline{\text{oms}}$ facies R in ea 2°] *om* V 22, 23 a subsolano] absolano R 23 usque] & usque V* cognoscet] V*corr*; cognoscit RV* 26 factus est] + inquit V (*sic*)

RV *terea fili hominis profetare et confirma faciem tuam ad Hierusalem, respice in sancta eorum, et profetabis super terram Israhel. haec dicit Dominus, Ecce ego educam gladium meum de uagina sua, et disperdam de te iniquum et iniustum. sic exiet gladius meus de uagina sua super omnem carnem a Subsolano usque ad Aquilonem, et sciet omnis caro quia ego sum Dominus, qui emisi gladium meum de uagina sua, non egredietur ultra. Confirma* inquit *faciem tuam* [Eze xx 46] *super Theman et respice in Dagon,* et interpretatus est dicens: *confirma faciem tuam ad Hierusalem et respice in* [*Ib* xxi 2] *sancta eorum,* et ostendit non omnem Hierusalem dicens: *disperdam de te iniquum et iniustum,* et ita futurum genera- [*Ib* 3] liter ait: *sic exiet gladius meus super omnem carnem a Sub-* [*Ib* 4] *solano usque ad Aquilonem.* ostendit in Hierusalem esse Theman, quam illic Deus interficiet et Dagon et omnia execrabilia gentium, operante filio Dauid Salomone in filiis suis. quae etiam euidenter deiecta templa Dei et demolita atque spiritaliter exusta proiecit in torrentem, id est saeculum, qui nascitur filius Dauid Iosias, ut disrumpatur altare in Bethel, sicut scriptum est: *Altare altare, haec dicit Dominus: ecce* [3 Regn xiii 2] *filius nascitur domui Dauid, Iosias nomen illi.*

Nineue ciuitas alienigenarum bipertitae Ecclesiae figura est, sed quia ordine lectionem interpretando persequi longum est, sat erit id quod in speciem conuenire non potest dici. *Erat* inquit *Nineue ciuitas magna Deo,* cum esset [Ion iii 3] aduersa Deo, ut metropolis Assyriorum quae et Samariam deleuit et omnem Iudaeam semper obpressit. sed in figura Ecclesiae praedicante Iona, id est Christo, omnis omnino liberata est. eadem Nineue omnino in sequenti profetia peritura describitur, cui praedicans Dominus *signum* est [cf Mt xii 40]

1 prophetare RV*; propheta V^a 2 respice in] respiciens V prophetabis RV 4 iniquum] inimicum V 8 egredietur] regredietur V* *sed supr ras* inquid V* 11 omnem hierusalem] omne××××××× V* 12 iniquum] inimicum V et ita] ita V 15 interficiet] interfecit V 17 quae] qua V 18 qui] V*; q̊ V*corr* 21 nascetur V 22 alienarum V bipertito R 23 ordinem R 24 sat] satis V specie V 25 dici] dicere V inquid V magna deo] magna d̅i̅ R; magna ad̅o̅ V 27 *post* deleuit *ras in* V oppressit V 28 omnino] *pr* omnis R 29 proph&ia R; propheta V 30 cui] cum R est] *om* R

Ionae in uentre ceti. atque ut et ipse profeta ostendat non RV
esse illam ciuitatem specialem, interponit aliqua quae speciei
Nah iii 3 modum excedant. *Non erat* inquit *finis gentilibus illius,*
Ib 16 cum esset ciuitas unius gentis. et iterum: *Multiplicasti*
mercatus tuos super astra caeli, id est super Ecclesiam. et
Ib 19 iterum: *Super quem non euenit malitia tua semper?* numquid
potuit unius ciuitatis malitia super omnem hominem aut
semper uenisse, nisi illius quam Cain fratris sanguine funda-
cf Ge iv 17 uit *nomine filii sui,* id est posteritatis?

Manifestius adhuc docet profeta Ecclesiam esse Nineue.
Soph ii 13–iii 5 *Et extendet* inquit *manum suam in Aquilonem*—id est populum solis alienum aduersum Meridiano—*et perdet Assyrium, et <ponet> illam Nineue exterminium sine aqua in desertum, et pascentur in medio eius greges, omnes bestiae terrae. et chameleontes et hericii in laquearibus eius cubabunt, et bestiae uocem dabunt in fossis eius, et corui in portis eius, quoniam cedrus altitudo eius. ciuitas contemnens quae habitat in spe, quae dicit in corde suo Ego sum, et non est post me adhuc! quomodo facta est in exterminium pascua bestiarum! omnis qui transit per illam sibilabit, et mouebit manus suas. O inlustris et redempta ciuitas, columba quae non audit uocem, non recepit disciplinam. in Domino non est confisa, et ad Deum suum non adpropinquauit, principes eius in ea ut leones frementes, iudices eius ut lupi Arabiae non relinquebant in mane. profetae eius spiritu elati uiri contemptores, sacerdotes eius profanant sacra et conscelerant legem. Dominus autem iustus in medio eius non faciet iniustum.*

1 co&i RV   propheta RV   ostendat] V*; ostendit V*corr*   3 inquid V   gentilibus] genti gentibus R   6 euenit] uenit V   9 posteritas R*   10 profeta] R[a] (*sic*); profecta R*; propheta V   11 inquid V   12 aduersus V   meridianum V*corr*   perdat R   13 ponet] *addidi*; θήσει LXX   illam nineue] illa nineue R; illud nineue V   sine] siue V   14 greges] gentes R; gregis V   15 cameleontii V   hericii] ericii R; hirci V   19 exterminio V   pascua] ciuitas R   20 sibilauit R   21 inlustras V*   22 audit] RV*; audiuit V*corr*   23 deum] dn̄m V   24 eius 1°] *om* V*   in ea ut] ineant R   25 relinquebant] relinquebunt V*; relinquent V[a]   prophetae RV   spiritu elati] in spu uelati R   26 profanant] prophetant V   27 medio] templo V   faciet] facit R

RV Aegyptus item bipertita est. *Ecce* inquit *Dominus sedet* [Esai xix 1] *super nubem leuem et uenit in Aegyptum.*—nubes corpus est spiritale post baptisma et claritas filii hominis; primus est enim aduentus Domini iugiter corpore suo uenientis, sicut dicit: *A modo uidebitis uenientem in nubibus caeli.*—*Et com-* [Mt xxvi 64; Esai xix 1—3] *minuentur manufacta Aegypti a facie illius, et cor ipsorum minorabitur in illis. et exurgent Aegypti super Aegyptios, et expugnabit homo fratrem suum et homo proximum suum,* et expugnabit *ciuitas supra ciuitatem,* et exurget id est Aegyptus super Aegyptum, *et lex supra legem,* sensus scilicet diuersitate sub una lege, *et turbabitur spiritus Aegyptiorum in ipsis, et cogitationes eorum dispargam.* et postquam nunc generi speciem nunc genus speciei miscuisset adiecit dicens: *Die autem illo erit altare Domini in regione Aegyptiorum, et* [Esai xix 19, 20] *tituli ad terminos eius Domino. erit autem in signum in aeternum Domino in regione Aegyptiorum.* non dixit Decebit esse altare ad terminos Aegypti in aeternum, sed Erit.

Ezechiel uero apertius ostendit totum mundum esse Aegyptum dicens: *O dies! quia prope est dies Domini, dies* [Eze xxx 2—] *finis gentium erit. et ueniet gladius super Aegyptios.* et iungit speciem: *Et erit tumultus in Aethiopia, et cadent uulnerati in Aegypto, et cadent fundamenta eius, Persae et Cretes et Lydii et Lybies et omnes commixticii, et filii testamenti mei gladio cadent in ea cum ipsis.* Hoc autem factum est, cum post excidium Hierusalem descenderent in Aegyptum et occiderentur illic a Nabuchodonosor secundum Hieremiae profetationem. fiet autem et generaliter nouissimo die, quando cum Aegyptis filii testamenti ceciderunt, Aegyptiorum more uiuentes.

Item per Ezechielem minatur Deus regi Aegyptiorum et

3 baptismum V*corr* fili V 6 facie] facie×× V* 7 minorabitur] R[a]; inmorabitur R* aegypti] RV (*sic*) 8 et homo proximum suum] *om* R 9 expugnabit] pugnauit V*; -bit V*corr* supra] super V id est] RV*; *om* V*corr* 12 dispergam RV, *cf pp* 45[5], 52[21] nunc] *om* V* 15 in signum] *om* in R 16, 17 decebit] licebit V 18 hiezechiel R; ezechihel V 21 in] *om* V 23 cr&aes R lidii & libii V commisticii V* 26 et occiderentur] ut occiderent R nobocodonosor R; naboc- R[a] 27 prophetationem RV 28 aegyptis] RV*; aegyptiis V*corr* ceciderunt] R*V*; ceciderint R*corr* V*corr* 29 more] morte V* 30 ezechihelum RV*corr*; ezechielum V*

RV

eius multitudini, quod essent terribiles in sanctos, inter incircumcisos deputari, quod non conuenit nisi in eos qui Eze xxxii 32 sibi circumcisione, id est sacris, blandiuntur. *Quoniam* igitur *dedit timorem suum super terram uitae, dormiet in medio incircumcisorum cum uulneratis gladio Farao et omnis multitudo eius cum ipso, dicit Dominus.* item illic a genere ad Eze xxxii 3–15 speciem: *Haec dicit Dominus, Circumiaciam super te retia populorum multorum, et extraham te in hamo meo, et extendam te super terram. campi <replebuntur> tui, et constituam super te omnes aues caeli, et saturabo omnes bestias uniuersae terrae, et dabo carnes tuas super montes, et satiabo sanguine tuo colles, et rigabitur terra ab his quae de te procedunt. a multitudine tua in montibus uepres inplebo abs te, et cooperiam caelum cum extingueris, et obscurabo astra eius; solem in nube contegam et luna non lucebit lumen eius. omnia quae lucent lumen in caelo obscurabuntur super te, et dabo tenebras super terram tuam, dicit Dominus.* iungit speciem: *Et exasperabo cor populorum multorum, cum ducam captiuitatem tuam in nationes in terram quam non noueras.* excedit speciem: *Et contristabuntur super te multae nationes, et reges earum mentis alienatione stupebunt cum uolabit gladius meus super facies eorum in medio eorum, †erit ad† ruinam suam ex die ruinae tuae.* redit ad speciem: *Quoniam haec dicit Dominus, Gladius regis Babylonis uenit tibi in gladiis gigantum, et deiciam uirtutem tuam, pestes a nationibus omnes, et perdent contumeliam Aegypti et conteretur omnis uirtus eius.* in genus: *Et perdam omnia pecora eius ab aqua multa, et non*

1, 2 inter circumcisos V 4 uitae dormiet] uitae dormir& V*; *om* uitae V*corr* 5 cum uulneratis] *scripsi*: cum uulneratus R; uulneratus V pharao R 6 item] et V *supr ras* 7 circumiacium V* super te retia] super tertiam V 8 extrahunt V* hamo meo] amoneo V*; amo meo V*corr* 9 replebuntur] *suppleuit Sabat.; om* RV 11 montes] o̅m̅s̅ R 13 implebo V 15 luna] R* lunae R*corr* V 16 lumen] V*; lumina R; lumine V*corr*; *πάντα τὰ φαίνοντα φῶς* LXX super te] *om* V 18 ducū V* *vid* 19 tuam] tuae V* 21 alienationes R uolauit R 22 erit ad ruinam] RV: *cf p* 45[12]; *προσδεχόμενοι τὴν πτῶσιν* LXX 23 tuae] suae R ad] in V 24 babilonis V in gladiis] gladius R 25 deieciam R pestis R omnis R 26 contumelia R eius] eòrùm eius V (*sic*) 27 eius ab] *om* V

RV *turbabit eam pes hominis ultra, et uestigium pecorum non cal-
cabit eam. tunc requiescent aquae eorum, et flumina eorum
ut oleum abibunt, dicit Dominus.* species: *Et dabo Aegyptum
in interitum, et desolabitur terra cum plenitudine sua et dis-
pargam omnes inhabitantes eam.* genus: *Et scient quia ego
sum Dominus. Operiam* inquit *caelum cum extingueris, et* Eze xxxii 7, 8
*obscurabo astra eius; solem in nube contegam, et luna non
lucebit lumen eius. omnia quae lucent lumen in caelo obscura-
buntur super te, et dabo tenebras super terram tuam.* in pas-
sione Domini non in terra Aegypti tantum fuerunt tenebrae, cf Lc xxiii 45
sed in toto orbe. sed nec capta Aegypto obstipuerunt
gentes, *expectantes ruinam suam ex die ruinae* eius. Eze xxxii 10

Nam et de Sor scriptum est: *Haec dicit Dominus ad Sor,* Eze xxvi 15—18
*Nonne a uoce ruinae tuae in gemitu uulneratorum, dum inter-
ficiuntur gladio in medio tui, commouebuntur insulae? et
descendent a sedibus suis omnes principes maris, et auferent
mitras et uestem uariam suam despoliabunt se. in stupore
mentis stupebunt et timebunt in interitu tuo, et ingemescent
super te, et accipient super te lamentationem, et dicent tibi:
Quomodo destructa est de mari ciuitas illa laudabilis, quae
dedit timorem suum omnibus inhabitantibus in ea! et time-
bunt insulae ex die ruinae tuae.* iterum de eadem: *In die* Eze xxvii 27—36
*ruinae tuae ad clamorem uocis tuae gubernatores tui timore
timebunt, et descendent de nauibus omnes remiges tui, et uec-*
59 *tores et proretae maris super terram stabunt, et ululabunt
super te uoce sua, et clamabunt amarum super te, et inponent
super caput suum terram, et cinerem sternent, et accipient
super te lamentationem filii eorum, lamentam Sor: Quantum*

4, 5 dispargam] V*; dispergam RV*corr* 5 eam] in ea V 6 operam inquid V* extinguaeris V* 7 luna] *scripsi, uid supra*; lunę R; lunae V 8 lucent lumina R 8, 9 obscurabunt V 11 obstupuerunt R 12 expectantes] expugnantes R 13 sor] soor V scriptum] *pr* sic V 14 a uoce ruinae tuae] a ruina&uae V 15 insulae] in sole V* 16 descendent] discedent V 17 uariam suam] aurium suum V dispoliabant V*; -bunt V*corr* 18 stupebunt...inge(miscent)] R *supr ras* 20 quae] qui V 22 insulae] insylę R 23 gubernatoris R 23, 24 timore...remiges tui] *om* R 26 uocem suam RV 28 filii eorum] *scripsi ex* LXX; filiorum RV lamentam] lamentum V sor] R *semp*, V *hic*

inuenisti mercedem de mari! satiasti gentes multitudine tua, et a commixtione tua locupletasti omnes reges terrae. nunc autem contrita es in mari, in profundo aquae commixtio tua, et omnis congregatio tua in medio tui. ceciderunt omnes remiges tui, omnes qui inhabitant insulas contristati sunt super te, et remiges eorum mentis alienatione stupuerunt, et lacrimatus est uultus eorum super te. mercatores de gentibus exibilabunt te; perditio facta es, et ultra non eris in aeternum, dicit Dominus. numquid in unam insulam conueniunt quae dicta sunt, aut sola potuit locupletare omnes reges terrae? sed aliqua relinquimus locis oportunis, quibus etsi strictim dicantur uideri possunt. RV

Tyrus bipertita est, sicut per Esaiam, qui post multa
Esai xxiii 15—17 speciei et generis hoc quoque adiecit dicens: *Erit post septuaginta annos Tyrus sicut canticum fornicariae. accipe citharam, uagulare, ciuitas fornicaria oblita; bene citharizare, multa canta, ut tui commemoratio fiat. et erit post septuaginta annos respectionem faciet Deus Tyri, et iterum restituetur in antiquum <, et erit commercium omnibus regnis terrae>.* numquid credibile est uniuersa regna terrarum Tyrum uenire negotiandi causa? quod si ueniant, quae utilitas praedixisse
Ib 17 futura Tyro *commercia omnibus regnis terrae,* si non Tyrus Ecclesia est in qua orbis terrarum negotium est aeternae uitae?
Ib 18 sequitur enim et ostendit quod sit eius negotium dicens: *Et erit negotiatio eius et merces sancta Domino. non enim illis colligitur, sed illis qui habitant in conspectu Domini. omnis negotiatio eius edere et bibere et repleri in signum memoriale in conspectu Domini.* si ergo negotiatio eius sancta Domini, quomodo potest omnibus esse regnis, nisi ubique fuerit ista Tyrus?

1 mercede R 3 contrita] contristata V 4 congratio R 5 insulas] siluas R 7 mercatores] + eorum V 7, 8 exhibilabunt V*; exsibilabunt Vcorr 8 te] & R es et] est V*; es Vcorr 11, 12 dicuntur V 13 iesaiam Rcorr 15 fornicariae] fornicari R 16 cytharā V uagulare] R, ῥέμβευσον LXX; angulare V citharizari R; cytharizare V 17 multa] + cantica V 18 facit dns R 19 et erit... terrae] *om* RV 20 tyrum] tyro R 22 futuro R commertia R 23 qua] quo R orbis] omne V 25, 27, 28 negotiatio] negotia R 25 mercis RV* 27 aedere V* memoriale] memoriae V 29 regni V

RV Sequitur enim et aperte ostendit quid sit Tyrus dicens: *Ecce Dominus corrumpet orbem terrarum et uastabit illum et* (Esai xxiv 1–13) *nudabit faciem eius. disparget eos qui inhabitant in eo, et erit populus sicut sacerdos,*—num illius orbis cuius negotiatio sancta Domino?—*et famulus sicut dominus et famula sicut domina. et erit emens sicut uendens, et qui debet sicut ille cui debetur, et qui fenerat sicut ille qui feneratur. quia corruptione corrumpetur terra et uastatione uastabitur terra, os enim Domini locutum est ista. planxit terra, corruptus est orbis terrae, planxerunt alti terrae. terra autem facinus admisit propter eos qui habitant in ea, quia transierunt legem et mutauerunt iussa, testamentum aeternum. propterea ergo maledictio comedit terram, quia peccauerunt qui inhabitant in ea. propter hoc egentes erunt qui inhabitant terram,*—numquid illi egentes esse possint, quibus in *omnibus regnis terrae* (cf Esai xxiii 18) *negotiatio* est *edere et bibere et repleri,* non quodam tempore, sed *in signum memoriale in conspectu Domini?*—*et relinquentur homines pauci. lugebit uitis, lugebit uinum, gement omnes quorum iucundatur anima. cessauit iucunditas tympanorum, cessauit inpudicitia et diuitiae impiorum.* numquid sanctorum cessabit uox citharae? *confusi sunt, non biberunt uinum, amarum factum est sicera eis qui bibunt illud. deserta est omnis ciuitas, claudent domos ne introeant. ululate de uino ubique, cessauit omnis iucunditas terrae, et relinquetur ciuitates desertae, et domus derelictae peribunt. haec omnia erunt terrae in medio gentium.* si *deserta est omnis ciuitas,* quae sunt gentes in quarum medio ista sunt?

3 eos] + his V disperget RV, *cf pp* 45[5], 52[21] 4 num] numquid R negotio R 6 uendens] *pr* et V quid debet V* 8 et] e V* 9 ista] haec V corruptus] curuatus V 10 admisit] amisit V 11 inhabitant V* *vid* quia] qui R 12 iussa testamenti aeterni V 13 comed& R habitant V*corr* 14 propter hoc] numquid illi R erunt] erant V 15 possunt V 16 negociatio R 17 memoriale] memoriae V 18 gemant V 19 iocundator V*, iocundatur V*corr* 19, 20 cessauit] *scripsi*, πέπαυται LXX; cessabit RV *utroque loco* 19 iocunditas V 19, 20 tympanorum] tympano cum V 22 uinum] RV*corr*; ×××× V* eis] illis V deser×o V* 23 claudent domos] plaudent oms V 23, 24 de uino] diuino V 24 cessabit V iocunditas V 27 sunt 2°] faciant V

Etsi aliqua horum uidentur et iam perspicue fieri, tamen RV
omnia spiritalia sunt. omnem ciuitatem desertam spiritaliter mortuam dicit, sed Tyri illius meretricis, non cuius est
Esai xxiv 6 negotiatio sancta toto orbe. quod autem dixit *relinquentur homines pauci*—saluo utique statu—eorum qui peribunt. pauci relinquuntur ex eis quos spiritaliter mortuos dicit, qui per recordationem uixerint, quos Ecclesia non interfecerit, sicut multis in locis legimus. sed quia propositum nobis implendum est duobus contenti sumus exemplis. minatur Deus ignem ex igni Israhel regi Assyriorum, id est aduerso corpori, et dicit
Esai x 16—19 arsurum uelut stipulam, paucosque ignem fugituros. *Mittet* inquit *Dominus Sabaoth in tuum honorem ignominiam, et in claritatem tuam ignem ardentem, †et ardebit† lumen Israhel †et erit ibi† ignis, et sanctificabit illud in flamma ardente*—scilicet *lumen Israhel—et manducabit quasi faenum siluam. in illo die ardebunt montes, et per praeripia fugient, quasi qui fugit a flamma ardenti. et qui remanserint ab illis erunt numerus, et puer scribet illos. Qui remanserit* inquit *ab illis*, non ab igni, non enim potest ignis qui conburit ardere; qui autem ex conbustis superauerint ignis efficientur. et in Zacharia legimus illos remanere quos Ecclesia non occiderit, quod ad se conuertantur; ceteros uero spiritaliter cruciatibus interficere, si quidem *stantibus* oculos eruat, et *carnes tabes-*
Zech xiv 11—16 *cere* faciat. *Habitabit* inquit *in Hierusalem confidens. et*

1 et iam perspicue] imperspicue V*; perspicue V*corr* 3 est] *om* V 4 negociatio R tota R quod autem dixit] R; ·hierusalem· ihs autem V (*sic*), *fortasse omnia a prima manu* 5 peribunt] perimunt[r] V 6 relinquuntur] relinquentur V 7 uixerunt V ecclesia] ecclesiasticus V interficerit R sicut] si V 8 praepositum V nobis] orbis V 10 assiriorum V 10, 11 dicit arsurum uelut] dicitur syrum uel ad V* (dicit ad V*corr pro* dicitur) 11 fugituros] futurus V 12 tuum honore ignominia V* *vid* 13, 14 et ardebit...ignis] *debebat esse* 'ardebit. et erit lumen Israhel ut ignis' 14 erit ibi] V*corr*; ardebit V* *vid*; erit tibi R scificauit R flammam ardentem R 15 manducauit R 16 praeripia] precipitia V 17 fugit] fugiat R ardente V 19 non ab igni] *om* V comburit R 20 superauerit R et] *om* V 21 remanere] remeare V 22 cruciantibus R 23 oculos seruat R 24 hierusalem] irl V

RV *haec erit strages qua caedet Dominus populos, quotquot militauerunt aduersus Hierusalem: tabescent carnes eorum stantibus eis super pedes suos, et oculi eorum fluent a foraminibus eorum, et lingua eorum tabescet in ore eorum. et erit in illa die alienatio magna super illos, et adprehendet unusquisque manum proximi sui, et implicabitur manus eius manui proximi eius,*—id est caecus caecum ducens. *et Iudas proeliabitur in Hierusalem, et colliget uires omnium populorum, aurum et argentum et uestem in multitudinem nimis. et haec erit strages equorum et mulorum et camelorum et asinorum et omnium pecorum quae sunt in castris illis, secundum stragem istam. et erit quicumque relicti fuerint ex omnibus gentibus uenientibus super Hierusalem, et ascendent quotquot annis adorare regem Dominum omnipotentem, celebrare diem festum scenopegiae.*

Aelam alienigenarum est. huic speciali iungit generalem, monstratque bipertitam. *Haec dicit Dominus, Confringantur* Hier xxv 35–39
arcus in Aelam principatus eorum. excedit speciem: *Et superducam quattuor uentos a quattuor cardinibus caeli, et dispergam illos per omnes uentos caeli, nec erit gens quae illuc non ueniat, quae expellat Aelam.* redit in speciem: *Et terrebo illos coram inimicis eorum qui quaerunt animas eorum, et superducam in eos secundum iram indignationis meae, et mittam post eos gladium meum, donec consumat eos.* iungit genus: *Et ponam sedem meam in Aelam, et perdam*

1 haec] V*corr*; ha×× V* cedet V dominus] d̅s V quodquod V* 2 hierusalem] i̅r̅l̅ V 4 eorum 1°] suis V linguae...tabescent R 5 illos] eos V adprehendit V* 6 implicabitur] implebitur V 8 praeliabitur R uires] uiros V 9 aurum] *pr* et V in multitudine nimia V[a] 10 haec] *om* V*corr* mulorum et] multorum V 11 pecorum] *om* R illis] illius R 13 gentibus] *om* V*; *add in mg* quotquot] quodquod V* 14 dominum omnipotentem] *scripsi*; i̅h̅m̅ d̅m̅ potentem R; d̅n̅m̅ d̅m̅ o̅mipotentem V caelebrare V 15 scenophegiae R; scinofegiae V*; scenofegiae V*corr* 16 elam V *hoc loco* huic] hic V 17 monstrat quae V (*sic*) confringantur] confringānair V 18 in] *bis scripsit* V* excedit] *pr* et V et] *om* V 22 eorum] R *supr lin* 23 secundum] secum R

RV (M) *inde regem et potentes; eritque in nouissimis diebus auertam captiuitatem Aelam, dicit Dominus.* numquid credendum est non fuisse gentem quae non uenerit ad expugnandam Aelam, aut illic sedem Domini, cuius captiuitatem auertit, nisi Ecclesiae sit figura?

Aliquae uero species sinistrae tantum sunt, ut Sodoma, (Esai i 10) sicut scriptum est: *Audite uerbum Domini principes Sodomorum,* (Ap xi 8) et: *Quae uocatur spiritaliter Sodoma et Aegyptus, ubi et Dominus eorum cruci fixus est.* ex his Sodomis exiet Loth, (2 The ii 3) quod est, *Discessio,* ut *reueletur homo peccati.* Babylon ciuitas aduersa Hierusalem totus mundus est, qui in parte sua, quam in hac Hierusalem habet, conuenitur. (Esai xiii 1) *Visio* inquit *aduersus Babyloniam,* et dicit aduersum orbem terrarum uenturos sanctos Dei milites. (Esai xiii 2–18) *Tollite signum et exaltate uocem illis. nolite timere exhortamini manus, aperite magistratus, quia ecce ego praecipio. sanctificati sunt, et uoco eos; gigantes ueniunt iram meam lenire, gaudentes simul et iniuriam facientes. uox multarum gentium in montibus similis gentium multarum, uox regum et gentium collectarum,* cum Babylonem gens et rex Medorum euerterit. sequitur enim et dicit qui sunt isti reges, et quae Babylon. *Deus Sabaoth praecepit genti bellatrici uenire de longinquo de summo fundamento caeli, Deus et bellatores eius corrumpere uniuersum orbem terrae. ululate, proximus est enim dies Domini, et contritio a Deo aderit. propter hoc omnes manus resoluentur, et omnis anima hominis trepidabit. turbabuntur legati, parturitiones*

1 regem] V*corr*; regen×× V*; reges R eritque] erit V auertam] a&ernam V 3 quae] qui R uenerit] nouerit V 4 auertit] uertit V 5 ecclesiae] ecclesiasticus V*; ecclesiastica V*corr* figurae R 6 aliquae] quae V 7 audit V* 7, 8 sodomorum] sodomam V* 8 uocatur] secatur V 11 aduersa] aduersus V qui] *om* V 12 hierusalem habet] israhel haec V inquid V* 13 babyloniam] babylonem V aduersus V 14 exaltate] exultate V uocem] uicem V 15 illis] illius R 16 sanctificati] *pr* qui R uoco eos] uocē V 17 ueniant R lenire] *cf Cyp* 785[14]: linire V; mitigare R 18 similis] similes V 19 collecturum V* cum babylone V 20 euerterit] euenerit R 21 sunt] sint V precipit R 22 fundamenta V 26 legati] ligati R

RV (M) *enim illos habebunt quasi mulieris parturientis, et patientur circumstantiam; alius ad alium expauescent, et facies eorum sicut flamma commutabuntur. ecce enim dies Domini insanabilis uenit indignationis et irae, ponere orbem terrarum desertum, et peccatores perdere ex eo.* diem Domini ex quo passus est dicit, ex quo spiritaliter interficitur mundus, interficiente exercitu Dei, dum eius lumen iniqui non uident, sicut sequitur dicens: *Stellae enim caeli et Orion et omnis ornatura caeli lumen non dabunt, et tenebrescet oriente sole † lumen et † non permanebit lumen eius. et infligam orbi terrae mala et iniustis peccata eorum, et perdam iniuriam scelestorum et iniuriam superborum humiliabo. et erunt qui remanserint*—id
60 est quos supradicti milites non occiderint—*honorati magis quam aurum quod non tetigit ignem, et homo honoratus erit magis quam lapis ex Sufir. caelum enim indignabitur et terra commouebitur a fundamentis suis propter animationem irae Domini, in die qua aderit indignatio eius.* iungit speciem: *Et erit qui relicti sunt quasi capreola fugiens, et sicut ouis errans et non erit qui colligit, ut homo ad populum suum conuertatur, et uenire in tribum suum festinet. qui enim inciderit superabitur, et si qui collecti sunt gladio cadent. et filiae eorum in conspectu eorum †cadent†, et domos eorum diripient, et uxores eorum habebunt. ecce excito uobis Medos, qui non computant pecuniam, neque auro opus est illis.* subtiliter adstringit genus; cui enim hosti non opus est auro nisi Eccle-

1 enim] *om* V   mulieres parturientes R   patientur] parietas V   2 circumstantia V   aliam V   6 interficietur R   8 sequitur] seruentur V   caeli] *om* R   et orion] exteriore V   omnis] omnes V   ornatura] *conieci, cf. Roensch* 42: creatura R; ex ea rura V; ὁ κόσμος LXX   9 tenebrisc& R; tenebrescit V   oriente sole lumen] R; *om* V, *spatio relicto circiter xxv litterarum*   9, 10 lumen et...eius] καὶ ἡ σελήνη οὐ δώσει τὸ φῶς αὐτῆς LXX   10 orbi] mortui V   13 supradicti] supputadicti V   occiderit V   14 homo] *pr* non V   erit] fuerit R   15 sufir] sophyr R   16 suis] *om* V   propter] propterea V   aminationē R   17 indignatio] *cf* LXX; indignationis RV   18 capriola V   19 colligat V   20, 21 incederit V   21, 22 filiae earum V* *vid*   22 domus V   24 conputant V   25 adstringit] *scripsi*; aut stringit R; item inserit V (M)   hosti] ostis V; hostis M   auro] + et argento V   ecclesiae] ecclesiasticus V

siae quae spiritali fruitur uita? *Sagittationes iuuenum con-* RV
fringent, et filiis uestris non miserebuntur, et super nepotes uestros non parcent oculi eorum.

Omnia spiritaliter, sicut de eadem Babylonia scriptum
Ps cxxxvi 9 est: *Felix est qui obtinebit et conlidet paruulos tuos ad petram.* neque enim regem Medorum quod obtinuerit aduersum Babylonem dixit felicem, et non Ecclesiam quae *obtinet et conlidet* filios Babylonis *ad petram* scandali. *obtinet* autem, sicut
2 The ii 7 scriptum est: *Qui obtinet modo, donec de medio fiat.* et post multa speciei et generis in clausula periochae aperte ostendit omnes gentes esse Babylonem et eas *in terra* atque *in monti-*
Esai xiv 22—27 *bus* suis, id est in Ecclesia, perdere. *Haec dicit Dominus, Ponam Babylonem desertam, ut inhabitent hericii in illa, et erit in nihilum, et ponam illam luti uoraginem in perditionem. haec dicit Dominus Sabaoth dicens, Quomodo dixi sic erit, et quomodo cogitaui sic perseuerabit, ut perdam Assyrios in terra mea et in montibus meis, et erunt in conculcationem. et auferetur ab eis iugum eorum, et gloria ab umeris eorum auferetur. haec cogitatio quam cogitauit Dominus in orbem terrae totum, et haec manus alta super omnes gentes orbis terrae. Deus enim sanctus quod cogitauit quis disparget, et manum illam fortem quis auertet?* quotienscumque autem post excidium minatur ruinae ciuitatis habitationem bestiarum et auium inmundarum, spiritus inmundos dicit habitaturos in hominibus quos Spiritus Sanctus deseruerit. non enim hanc iniuriam possunt interfecti habitatores aut ruina sentire.

1 spiritali] spiritalit~ V 5 qui] quod R optinebit V collidebit V tuos] suos R 6 aduersus V 7 ecclesiam] aecclesiasticus V collidet V 8 optinet V 9 qui] quod R 10 specie V in clausula periochae] *scripsi*; in clausa perichae R; clausula periocae V 10, 11 omnes ostendit omnes V*, omnes 2° *nunc eras* 13 desertum V ericii V 14 illam] illud V 16 quomodo] quem ad modum V perseuerauit R 17 conculcatione V 18 aufertur V ab] R *supr ras* humeris V 20, 21 orbis terrae] R *supr ras* 21 disparget] dispergit R; par disgit V (*sic*) et] *om* R 22 quotiescumque R 24 et auium inmundarum] *om* V 25 sp̄s sp̄s V (*sic*) deseruit R 26 ruinam R

RV (M) *Sermones* inquit *Amos, quos uidit super Hierusalem;* et [Am i 1] coepit: *In tribus impietatibus Damasci et in quattuor non* [Ib 3] *auersabor eam, eo quod secabant serris ferreis in utero habentes.* et iterum: *In tribus impietatibus Idumaeae et in quattuor* [Ib 11] *non auersabor eam propter quod persecutus est in gladio fratrem suum.* et multas alias ciuitates alienigenarum in Ecclesiae figuram conuenit. ubicumque autem Idumaeam, Theman, Bosor, Seir nominat, fratres malos significat; sunt autem possessiones Esau. *serras* uero *ferreas* homines dicit duros et asperos, qui *secant* parturientes Ecclesias.

Item omnes gentes quae sub caelo sunt in ciuitate Dei iram Dei bibere et illic percuti Hieremias testatur dicens: *Sic dicit Dominus Deus Israhel, Accipe calicem uini meri de* [Hier xxxii 15—29] *manu mea, et potabis omnes gentes ad quas ego mitto te, et uoment et insanient a facie gladii, quem ego mitto in medio illarum. et accepi calicem de manu Domini, et potaui gentes ad quas misit me Dominus ad ipsas: Hierusalem et ciuitates Iudae et reges eius et principes eius, ut ponerentur in desolationem et in deuastationem et in sibilationem; et Farao regem Aegypti et pueros eius et potentes eius et uniuersum populum eius et omnes promiscuos eius; et reges omnes alienigenarum, Ascalonem et Gazam et Accaron et quae contra faciem Azoti; et Idumaeam, et Moabitatem, et filios Ammon, et regem Tyri et regem Sidonis, et reges qui trans mare sunt, et Dedan et Theman et Bosor, et omnem circumtonsam a facie, et omnes promiscuos qui commorantur in deserto, et omnes reges Aelam, et omnes reges Persarum, et uniuersos reges a Subsolano qui longe et qui iuxta sunt, unumquemque ad fratrem suum, et omnia regna terrae quae supra faciem terrae sunt. et dices illis: Sic dicit Dominus omnipotens, Bibite et inebriamini et uomite,*

2, 4 quatuor R 4 idumeae RV* 7 idumæam RV*corr* 9 autem] R*; aut R[a] 11 quae] qui R in ciuitate Dei] *om* R 12 bibere] uiuere V* 15 uoment] uenient R 16 accipi R 18 et reges] *om* et R 18, 19 desolatione...deuastatione ...sibilatione V 19 pharao regi R 20 et 3°] *om* V 21 promiscuos] praemiscuos V 22 ascalonem] asalonem V* 23 idumeam V* moabitem V 24 sidoni R 25 a faciae V* 26 prȩmiscuos RV aelam] helam R; elam V 29 supra] super V 30 sic] haec V

et cadetis et non surgetis a facie gladii, quem ego mitto in RV
medio uestrum. et erit si noluerint accipere calicem ita ut
bibant, dices: Sic dicit Dominus, Bibentes bibetis, quia in
ciuitate in qua inuocatum est nomen meum super ipsam
incipio uexare uos, et uos purgatione non eritis purgati, quia
Hier xxxii 18 *gladium ego inuoco super inhabitantes super terram. Potabis*
inquit *Hierusalem, ciuitates Iudae et reges eius et principes*
Ib 26 *eius;* deinde dicit: *Et uniuersa regna terrae quae super faciem*
terrae sunt, ut ostenderet ab speciali Hierusalem transitum
fecisse ad generalem, in qua sunt omnes gentes terrae quas
Ib 29 illic Deus percutiet, sicut et interpretatus est dicens: *Quo-*
niam in ciuitate in qua inuocatum est nomen meum in ipsa
incipio uexare uos, et uos purgatione non eritis purgati. num-
quid Hieremias, cum esset in corpore, qui de Iudaea et
carcere numquam nisi in Aegyptum tractus, perspicue adiecto
mero in calice ut potum dare omnibus gentibus quae sub
caelo sunt, aut nunc praeter Ecclesiam profetat? quodsi
tunc quoque et nunc in Ecclesiam locutus est, manifestum
est et omnes gentes illicubi Hieremias loquitur conueniri in
principali eorum parte. si quid enim summum Satanas in
corpore suo, si quid dextrum, si quid graue habet, caelestibus
miscuit ut bellantium est mos fortibus fortes opponere. unde
cf Eph vi 12 apostolus dicit *non* esse sanctis *pugnam aduersum* humana,
sed aduersus spiritalia nequitiae in caelestibus.

1 caditis R 2 erit] erint V (*sic*) 6 ego...in(habitantes)] *supr ras in* R terram] terrā ammon R 7 iuda R 13 purgationē R eritis] estis R 13, 14 numquit V* 14 iudaea et] iudeae V 15 aiecto V 16 ut] id V dare] RV: *fortasse pro* daret, *sed cf Roensch* 445; *Priscillian* 42[1] quae] qui R 17 praeter] per V 17, 18 profetat...ecclesiam] *om* R 17 prophetat V 18 ecclesia V locutus] R (*sic*); locus V 20 enim] *om* R 20, 21 in corpore...graue] si quid graue si quid dextrum in suo corpore V 22 est] *om* R 23 pugna V aduersum] aduersus V humana] humanitatem V

24 caelestibus] + EXPLICIT DE SPECIE | ET GENERE | INCIPIT DE TEMPORIBVS | REGVLA R (*rubro*); + EXPLICIT DE SPECIAE. ET GENERE. AMEN || INCIPIT DE TEMPORIBVS. LIB | QVINTVS V

V. De temporibus.

RV [D] (M) Temporis quantitas in Scripturis frequenter mystica est tropo synecdoche, aut legitimis numeris, qui multis modis positi sunt et pro loco intellegendi; synecdoche uero est aut a parte totum, aut a toto pars.

Hoc tropo cccc annos seruiuit Israhel in Aegypto. nam § D §dicit Dominus Abrahae: *Sciens scies quia peregrinum erit semen tuum in terra non sua, et dominabuntur eorum et affligent annis cccc;* (Ge xv 13) Exodi autem Scriptura dicit cccc xxx annos (cf Ex xii 40) fuisse Israhel in Aegypto. an non omne tempus seruiuit? quaerendum ergo, ex quo tempore: quod inuenire facile est. dicit enim Scriptura non seruisse populum, nisi post mortem ¶ D Ioseph.¶ *Mortuus est* inquit *Ioseph et omnes fratres eius et omnes saeculi illius, filii autem Israhel creuerunt et multiplicati sunt et cydaei fuerunt et praeualuerunt nimis, multiplicabat autem eos terra. exsurrexit autem rex alter super Aegyptum qui ignorabat Ioseph, et dixit genti suae: Ecce gens filiorum Israhel magna multitudo, et ualent super nos; uenite ergo circumueniamus eos.* (Ex i 6–10) § D §si autem post mortem Ioseph coepit seruire populus, ex cccc et xxx annis, quibus in Aegypto moratus est, deducimus LXXX annos regni Ioseph —regnauit autem a xxx annis usque in cx,—et erunt reliqui (cf Ge xli 46 l 22)

2 temporis] temporum V *supr ras* M mystica est] mysticae sunt R 3 tropo synecdoche] M *Eug* 872; tropo ϹΥΝЄΚΔΟΚЄ *Aug cod Pal* 188; ·ΤΡΟΠѠϹΥΝЄΚΑѠΚΗ· R; tropo sinedoche V 4 synecdoche] ·ϹΥΝЄΚΑѠΚΗ R; sinedoche V est] *post* totum VM 6 cccc] quadringentos V *et sic semper* annos] *om* R 7 dictum est Abrahae peregrinum: *sic incipit D; uid Introd p* xx dominus] d̄s V scies] scieᶏs V (*sic*) 8, 9 adfligent eos VM 9 annis] annos *D* exodo *D* cccc et xxx *D* 10 Israhel] *om* V in aegyptum *D* an...seruiuit] *om D* 11 ergo] + est *D* facile est] *om* est *D* 12 enim] d̄n̄s R 13 mortuus...ioseph] *om* V 15 cydaei] cydei R; cythei V; χυδαῖοι LXX nimis] *om* V 19, 20 quod si tunc coepit: *sic rursus incipit D* 20 cccc et xxx] *D*; quatrigentis & triginta R; quadringentis & triginta V quibus] *pr* ex V 21 moratus] demoratus V diducimus V*corr* LXXX] septuaginta *D* 22 autem] enim V xxx annis] quadragesimo anno *D*, *sed cf p* 64[13] cx] centesimo decimo *D*

seruitutis Israhel anni CCCL, quos Deus dixit CCCC. si autem RV
omni tempore peregrinationis suae seruiuit Israhel, plus est [D] (M)
quam Deus dixit; si ex morte Ioseph secundum Scripturae
sanctae fidem, minus est. quo manifestum est centum a toto
partem esse, nam post CCC annos pars aliorum centum anni
sunt: propterea dixit CCCC annos.

Sic in omni summa temporis, ut puta post nouem dies
prima hora decimi diei dies est, aut post nouem menses
Sap vii 1, 2 primus dies mensis est, sicut scriptum est: *In utero matris
figuratus sum caro decem mensuum tempore coagulatus in
sanguine.* sicut autem in prima parte cuiusque temporis
totum tempus est, ita et nouissima hora totus dies est,¶ aut ¶ *D*
reliquiae mille annorum mille anni sunt. sex dies sunt
mundi aetas, id est sex milia annorum. in reliquiis sexti diei,
id est M annorum, natus est Dominus, passus et resurrexit.
itidem reliquiae M annorum dictae sunt mille anni primae
resurrectionis. sicut enim reliquiae sextae feriae, id est tres
horae, totus dies est, unus ex tribus sepulturae Domini, ita
reliquiae sexti diei maioris quo surrexit Ecclesia totus dies
Mt xii 40 est, id est M anni. hoc enim tropo constant *tres dies et tres
noctes.* noctis autem et diei XXIIII horae unus dies est, nec
adiciuntur noctes diebus nisi certa ratione. alias dies solos
cf Gal i 18 dicimus, sicut Apostolus dicit mansisse apud Petrum diebus
XV: numquid opus erat dicere totidem et noctibus? sic 61
Ge i 5 enim scriptum est: *Vespera et mane dies unus.* quod si nox

1 israhel] *om DM* anni CCCL] anni ·CCCCL· R; annis trecentis quinquaginta V* (anni trecenti...V*corr*); anni CCCLX *D* quos] quod V 2 omni tempore] omnem tempus V*; omne tempus V*corr* israhel] *om D* 3, 4 secundum...fidem] *om D* 4 quo manifestum est] quos manifestatum *D* 6 CCCC] quadringintos V*D* 7 sic] si hic V 8 prima...dies] *om* V diei dies] *om* dies *D* 9 mensis] + decimus V; *pr* mensis M 10 decem mensuum tempore] decimmensū V; decem mensium *D* coagulatus] + sum *D*M 11 autem] enim *D* cuiusque temporis] cuiusquam temporis *D*; cui: temporis M; temporis cuiusq· temporis cuiusq· V (*sic*) 12 totum] *om* V est 1°] *om D* ita et] R*D*M; ita in V nouissima] R*D*; + ut nouissima VM dies sit VM 13 sunt 1°] sint VM 14 sex milia] V; $\overline{\text{VI}}$· R reliquis V* 15 M] mille V *semper* 16 itidem] idem V 19 surrexit] resurrexit V 20 id est] *om* V constat V 21 horae] hore R unus dies] unum tempus V 22 alias] RV[b]; alius V 23 aput V* 25 uespere R

RV et dies unus dies est, nouissima hora diei et totum diem et noctem transactam retinet. similiter et nouissima hora noctis totam noctem et diem futuram: hora enim pars est utriusque temporis. hora qua sepultus est Dominus pars est sextae feriae cum sua nocte quae transierat, et hora noctis in qua resurrexit pars est inminentis diei. ceterum si neque in die praesenti nox est praeterita neque in nocte praesenti dies crastinus, non die resurrexit Dominus sed nocte. quoniam dies ab ortu solis est, sicut scriptum est: *Luminare maius initium* [Ge i 16] *diei;* Dominus autem ante solis ortum resurrexit. nam Marcus dicit: *Oriente sole,* non orto sed *oriente,* id est ad [Mc xvi 2] ortum eunte; Lucas autem: *Diluculo.* sed ne de hac locutione [Lc xxiv 1] ambigeretur alteri euangelistae aperte noctem fuisse testantur. nam Matheus nocte dicit uenisse mulieres ad monu- [cf Mt xxviii 1] mentum et uidisse Dominum, Iohannes uero *cum adhuc tene-* [Ioh xx 1] *brae essent.* si autem Dominus ante solem, id est ante initium diei resurrexit, nox illa pars est inlucescentis diei. quod et competit operibus Dei, ut non dies obscuretur in noctem sed nox lucescat in diem. ipsa enim nox inluminatur et efficitur dies, quod est figura eorum quae facturus erat in Christo, *quoniam Deus qui dixit de tenebris lumen fulgere* [2 Co iv 6] *fulsit in cordibus nostris,* qui inluminauit tenebras, sicut scriptum est: *Tenebrae tuae sicut meridies erunt,* et: *Nox tran-* [Esai lviii 10 Ro xiii 12, 13] *siuit, dies autem adpropinquauit; sicut in die decenter ambulemus.* prius est enim quod carnale est, *deinde quod spiritale.* [1 Co xv 46]

Dies ergo primus et nouissimus a toto pars est. solus medius plenus fuit a uespera in uesperam secundum Dei conditionem atque praeceptum, sicut Mosi dicit in Leuitico *a uespera in uesperam* obseruari diem sabbatorum. quidam [Lev xxiii 32] autem putant ex die computandum, quoniam Dominus tres [cf Mt xii 40] dies et noctes dixit, non tres noctes et dies. sed hoc non

1 unus dies] unum tempus V diem totum V 2 transactum V* 3 noctem] *om* V futurū V 5 quae] qui R 5, 6 in qua] quae V*; qua V*corr* 6 imminentis R 12 deluculo R loquutione R 13, 14 alter euangelista...testatur R 13 noctem] nocte V 17 est] erat V inluciscentis RV 18 obscuraretur V 19 diem] die V 20 facturus] facta V 24 adpropinquabit V die] diem V 27 dei] VR*corr*; di×m R* 28 moysi V in leuitico] *om* V 29 obseruari] obscuraui V 30 putant] dicunt V

longa ratione destruitur. si enim ex die initium sepulturae, RV in nocte finis; si autem in die finita est, a nocte coepit. nam si dies utrimque concluditur, plus erit unus dies. Dicunt praeterea non posse in die noctem esse praeteritam nec in nocte diem futurum, sed separatos tres dies et noctes oportere adsignari, computantes primum diem quo cruci fixus est, alterum trium horarum separatarum, tertium sabbati—erit dominicus dies quartus! qui autem hanc circumuentionem uitant consentiunt a nocte quidem computandum, sed noctes a diebus debere separari, dicentes in tribus horis tenebrarum inportunarum primam noctem, alteram sabbati, tertiam inlucescentis dominici. noctes quidem ueluti tres sunt, sed dies duo: primus in tribus horis post tenebras, secundus sabbati! non enim qui separatos dies promittit potest dicere in nocte qua resurrexit fuisse diem futurum. quod si in id consensit, consentiat necesse est in reliquis diei sextae feriae fuisse noctem praeteritam. quasi tenebrae inportunae fuerunt, tres tamen horae lucis eiusdem sunt diei, nec amiserunt ordinem suum, quo minus pars esset diei ac noctis suae. taceo tres horas tenebrarum noctem esse non potuisse, quod praeter ordinem fuerint conditionis Dei. quicquid enim signi est non turbat elementorum rationalem
cf Ios x 7; 4 Regn xx 11 cursum. non enim quia stetit sol et luna in diebus Hiesu et Ezechiae solus sol reuersus est; aliquid cursus inter solem et lunam mutilatum est et detractum uel additum diei ac nocti, et noua exinde coepit temporum aut neomeniae supputatio,
Ge i 14 quam statuit Deus in sole et luna esse *in tempora dies et annos,* sicut in Genesi scriptum est. multo magis in illo die nihil turbatum est, cui non sunt adiectae tres horae tenebra-

2 in noctem R si autem finis R 3 utrimque] utrumq. RV 4 noctem esse] *tr* V 5 in noctem V* *vid* 7 separatarum] reparatarum V 8 dominicus] dn̄i V 12 inluciscentis V* dominice V*; dominicae V*corr* uelut R 14 separatos] separatus V* promittit] R; promit V*corr*; promit××× V* 16 consensit] consentit V reliquiis V*corr* 17 quasi] quae si V*corr* 19 amiserunt] admiserunt V 20 horas] horae V* 22 signi] signis R rationalem] rationale R; rationabilem V 23 in diebus] *om* in V ih̄u RV et 2°] aut V 25 additum] addictum V* ac] aut V 27 in solem et lunam V tempora] temporum V

[RV] rum ut essent XV horarum, sed pars ipsius diei obscurata est [[Eug] (M)] —sexta in nonam. quod si non solem obscuratum et rursum ostensum diem dicimus, quod nomen, quem ordinem damus ipsi diei qui fuisse dicitur inter sextam feriam et sabbatum, nisi bis sabbatum fuit et ebdomadas illa octo dies habuit? certe, si contentio ratione minime sedari potest, compendio probamus tres horas tenebrarum non pertinere ad sepulturam Domini, eo quod adhuc uiueret. non enim potuit esse *in* [Mt xii 40] *corde terrae* nisi ex quo mortuus est et sepultus est, quod factum est in tribus horis sextae feriae intra duodecimam. quoniam post occasum solis non licebat Iudaeis sepelire, cum esset cena pura initium sabbati, sicut Iohannes dicit: *Illic* [Ioh xix 42] *ergo propter cenam puram Iudaeorum, quoniam proximum erat monumentum, posuerunt Iesum.* dies autem noctibus dignitate non nouitatis ordine praeferuntur, ut omnes masculi primogenitis, sicut dictum est: *Genuit filios et filias et* [cf Ge v 4] *obiit,* cum contra legem sit naturae ut omnes illi masculos primum genuisset. nobis autem totum tempus dies est; omnia noua sunt, figurae transierunt.

Ex legitimis numeris sunt septenarius, denarius, duodenarius. idem autem est numerus et cum multiplicatur, ut LXX, DCC; uel totiens in se, ut septies septeni uel decies deni. sed aut perfectionem significant, aut a parte totum, aut simplicem summam. perfectionem, ut VII spiritus Ec- [cf Ap i 4] [§¶ Eug 873] clesiae, aut ut dicit: § *Septies in die laudabo te,*¶ aut: *Septies* [Ps cxviii 164] [Lc xviii 30] *tantum recipiet in isto saeculo.* similiter decies, ut alius euangelista dicit: *Centies tantum recipiet in isto saeculo.* et [Mc x 30]

1 esset V 1, 2 xv horarum...nonam] quindecim nam V 4 inter sextam] interfectam V* ; intersectam V*corr* et sabbatum] et sabbatorū V 5 nisi bis sabbatum] nisi si uis sabbatum V ; nisi sabbata R ebdomadas] ebdomada V 6 si] sic V compedio R 8, 9 in cor V 9 est et] uel V 10 horis sextae] hore sexte V duodecima V 12 cena pura] caena pura R ; pura cena V* (pura caena V*corr*) initiu× V* sabbatis V 13 caenam R 14 erat] fuerat V 15 nouitatis ordine] nouitaordinē R*, *mox corr* 17 cum] quod V 20 numeri sunt V* 21 autem est] *tr* V 22 septuaginta uel septingenti V toties R septeni] .VII. R uel] aut V 23 a toto partē R, *uid infra* 24 aut] MV*corr* ; ut V* ; aūt R (*sic*) ut] & V* 24, 25 ecclesiae] + septem V 25 laudabo te] V *Eug* ; laudē dixit tibi R ; laudem dixit M 26 decies] denarius VM

Danihel angelorum et caeli uel Ecclesiae innumerabilem RV
Dan vii 10 multitudinem denario numero complexus est dicens: *Milies* (M)
milia apparebant illi et decies milies decies milia circumsiste-
Ps lxvii 18 *bant.* et Dauid *Currus* inquit *Dei decies milies tantum.* et
Ps civ 8 de omni tempore Dauid: *In mille saecula.* item per duode-
cf Ap vii 4 narium de omni Ecclesia dictum est CXLIIII. et duodecim
Mt xix 28 tribus omnes gentes, sicut: *Iudicabitis XII tribus Israhel.* a
parte totum est, quoniam certum tempus legitimis numeris
Ap ii 10 difinitur ut in Apocalypsi: *Habebitis pressuram X dies,* cum
significet usque in finem. LXX autem annos in Babylone
idem tempus esse importunum est nunc probare.

Praeter legitimos etiam numeros, quodcumque tempus in
quodcumque numero frequenter breuiauit Scriptura, sicut
supradictum tempus Hora appelatum est, dicente apostolo;
1 Ioh ii 18 2 Co vi 2 *Nouissima hora est*; et Dies, sicut: *Ecce nunc dies salua-*
(Esai lxi 2) Lc iv 19 *tionis*; et Annus, sicut per Esaiam: *Praedicare annum*
Domini acceptabilem. quoniam non ille quo Dominus prae-
dicauit solus fuit acceptabilem, sed et iste quo praedicat,
2 Co vi 2 sicut dictum est: *Tempore accepto exaudiui te,* quod aposto-
lus interpretatur: *Ecce nunc tempus acceptabile.* finis de-
Lc iv 19 nique huius anni diem iudicii iunxit dicens: *Praedicare*
Ps lxiv 12 *annum acceptabilem et diem retributionis.* et Dauid *Bene-*
dices inquit *coronam anni bonitatis tuae.*

Aliquando hora dies et mensis annus est, sicut in Apoca-
Ap ix 15 lypsi: *Parati in horam et diem et mensem et in annum,* quod
Ib 10 est tres anni et dimidius. ibidem, menses pro annis: *Datum*
est ei laedere homines mensibus quinque. aliquando dies
Ap xi 3 denario numero C dies sunt, sicut in Apocalypsi: *Dies MCCLX,*
nam milies ducenties centies et sexagies centeni centumui-

2 milies] mille V 3 apparebunt V milies] milias R decies milia] denaria V 4 currus] cursus R 8 totum est] toto V*; totum V*corr* certum] centum V 9 ut] *om* R apocalypsin V x] decim V* 10 annos] *om* V babylonē R 15 sicut] *om* R* 15, 16 saluationis] salutationis V; salutis M 17 domini] dnm V*; dno V*corr* 21 diem] idem V 22 annum] + dni V 23 bonitatis] benignitatis V 24, 25, 28 in apocalypsin V 25 et in] *om* in V 26 dimidium V menses] mensis R 27 laedere] ledere RM; delere V mensibus] menses V 28 centum dies V 29 et] *om* V centini R centumuiginti] centies R

RV (M) ginti sex milia dies sunt, qui fiunt anni CCCL mensibus tricenorum dierum. ibidem, unus mensis denario numero centum
menses sunt, ut: *Ciuitatem sanctam calcabunt mensibus XLII*, Ap xi 2
nam XLII centeni $\overline{\text{IIII}}$ et CC menses sunt, qui sunt anni CCCL.

Tempus aut annus est aut centum anni, sicut *Tempus et* Ap xii 14
tempora et dimidium temporis, quod est aut tres anni et
dimidius aut CCCL. item unus dies aliquando centum anni
sunt, sicut de Ecclesia scriptum est iacere *in ciuitate ubi et* cf Ap xi 8, 9
Dominus eius *cruci fixus est tres dies et dimidium*, et: *Oportet* Mt xvi 21
*filium hominis Hierusalem ire, et multa pati a senioribus et
principibus sacerdotum et scribis, et occidi, et post tres dies
resurgere*; ipse enim tertio surrexit.

Generatio aliquotiens et C anni sunt, sicut Dominus dicit
Abrahae: *Quarta autem generatione reuertentur huc.* in Ge xv 16
Exodo uero non de seruitutis sed de totius peregrinationis
tempore dictum est: *Quinta autem generatione ascendit* Ex xiii 18
populus ex Aegypto, id est post CCCC et XXX annos. item
62 generatio aliquotiens X anni sunt, sicut Hieremias dicit:
Eritis in Babylonia usque ad generationes VII. Baruch vi 2

Ternarium numerum eundem esse, qui et denarius,—id
est plenus,—in Euangeliis deprehenditur. nam Matheus cf Mt xxv 14 ff
dicit tribus seruis creditam Domini substantiam; Lucas uero
X, quos X in tres redigit, dum et ipse a tribus dicit exactam cf Lc xix 13 ff
rationem.

Aliquotiens unus dies M anni sunt, sicut scriptum est:
Qua die gustaueritis ex arbore morte moriemini. et VII dies Ge ii 17
primi $\overline{\text{VII}}$ anni sunt; sex diebus operatus est Dominus *et* Ge ii 2, 3
*requieuit ab omnibus operibus suis die septimo, et benedixit et
sanctificauit illum.* Dominus autem dicit: *Pater meus usque* Ioh v 17
nunc operatur. sicut enim mundum istum sex diebus operatus est, ita mundum spiritalem, qui est Ecclesia, per sex
milia annos operatur, cessaturus die septimo quem benedixit,
fecitque aeternum.

1 fiunt] sunt V 1, 2 trecenorum V*; trigenorum V*corr* 7 centum] V[a]; centeni V*; *om* R 12 tertio] + die V 13, 18, 25 aliquoties R 14 reuertetur V huc] hoc V* 15 sed de totius] *om* R*; *add* R[a] 20, 21 id est plenus] idē plenius V 21 in euangelio V 27 dominus] $\overline{\text{ds}}$ V 30 nunc] modo V 31 ecclesiam V* *vid* 32 operatur] operator R 33 aeternum] *pr* in R

Hoc est quod Dominus inter cetera mandata nihil aliud crebrius praecepit, quam ut obseruemus et diligamus diem sabbatorum. qui autem praecepta Dei facit sabbatum Dei diligit, id est septimum diem quietis aeternae. propterea Deus hortatur populum non intrare portas Hierusalem cum onere in die sabbati, et minatur portis et intrantibus per eas RV
Hier xvii 19–27 et exeuntibus, sicut Hieremiae mandat dicens: *Vade sta in portis filiorum populi tui, in quas ingrediuntur reges Iuda et egrediuntur, et in omnibus portis Hierusalem, et dices ad eos: Audite uerbum Domini qui intratis in portas istas. haec dicit Dominus, Custodite animas uestras, et nolite tollere onera in die sabbatorum et nolite exire portas Hierusalem et nolite efferre onera de domibus uestris in die sabbatorum, sicut mandaui patribus uestris; et non audierunt in auribus suis, et indurauerunt ceruicem suam super patres suos, ut me non audirent neque percipirent disciplinam. eritque si me audieritis, dicit Dominus, ut non inferatis onera per portas ciuitatis huius in die sabbatorum, ut non faciatis omne opus uestrum, et sanctificetis diem sabbatorum, et intrabunt per portas ciuitatis huius reges et principes sedentes in sede Dauid et ascendentes in currus et equos, ipsi et principes eorum, uiri Iuda et qui inhabitant Hierusalem. et habitabitur ciuitas haec in aeternum, et uenient de ciuitatibus Iuda et †ciuitatibus† Hierusalem, et de terra Beniamin et de terra campestri et de terra quae ad Austrum, adferentes holocausta et incensa et manna et tus, ferentes laudationem in domum Domini. et si me non audieritis ut sanctificetis diem sabbatorum, ut non portetis onera neque intretis per portas Hierusalem in die sabbatorum, et succendam ignem in portis eius, et consumet itinera Hierusalem et non extinguetur.* sufficeret breuiter mandasse non
Hier xvii 21 operari sabbatis; ut quid *Nolite inferre onera per portas Hierusalem?* aut si opus erat et operis speciem dicere, quid

1 hoc] id V 10 in] *om* V 13 efferre] ferre V 14 audierunt] obaudierunt V 16, 17 audieritis] quesieritis R 17 honera V 21 ęquos R; equus V* et qui] *om* et V 23 ciuitatibus 2°] *pr* de R; κυκλόθεν LXX 25 olochausta V 26 domum domini] domum R; domodn̄i V 28 in die sabbatorum] *om* V 29, 30 hierusalem] + in die sabbatorū· R 31 honera V 32 dicere quid] diceret id V

RV *Nolite inferre per portas?* non enim aliqui per muros et tecta infert onera in ciuitatem.

Hierusalem bipertita est, et portae eius bipertitae. per portas inferorum exitur de Hierusalem sancta, et per easdem intratur in maledicta. qui autem per portas intrant caeli intrant in aeternam Hierusalem, ut *reges in curribus et in* (cf Hier xvii 25) *equis sedentes in sede Dauid,* sicut per Esaiam: *Adducent* (Esai lxvi 20) *fratres uestros ex omnibus gentibus donum Domino cum equis et curribus in splendore mulorum cum umbraculis in sanctam ciuitatem.* sanctae portae ciuitatis Hierusalem Christus est, et uicarii eius custodes legis, *interficientes* uero *prophetas et* (cf Mt xxiii 37) *lapidantes missos ad se.* porta diabolus est, et uicarii eius pseudoapostoli praedicatores legis, *claues regni caelorum* (cf Mt xvi 18, 19) alto sensu abscondentes. ipsi sunt *portae* quae *non uincunt Ecclesiam,* quae *supra petram fundata est,* quoniam *firmum* (cf Mt vii 25; 2 Tim ii 19) *fundamentum Dei stat,* sicut scriptum est: *Cognouit Dominus qui sunt eius.* si quis autem per praecepta praesidentium (cf Mt xxiii 2 ff) *cathedrae Mosi* introiit, per Christum intrat—ipsius enim sunt praecepta, ipse exponit onus peccatorum suorum—, et sine illo intrat in requiem sabbati. si quis uero non per praecepta sed per facta praesidentium cathedrae intrat, fiet *filius gehennae* magis quam illi, et requiescentibus uniuersis (Ib 15) qui ante sabbatum manna collegerunt, ille cum onere suo (cf Ex xvi 28 ff; cf Nu xv 30) inuenietur in die sabbati, in quo non est manna colligere neque onus exponere. quia nolunt audire uocem filii Dei clamantis in Ecclesia et dicentis: *Venite ad me omnes qui* (Mt xi 28) *onerati estis, et ego uos requiescere faciam.*

Isti sunt fures qui non per ianuam ueram sed per portas (cf Ioh x 1 ff) suas intrant in suam Hierusalem, et succendet Deus *ignem* (Hier xvii 27)

2 infert] inferre V honera V 5 autem] aut R 6 aeternam] aeterna R; aeternū V 8 fratres uestros] ff̄ V (*sic*) domino] d̄o V 9 splendorem R mulorum] multorum R; multarum V 10 sanctae portae] *tr* V ciuitati V 11 uicari V* 12 diabolus] R**vid* V; diaboli R*corr* uicarius V 14 uincant V 15 supra p&ra R 16 dominus] d̄s V 17 praesidentium] praesentiū V 18 moysi V 20 intrat] *pr* non V[b] 21 cathedrae] cathedra R; cathedrae moysi V fiet] *om* V 22 illi] ipsi V 23 colligerunt V* onere] honore V*; honere V*corr* 24 inueniatur V 29 succendit V

RV (M)

in portis Hierusalem, et conburet *itinera* eius *et non extinguetur.* ignis enim qui specialis Hierusalem portas exussit extinctus est; apostolus autem sabbatum et alia legis man- [Col ii 16] data figuram esse futuri sic ait: *Nemo ergo uos iudicet in cibo et potu aut in parte diei festi aut neomeniae aut sabbatorum, quod est umbra futuri.*

Multis in locis unius temporis diuersi euentus in speciem separatim descripti duo tempora fecerunt, quasi ex ordine se insequentia; in genere autem uno tempore est uterque [Ge xli 26 ff] euentus. sic XIIII anni sub Ioseph ubertatis et sterilitatis VII anni sunt tantum, id est omne tempus a passione [Ib 46] Domini, in cuius figura factus est Ioseph dominus Aegypti cum esset XXX annorum; qui sunt itaque nobis VII anni ubertatis et saturitatis, id est ceteris VII sterilitatis et famis. [cf Lc vi 20 ff] isto enim tempore minatur Dominus diuitibus famem, pauperibus uero saturitatem promittit. haec bona et mala duplicis temporis uno tempore futura testatur Scriptura Exodi, qua [cf Ex x 23] manifestum est omnium plagarum Aegypti inmunem fuisse Israhel, et per tres dies tenebrarum lumen habuisse. quod nunc spiritaliter geritur, sicut Deus eidem Faraoni postea [Eze xxxii 8] comminatus est dicens: *Dabo tenebras super terram tuam.*

Aliquotiens unum tempus in multas diuidet partes, quarum singulae totum tempus sint. sic annus quo fuit Noe in arca diuiditur inter omnes numeros. quotiens tamen temporum mentio est, quaternarius numerus specialiter tempus est a Domini passione usque in finem. quaternarius est autem quotiens aut plenus est, aut post tertium pars quarti ut CCCL aut tres et dimidium. ceteri uero numeri pro locis intellegendi sunt; signa sunt enim, non manifestae [Ge vii 4] definitiones. XL ergo dies diluuii tempus est. nam isti sunt

1 comburet V 4 uos] *om* V 8 descripti] describit V* *vid*; describi V*corr* ordi×ne V *nunc* 10 anni] annis V iosephx V* 11 a] *om* V 12 figuram R 14 id est] idem V ceteri V septem sterelitatis R 16, 17 promittit. haec...futura testatur] *sic diuidit* R; V *iungit* promittit *et* haec, *et disiungit* futura *et* testatur 17 qua] quia V 20 pharaoni R 22 aliquoties R unum] ·I· R 24 archa R 24, 27 quoties R 27 est autem] *om* est R 28 CCCL] CCL R; trecenti quadraginta V aut] aūt· R dimidio V numeri] nam V 29, 30 manifeste definitionis R; manifeste definitiones V 30 dies diluuii] *tr* V tempus] *pr* totum V

RV (M) CCCC anni in Aegypto, et XL anni in heremo, et XL dies ieiunii Domini et Moysi et Heliae, quibus in heremo ieiunat Ecclesia, id est abstinet a mortuorum uoluptatibus; id est XL dies quibus manducat et bibit Ecclesia cum Domino post [cf Ac i 3, 4] resurrectionem, id est XL anni quibus erat Ecclesia *manducans* [3 Regn ii 46 a] *et bibens* sub Salomone, pace undique uersum profunda, premente tamen eodem bipertito Salomone, sicut eadem Ecclesia dicit: *Pater tuus oppressit nos.* [3 Regn xii 24 p] XL dies fuit aqua [cf Ge vii 17] statu suo et totidem defecit dies, et defectio aquae decimo [Ge viii 6] mense, id est perfecto tempore, conpletur. sed in genere non ita est, ut quodam tempore inualescat et deinde deficiat: quoniam quo tempore inualescit carnaliter eodem deficit spiritaliter, ut ipsa elatio sit defectio usque dum perficiatur tempus, sicut mundus regnans ponitur sub pedibus Ecclesiae, id est filii hominis. qui sunt itaque XL dies, id est CL, in [cf Ge vii 17, 24] Ezechiel; namque XL diebus exsoluit peccata Iuda, et Israhel [cf Eze iv 4—6] CL, quod est unum atque idem. et *septimo mense sedit arca,* [Ge viii 4] idem tempus; et *deficiebat aqua usque in decimum mensem,* [*Ib* 5] idem tempus. exiuit de arca duodecimo mense; hic est [cf *Ib* 6] *annus* libertatis *Domini acceptabilis,* quo conpleto manifesta- [cf Lc iv 19] bitur Ecclesia mundi pertransisse diluuium.

Vnaquaeque pars huius anni idem annus est. quale si diceret, Exiuit de arca quadragesimo die, aut, Mense septimo aut decimo; sunt enim istae partes recapitulationis ab initio usque in finem. sicut ab Adam usque Enoc, id est Ecclesiae translationem, VII generationes, quod est omne tempus;

1 cccc] quadrigenti V 2 heliae] eccla V heremo] herimo R; eccla V ieiunant V 3 id est 2°] idem V 4 dies] dieb. V* 5 id est] *om* V anni] annis V*; annis Vcorr (=anni sunt) 6 uersum] uessum R profunda] *om* R; profundi V* *vid* 7 praemente R eodem] eo V 8 dic& V 9 statu] *pr* in VM dies] ubis V*; ut bis V[b] 9—12 decimo...quo tempore] R *supr ras* 10 compleretur V 12 quo tempore] tempore V*; tempore quo V*corr* defecit RV* 14 sicut] sic VM regnans] repugnans M 15 id est 1°] V*; *exp* V[a] fili V* id est 2°] idem V 16 hiezechiel R; ezechihel V diebus] dies V 17 idem...arca] *om* R 20 completo V 22 idem] id est RM 23 exiuit] exiit V 24 decimo] *add* EXPLICIT LIBER QVINTVS • || INCIPIT LIBER • VI • DE RECAPI|TVLATIONE • V sunt...recapitulationis] Recapitulationis sunt enim ista partes V (*sic*); sunt autem partes istae recap. M 25 enoch RM

rursum ab Adam usque ad Noe, id est mundi reparationem, x generationes, quod est omne tempus; et a Noe usque ad Abraham x generationes. nam et c anni quibus arca fabricata est omne tempus est quo Ecclesia fabricatur, et eo tempore in diluuio pereuntibus uniuersis gubernatur. RV [*Eug*] (M) 63

Quod prudentibus plenius inuestigandum data uia relinquimus; quoniam, ne copia Scripturae foret in interpretando et ea quae hunc intellectum forte impediunt remouendo, singula persequenda non putauimus alio properantes.

VI. De recapitulatione.

Inter regulas quibus Spiritus legem signauit quo luminis uia custodiretur, non nihil custodit recapitulationis sigillum ea subtilitate, ut continuatio magis narrationis quam recapitulatio uideatur.

Aliquotiens enim sic recapitulat: Tunc, Illa hora, Illo die, Eo tempore; sicuti Dominus loquitur in Euangelio dicens:
Lc xvii 29—32 § *Die quo exiit Loth a Sodomis pluit ignem de caelo et perdidit* §*Eug* 875
omnes; secundum haec erit dies filii hominis, quo reuelabitur. illa hora qui erit in tecto et uasa eius in domo non descendat tollere illa, et qui in agro similiter non reuertatur retro,
meminerit uxoris Loth.¶ numquid illa hora qua Dominus ¶ *Eug*
reuelatus fuerit aduentu suo non debet quis conuerti ad ea quae sua sunt et uxoris Loth meminisse, et non antequam reueletur? Dominus autem illa hora qua reuelatus fuerit

7 ne] nec R 7, 8 foret in interpretando] interpretando fore& V* (for& V*corr*) 8 remouenda V 9 singula persequenda] *posuit* V *ante* et ea quae... alio] alibi V

properantes] *add* EXPLICIT REGVLA | DE TEMPORIBVS | INCIPIT REGVLA | DE RECAPITVLATIONE R *rubro* (*de sectionum diuisione codicis quo usus est Aug non satis liquet*)

11 spiritus] sps (s *supr ras*) R legem] lege VM 13 ea] & R 15 aliquoties R 16 sicuti] sicut R 17 die qua VM (*cf Introd p* xxxviii) exiit] exiuit V 18 erit dies] R *Aug*; erunt dies V, *sed supr ras*; erunt omnes dies *Eug* fili V 19 illa hora] in illa hora *Eug* descendat] *Eug*; discendat V; descendet R 23 uxori V

RV (M) iussit ista obseruari, non solum ut abscondendo quaerentibus gratiorem faceret ueritatem, sed etiam ut totum illud tempus diem uel horam esse monstraret. eadem itaque hora, id est tempore, ista obseruanda mandauit, sed antequam reueletur: eadem quidem hora, sed in qua parte horae ratione cognoscitur.

Aliquotiens autem non sunt recapitulationes huius modi sed futurae similitudines, sicut Dominus dicit: *Cum uideritis* Mt xxiv 15, 16 *quod dictum est per Danihelem prophetam, tunc qui in Iudaea sunt fugiant in montes*, et inducit finem. quod autem Danihel dixit in Africa geritur, neque in eodem tempore finis. sed quoniam, licet non in eo tempore finis, in eo tamen titulo futurum est, propterea *Tunc* dixit, id est cum similiter factum fuerit per orbem, quod est *discessio* et *reuelatio hominis* cf 2 The ii 3 *peccati*. hoc genere locutionis dicit Spiritus in Psalmis: *Cum auerteret Dominus captiuitatem Sion facti sumus uelut* Ps cxxv 1—3 *consolati. tunc repletum est gaudio os nostrum et lingua nostra exultatione. tunc dicent in gentibus: Magnificauit Dominus facere cum illis, magnificauit Dominus facere nobiscum, facti sumus laetantes.* dicendum erat: Cum auerterit Dominus captiuitatem Sion, tunc dixerunt in gentibus; nunc autem: *Cum auerteret* inquit *tunc dicent in gentibus.* nos enim gentes quorum captiuitatem auertit. sicut et illorum in figuram tempus habemus dicentes: *Magnificauit Dominus facere cum eis, magnificauit Dominus facere nobiscum.* de similitudine itaque tempus suum et nostrum unum fecit et iuncxit dicens: *Tunc dicent in gentibus*, id est cum similiter gentibus fecerit.

Nec illud praetereundum puto, quod Spiritus sine mysteriis uel allegoria aliud sonare aliud intellegi uoluit, sicut per Iohannem: *Multi pseudoprophetae prodierunt in hoc mundo.* 1 Ioh iv 1—3

2 faceret] faciat R 7 aliquoties R recapitulationis V 9 danihelū V 11 dixit] *om* R in 2°] *om* V 12 quoniam] quo non iam R 15 loquutionis R 16 auerterit V 18 in gentibus] inter gentes V 20 dicendum erat] dicendo uera V 21 in gentibus] lugentibus V 23 et] *om* V 25 eis] illis V 25, 26 de similitudine] dissimilitudine R; per similitudinem M 27 iunxit V 30 alligoria R 31 multi] multa R hunc mundum V

RV (M) *in isto cognoscite Spiritum Dei: omnis spiritus qui soluit Iesum et negat in carne uenisse de Deo non est, sed hic de antichristo est, quod audistis quoniam uenit, et nunc in isto mundo praesens est.* numquid omnis qui non negat Iesum in carne uenisse Spiritum Dei habet? sed hanc negationem in opere non in uoce esse, ¶et unumquemque non ex pro- ¶M fessione sed ex fructibus intellegi debere, in omni ipsa epistula, qua non nisi de fratribus bonis et malis scripsit, 1 Ioh ii 3, 4 subtiliter admonet eodem genere locutionis, sicut dicit: *In isto cognoscimus quoniam cognouimus eum, si praecepta eius custodiamus. qui autem dicit quoniam cognouit eum, et mandata eius non seruat, mendax est.* numquid ex professione dixit intellegi fratrem qui Deum nescit, et non ex operibus? 1 Ioh ii 9 et iterum: *Qui dicit se in luce esse, et fratrem suum odit, in* 1 Ioh iv 20 *tenebris est usque adhuc.* et iterum: *Qui dixerit quoniam diligit Deum, et fratrem suum odit, mendax est.* si enim ut dicit diligit Deum, doceat operibus, adhaereat Deo, diligat Deum in fratre. si credit Christum incarnatum, quiescat cf Ioh i 14 odisse membra Christi. si credit Verbum carnem factum, quid persequitur Verbum in carne? si credit quod dixit Dominus: Mt xxv 40; cf Mt xviii 6 *Quamdiu fecistis uni ex istis fratribus meis minimis in me credentibus, mihi fecistis,* non operetur malum Christo in carne, id est in seruis eius, quoniam Dominus et Ecclesia cf Eph v 31, 32 *una caro* est. in qua carne si credit esse hominem, cur non diligit, aut—quod crudelius est—cur odit, sicut scriptum est: 1 Ioh iii 14, 15 *Qui non diligit* fratrem suum *permanet in morte,* et: *Qui fratrem suum odit homicida est?* aliud maius et euidentius signum agnoscendi antichristi non esse dixit, quam qui negat Christum in carne, id est odit fratrem. tale est autem quod

1 in isto] isto R spiritum] sps V 4 omnes V*M negant R 5 uenisse] uenire R 7 ipsa] *om* V 8 epistola V de fratribus] fratrib. R; de fructibus V 9 ammon& R; admonet V loquutionis R 14 odit frem suū V 16 diligit deum] diligo dnm R odit frem suū V 18 deum] dnm R fratrem RV 19 odisse] odire V verbum carnem] *pr* uerbum carnem factum quid persequitur in carne V carnem factum] carnefactum RV 20 si credit] *om* V 21 minixxmis V 24 non] *om* V* 26 suum] *om* V in mortem V* 27 et] aut V 28 agnoscendi] cognoscendi V antichristi R *plene* 29 christum] *om* V id est] idē V quod dicit] *om* R

RV dicit: *Quoniam qui non negauerit Christum in carne de Deo* [cf 1 Ioh iv 2] *est,* quale: *Nemo potest dicere Dominum Iesum, nisi in* [1 Co xii 3] *Spiritu Sancto,* cum multi dicant Dominum Iesum, ipso contestante: *Non omnis qui mihi dicit Domine Domine in-* [Mt vii 21] *troibit in regnum caelorum.* sed hoc loco apostolus neminem posse *dicere Dominum Iesum nisi in Spiritu Sancto* secundum conscientiam dixit, *secundum interiorem hominem* non secun- [Ro vii 22] dam solam professionem, ut ostenderet illis qui credunt Dominum Iesum nihil minus habere ab his qui charismatum generibus extolluntur, sed unum atque eundem Spiritum possidere omnem qui Iesum Dominum corde crediderit, id est operibus credidisse monstrauerit. *Nemo* inquit *potest* [1 Co xii 3–5] *dicere Dominum Iesum nisi in Spiritu Sancto. diuisiones autem charismatum sunt, idem autem Spiritus; diuisiones mysteriorum, et idem Dominus.*

Soluere autem *Iesum* est non facere quod Iesum fecisse [1 Ioh iv 3] confitetur, sicut idem Dominus dicit: *Qui soluerit unum* [Mt v 19] *ex mandatis istis minimis, et sic docuerit homines, minimus uocabitur in regno caelorum.* et quid sit *Soluerit* consequentibus aperit dicens: *Qui* autem fecerit *et sic docuerit.* hanc ergo negationem operum esse non uocis et Paulus apostolus confirmat dicens: *Deum scire confitentur, factis autem ne-* [Tit i 16] *gant.* et iterum: *Habentes deformationem pietatis, uirtutem* [2 Tim iii 5] *autem eius negantes.*

Hoc sensu dicit *quosdam* fratres *non sancte Christum* [Phil i 17] *praedicare,*—sed corde, nam uoce sancta praedicabant. consentit denique praedicationi eorum et mandat audiri dicens:

1 non] *om* V 2 est] RV*; *pr* non V*corr* potest] poterit V* dominum iesum] dn̄o ihū V*; dn̄s ih̄s V*corr* nisi in] *om* V* 4 omnis] omnes V 5 in regno R 6 iesum] + xp̄m V 8 credunt] dicunt V 9 charismatum] chrismatum V* 11, 12 id est] idē V 14 charismatum sunt] sunt carismatum V autem] uero V diuisiones] *pr* et V 15 mysteriorum] + sunt V 17 qui solueris V* 19 in regnū V 19, 20 ex consequentibus V 21 negationem] negotiationē R et] sed R* (*corr* R[b]) 22 deum] dn̄m V 23 et] ××et V deformationem] formam V 24 negantes] abnegantes V 25 hoc sensum V* non sc̄e xp̄m R; xp̄m non sc̄ae V 26 sancta] sc̄e V praedicabant] praedicabat R; praedicant V 27 audire R

RV [*Eug*]

Phil i 18 *Quid interest? omni modo siue per occasionem siue per ueritatem Christus adnuntietur.* Dominum autem Christum antichristus non uoto sed occasione praedicabat. alio tendens per Christi nomen ingreditur, quo sibi uiam sternat, quo sub Christi nomine uentri pareat, et his—quae turpe cf Mt xxiv 24, 26 est dicere—sanctitatis et simplicitatis nomen inponat, signis et prodigiis *cubiculorum* opera Christum esse adseuerans. 1 Ioh v 21 quos salubri cautione uitare admonet apostolus dicens: *Filioli, abstinete uos a simulacris.*

VII. De diabolo et corpore eius.

Diaboli et corporis eius ratio breuiter uideri potest, si id quod de Domino et eius corpore dictum est in hoc quoque obseruetur. transitus namque a capite ad corpus eadem Esai xiv 12–21 ratione dinoscitur, sicut per Esaiam de rege Babylonis: § *Quomodo* (§ *Eug* 876) *cecidit de caelo lucifer mane oriens! contritus est in terra qui mittit ad omnes gentes!* ¶ (¶ *Eug*) *tu autem dixisti in animo tuo: In caelum ascendam, super stellas Dei ponam sedem meam, sedebo in monte alto super montes altos in Aquilonem, ascendam super nubes, ero similis Altissimo. nunc autem ad inferos descendes in fundamenta terrae, et qui uiderint te mirabuntur super te et dicent: Hic est homo qui concitat terram, mouet reges; qui ponit orbem terrae totum desertum, ciuitates autem destruxit abductosque non soluit. omnes reges gentium dormierunt in honore, homo in domu sua; tu autem proiectus es in montes uelut mortuus abominatus cum omnibus*

2 autem] enim V 3 praedicat V 8 quos] quo R ammonet R 8, 9 filioli] fili V 9 simulacbris V (*sic*)

simulacris] *add* EXPLICIT DE RECAPITVLA|TIONE REGVLA | INCIPIT DE DIABVLI ET COR|PORE EIVS REGVLA R *rubro*; EXPLICIT • LIBER • SEXTVS || INCIPIT LIBER • VII • DE DIABOLO ET CORPO|RE EIVS V

11 corporis] *scripsi*; corpore R; corpori V ratio] *om* V 12 quod] q̄uo R *mox corr* 14 esaiam] R*V*; iesaiam R*corr*; isaiam V*corr* 15 de caelo] *ante* cecidit *Eug cod opt*; *post* lucifer V 19 ero] et ero R similes V* 20 discendes RV*corr*; diccendis V* uiderint te] *tr* R 24 dormierant V in honorē R domo V 25 omnibus] hominibus R*; ominibus R*corr* (*sic*)

RV *qui ceciderunt inserti gladio et descendunt ad inferos. quomodo uestimentum sanguine consparsum non erit mundum, ita nec tu eris mundus, quia terram meam perdidisti et plebem meam occidisti. non eris in aeternum tempus semen*
64 *nequam; para filios tuos interfici peccatis patris tui, ut non resurgant.* in rege Babylonis et omnes reges et omnis populus significatur, unum est enim corpus.

Quomodo inquit *cecidit de caelo lucifer mane oriens! con-* Esai xiv 12, 13
fractus est in terra qui mittit ad omnes gentes! tu autem dixisti in animo tuo: In caelum ascendam, super stellas Dei ponam sedem meam. diabolus hoc sibi non promittit; non enim sperat renitendo posse in caelum ascendere, qui ne deiceretur resistere non ualuit. multo magis ista homo sperare non
potest; tamen hominem esse sic dicit: *Hic est homo qui* Esai xiv 16
incitat terram. sed praeter hanc rationem qua neque diabolus neque homo sperare potest se posse in caelum ascendere et super stellas Dei sedens similem se Deo fieri, etiam ipsa Scriptura aliud inquirendum admonet. nam si in caelo et supra stellas Dei dicit sedem suam positurum, quomodo in monte alto sedebit aut super montes in Aquilone uel in nubibus, ut similis sit Altissimo? non enim Altissimus in huius modi habet sedem.

Caelum Ecclesiam dicit, sicut procedente Scriptura uidebimus. de hoc caelo cadit lucifer matutinus; lucifer enim bipertitum est, cuius pars sancta est, sicut Dominus dicit in
Apocalypsi de se et suo corpore: *Ego sum radix et genus Da-* Ap xxii 16, 17
uid et stella splendida matutina, sponsus et sponsa. item illic:
Qui uincit, dabo illi stellam matutinam, id est ut sit stella ma- Ap ii 26, 28
tutina sicut Christus, quem accepimus. pars ergo luciferi, id

1 discendunt RV* 2 conspersum RV*corr* 3 quia] qui R 5 tuos] tuo R interfice V ut] *om* R 6 in regem V 7 significatur] significatus V 9 est] *om* V 12 qui] quod R* deieceretur R 14 tamen] *pr* et V 15 qua] quam V 17 super] supra V 18 ammon& R in caelum V 19 supra] sup V 20 aquilonem V 21 enim] *om* R 22 huius modi] hui modi R* 25 cuius pars sancta est] *om* V 26 apocalysi R de se et] R*corr*; de sede & R*; de se & de se & V 26, 27 dauid & radix genus R 27 sponsus] sps RV: *sed cf p* 3[28] 28 uincit] uicerit R 29 luciferi] lucifer V

est aduersum corpus quod est diabolus reges et populus, cadit RV
de caelo et confringitur in terra. his regibus dicit Sapientia:
Sap vi 1–4 *Audite ergo reges et intellegite, discite iudices finium terrae,
praebete aures qui continetis multitudinem et placetis uobis in
turbis nationum. quoniam data est uobis potestas a Domino,
et uirtus ab Altissimo, qui interrogabit opera uestra, et cogitationes scrutabitur; quoniam cum essetis ministri regni illius
non recte iudicastis, neque custodistis legem.*

Rex ergo Babylonis totum corpus est, sed pro locis intel-
Esai xiv 12 legemus in quam partem corporis conueniat. *Cecidit de*
Ib 13 *caelo lucifer* in omne corpus potest conuenire; *In caelum
ascendam, super stellas Dei ponam sedem meam* similiter in
caput et maiores qui stellarum Dei, id est sanctorum, dominandum putant, cum ipsorum minores dominentur sicut
Ge xxv 23 scriptum est: *Maior seruiet minori.* huic Esau, id est fra-
tribus malis, sic dicit Dominus per Abdiam prophetam:
Abd 3, 4 *Exaltans habitationem suam, dicens in corde suo: Quis me
deducet ad terram? si exaltatus fueris sicut aquila, et inter
stellas ponas nidum tuum, inde detraham te, dicit Dominus.*

Esai xiv 13, 14 *Sedebo in monte alto super montes altos in Aquilonem,
ascendam super nubes, ero similis Altissimo. mons altus*
populus est superbus; *montes alti* singuli quique superbi, qui
adunati montem faciunt, id est corpus diaboli. multos enim
Ps xlv 3 esse montes malos sic dicit Scriptura: *Transferuntur montes*
Ps xvii 8 *in cor maris.* et iterum: *Fundamenta montium conturbata
sunt et commota sunt, quoniam iratus est eis Deus.* nam et si
corpus Domini id est Ecclesia mons dicitur, et singuli qui
Ps ii 6 Ecclesiam faciunt montes, sicut scriptum est: *Ego autem
constitutus sum rex ab eo super Sion montem sanctum eius*
Esai xiv 25 *adnuntians imperia eius.* et iterum: *Perdam Assyrios in*
Ps lxxi 3 *terra mea et in montibus meis.* et iterum: *Suscipiant montes*

1 populos V* 2 confrangitur R regibus] regulis V 6 interrogauit V 9, 10 intellegimus V 10 in quam] V*corr*: *om* in R; *om* quam V* 12, 13 in caput et] et caput V 13 maiore V* 14 minores] ininores R* *mox corr* 15 id est] *om* R 16 sic] sicut R 17 exultans R 18 terram] terras V 19 detraham te] *tr* V 20 monte alto super] *om* R aquilone RV* 22 superbi] *om* V 24 malos] V *supr ras* transferuntur] transferunt R; transferentur V 25 in corde V et] *om* V 26 eis] ei V 28 ecclesiam] ecc̄la V* 31 trã meã V

RV *pacem populo tuo et colles.* et iterum: *Montes exultabunt* Ps cxiii 4
uelut arietes, et colles uelut agni ouium. Deus in monte Sion
habet sedem et in montibus Israhel et in nubibus sanctis
suis, quod est Ecclesia, sicut scriptum est: *Timeat a facie* Zech ii 13
Domini omnis terra, quoniam exsurrexit de nubibus sanctis.
et iterum: *Nubibus mandabo ne pluant super eam imbrem.* Esai v 6
iterum: *Nimbus et nubes in circuitu eius.* et quod in monte Ps xcvi 2
Sion habitet sic dicit: *Cognoscetis quoniam ego sum Dominus* Ioel iii 17
Deus uester, habitans in Sion monte sancto meo. et diabolus
in monte sedet, sed Seir qui est Esau, id est fratrum malorum, quem montem Deus increpat per Ezechielem, et dicit
in laetitia uniuersae terrae desolaturum, quod aduersum Eze xxxv 14
Iacob inimicitias exerceat. ipse est mons, ipsi montes Aquilonis. in his diabolus sedet, et nubium caeli ueluti dominatur; hactenus se similem dicit Altissimo.

Duae sunt partes in Ecclesia, Austri et Aquilonis, id est
meridiana et septentrionalis. in parte meridiana Dominus
manet, sicut scriptum est: *Vbi pascis, ubi manes in meri-* Cant i 7
diano. diabolus uero in Aquilone, sicut dicit Dominus
populo suo: *Illum ab Aquilone persequar a uobis, et expellam* Ioel ii 20
illum in terram sine aqua,—id est in suos,—*et exterminabo faciem eius in mare primum, et posteriora eius in mare nouissimum,* quod est in populos primos et nouissimos. ad instar Ecclesiae fabricatus est iste mundus, in quo sol oriens non nisi per Austrum, id est meridianum, iter habet, et decursa Australi parte inuisibilis uadit in locum suum rediens. sic Dominus noster Iesus Christus sol aeternus partem suam percurrit, unde et meridianum uocat. Aquiloni uero, id est aduersae parti, non oritur, sicut idem cum in iudicium uenerint dicent: *Iustitiae lumen non luxit nobis, et sol non ortus* Sap v 6
est nobis; Timentibus autem Dominum *oritur sol iustitiae, et* Mal iv 2

1 tuo] *om* V 5 exsurrexit] exurgit V 6 et] *om* V nubibus] nub. V 8 cognoscitis V 11 hiezechielem R; ezechihelū V 12 in laetitiam R 15 actenus R 17 partē meridiana V* *vid*; partem meridianā V*corr* 18 sicut] *om* V pasces R 19 aquilonem V dicit dominus] d̅s̅ dicit V 20 a uobis et] RV*; ä uobis &̈ V[b] 21 terram] V*corr*; terra RV* suos et] suos sed R 27 dominus] ×et d̅n̅s̅ d̅s̅ V 28 et meridianum] meridianam R 30, 31 et sol...nobis] *om* V

sanitas in pinnis eius, sicut scriptum est. malis uero meridie (R) V
Esai lix 9, 10 nox erit, sicut scriptum est: *Dum sustinent ipsi lumen factae sunt illis tenebrae, dum sustinent fulgorem obscura nocte ambulauerunt; palpabunt sicut caecus parietem, et quasi cui non sunt oculi palpabunt, et cadent meridie quasi media nocte.*
Am viii 9 iterum: *Occidet sol meridie et tenebricabit super terram*¶ *dies* ¶ R
Mich iii 6 *luminis.* iterum: *Propterea nox erit uobis de uisione, et tenebrae uobis erunt ex diuinatione, et occidet sol super prophetas, et obscurabit super eos dies luminis.*

Huic populo ex Austro comminatur Deus, sicut per
Eze xxvii 26 Ezechielem Sor increpat dicens: *Spiritus Austri contriuit te.*
Can iv 16 si etiam confringere permittit, dicens: *Exurge Aquilo, et ueni Auster perfla hortum meum, et defluent unguenta mea,* exurgenti nequam spiritui resistit Spiritus Sanctus qui Domini hortum perflat, et eliciuntur unguenta, id est odor suauitatis offertur. et per Ezechielem iterum ex reliquiis populi mali sic dicit Deus adducere super populum suum
Eze xxxix 1–4 partem eiusdem populi, quod est mysterium facinoris: *Ecce ego super te Gog, principem Ros Mesoc et Tobel. et congregabo te et deducam te et ponam te a nouissimo Aquilone, et adducam te super montes Israhel; et perdam arcum tuum de manu tua sinistra, et sagittas tuas de manu tua dextera, et deiciam te super montes Israhel.* hoc autem geritur a passione Domini, quoadusque de medio eiusdem mysterii facinoris discedat Ecclesia quae detinet, ut in tempore suo detegatur impietas,
2 The ii 6–8 sicut apostolus dicit: *Et nunc quid detineat scitis, ut in suo tempore detegatur. mysterium enim iam operatur facinoris, tantum ut qui detinet modo, quoad usque de medio fiat; et tunc reuelabitur ille impius.* et in Hieremia legimus pecca-

1 pinnis] pannis V*; pennis V*corr* 2 erit] est V 3 dum sustinent] *om* V obscuram nocte R 4 quasi] V, *sed casu paene euanuit* 6 occidit RV tenebricabit] tenebriscauit R super terram] *add* FINIT LIBER TYCONII R *rubro: his uerbis desinit codex* 11, 16 ezechihelū V 11, 12 te. si] *conieci*: theis V (*sic*) 13 hortum] ortū V 14 exurgente...spm V* 15 domini] dm V* ortū V 16 iterum] idem V*; item V*corr* reliquis V* 21 te super] *scripsi*: super tem V*; super te V*corr* montes] montem V 28 qui] quid V* detinet] *scripsi*: detinens detinet V*; detinens ē detineat V*corr*: *cf Introd p* li

V tores Israhel in Aquilone conueniri, Domino dicente: *Vade* Hier iii 12
et lege sermones istos ad Aquilonem et dic, Conuertere ad me
domus Israhel, dicit Dominus. meridianum uero pars est
Domini, sicut et in Iob scriptum est: *A meridiana parte* Iob xi 17
germinabit tibi uita; Aquilo diaboli: utraque autem pars in
toto mundo.

Ascendam inquit *super nubes, ero similis Altissimo. nunc* Esai xiv 14–17
autem ad inferos descendes in fundamenta terrae. qui uide-
rint te mirabuntur super te et dicent: Hic est homo qui con-
citat terram, commouet reges, qui ponit orbem terrae totum
desertum. numquid in diabolum conuenit *Qui uiderint te*
mirabuntur super te, aut in regem nouissimum cum ad inferos
descenderit? ipso enim ad inferos descendente non erit qui
miretur mundo finito. non enim dicent: Hic est homo qui
incitauit terram, mouit reges et posuit orbem terrae totum
desertum, sed *Incitat* et *Commouet* et *Ponit.* hominem enim
totum corpus dicit tam in regibus quam in populis, cuius
hominis superbi partem cum Deus percutit et ad inferos
deicit dicimus: *Hic est homo qui incitat terram, commouet*
reges, scilicet sanctos.

Qui ponit orbem terrae totum desertum. inridentium uox Esai xiv 17
est, non confirmantium, sicuti: *Qui dissoluit templum et in* Mt xxvii 40
triduo illud suscitat! <et:> *Dixit enim: Fortitudine faciam,* Esai x 13, 14
et sapientia intellectus auferam terminos nationum, et fortitu-
dinem illarum uastabo, et comminuam ciuitates cum habitan-
tibus; et totam orbem comprehendam manu uelut nidum, et
uelut oua derelicta auferam, et non erit qui effugiat me aut
contradicat mihi. numquid ista quae sibi promittit ualet
65 implere? *Ponit* quidem *orbem terrae totum desertum,* sed Esai xiv 17
orbem suum; *Ciuitates autem destruxit,* utique sui orbis.
est enim bipertitus, mobilis et inmobilis, sicut <in> Para-
lipomenon: *Commoueatur a facie Domini omnis terra. etenim* 1 Par xvi 30
fundauit orbem terrae qui non commouebitur.

14 miretur] meretur V* 20 sanctos] $\overline{\text{scs}}$ V* (=sanctus) 22 sicuti] *conieci*: sicut ubi V*; sicut ibi V*corr* 23 et] *om* V 23, 24 fortitudinem...sapientiam V 25 comminu××× V* 31 in] *addidi*; *om* V 31, 32 paralypomenon V

[Esai xiv 17] *Abductosque non soluit.* potest istud in speciem conuenire, [V] quod captiuos in nullo relaxasset, sed inmitis raptu aestimans principari tota in eos uteretur potestate; quod [Zech i 15] obiurgat Deus dicens: *Ego quidem iratus sum modice, ipsi autem adiecerunt in mala.* uerumtamen in figuram generalitatis facta et dicta sunt, et spiritaliter implentur dum hi qui dominantur humilitatis subditos—aut temptationis causa uel merito sibi subditos—sine respectu pietatis atque communis conditionis affligunt, quibus non sufficit potestas, sed [Esai i 23] ea inmoderatius uti contendunt, quod culpat dicens: *Persequentes retributionem*, [Ps liv 21] et iterum: *Extendit manum suam ei in retribuendo.* parum est enim quod inimicus est; adhuc [Esai lviii 3] gestit et in subditum uindicare, sicut scriptum est: *Omnes subditos uobis conpungitis*; dissimulans odisse Dominum [Ps viii 3] *inimicum et uindicatorem,* quod per uindictam, quam soli [Ro xii 19] sibi Deus exceptauit, aliquid deitatis usurpet. *Scriptum est enim: Mihi uindictam et ego retribuam, dicit Dominus.*

[Esai xiv 18] *Omnes reges terrae dormierunt in honore, homo in domo sua. Reges* sanctos dixit, nam non omnes reges uel priuati in domo sua dormierunt, sicut sancti in domo quam delegerunt. [Ib 19] *Tu autem proiectus es in montes uelut mortuus abominatus, cum omnibus qui ceciderunt inserti gladio et descendunt ad inferos.* diabolo dicit *Proiectus es in montes,* in quibus sedet. denique non dixit Mortuus, sed *Velut mortuus abominatus*; adhuc enim uiuit, licet ipse in suis gladio perimatur et ad inferos descendat. sicut enim Dominus quicquid sui patiuntur se pati dixit, ita et diabolus ipse in suis inculcatur, [Pro xiv 28] ipse abominatus confringitur, sicut scriptum est: *In diminutione populi comminutio principis.* diabolus ab homine suo non separatur; nec homo in quo diabolus non est potest [Esai xiv 14; Ib 16] dicere: *Ero similis Altissimo,* nec de diabolo dici: *Hic homo qui incitat terram,* nisi in homine fuerit. sicut Dominus homo non dici potest nisi in homine, nec homo Deus nisi in

1 abductoque V* istud] V*corr*; inquit V* (*sic*) 2 captiuis V raptu] raptum V 7 temptationis] temptationib. V 10 culpat× V* 16 exceptabit V 17 uindicta V* *vid* 31 de diabolo] V*corr*; diaboli V*

V Christo. sed quid in quem conueniat pro locis obseruandum est.

Iterum <in> corpus ipsius diaboli conuenit dicens: *Sicut* Esai xiv 20, 21 *uestimentum sanguine consparsum non est mundum, ita nec tu eris mundus, quia terram meam perdidisti et plebem meam occidisti. non eris in aeternum tempus semen nequam; para filios tuos interfici peccatis patris tui, ut non resurgant.* hic ostendit non conuenire in speciem. rex enim Babylonis qui terram Domini uastauit et populum occidit, id est Nabuchodonosor, mundus obiit, in aeternum uiuit; corpori dicit sui cuiusque temporis parare quos genuerit interfici peccatis eius, quo ipse qui conuenitur genitus est. nouissimis enim rex non *filios* sed fratres habere potest, neque *uelut mortuus* cum ad inferos descenderit, sed mortuus.

Per Ezechielem sic Deus increpat regem Tyri, id est omne corpus aduersum: *Quoniam exaltatum est cor tuum, et* Eze xxviii 19 *dixisti: Deus sum ego, habitationem Dei habitaui in corde maris. tu autem homo es et non Deus, et dedisti cor tuum tamquam cor Dei. numquid sapientior es tu Danihele? sapientes non arguerunt te sapientia sua? numquid sapientia tua aut doctrina tua fecisti tibi uirtutem, et aurum et argentum thesauris tuis? numquid in multa doctrina tua et mercatu tuo multiplicasti uirtutem tuam <, et exaltatum est cor tuum in uirtute tua>? propterea haec dicit Dominus, Quoniam dedisti cor tuum sicut cor Dei, propter hoc ecce ego induco super te alienos, pestes ex gentibus, et exinanient gladios suos super te et super decorem doctrinae tuae, et uulnerabunt decorem tuum in perditionem, et deponent te, et morieris morte uulneratorum in corde maris. numquid dicturus es in conspectu interficientium te: Deus sum ego? tu uero homo es et non Deus; in multitudine incircumcisorum peribis in manibus alienorum, quia ego locutus sum, dicit Dominus. < et factus est sermo Domini ad me dicens: Fili hominis, accipe lamentum super*

3 in] *om* V diaboli] dicaboli V sicut] *pr* quomodo uenisti V; *constat* uenisti *ex* uesti(mentum) *ortum esse, et cf p* 71[1,2] 4 conspersum V*corr* 7 interfice V 9 uastabit V* 15 ezechihelū V 19 danihelo V 22 mercatu] V*corr; pr* in V* 23, 24 et exaltatum...tua] *om* V; *suppleui ex p* 79[24] 26 alienos] alienas V; *cf infra p* 79[35] 31 multitudinem V 32 *seq* et factus est...dominus] *om* V; *suppleui ex p* 80[26] *ff*.

principem Tyri, et dic illi: haec dicit Dominus,> Tu es V *signaculum similitudinis, et corona decoris in deliciis paradisi Dei fuisti, omnem lapidem optimum habens in te alligatum,—sardium <et> topazium <et> smaragdum et carbunculum et saffirum et iaspin et argentum et aurum et ligyrium et achaten et amethystum <et> chrysolithum et beryllum et onychinum,—et auro replesti thesauros tuos et apothecas tuas <in te. ex qua die creatus es tu> cum cherubim posui te in monte sancto Dei, fuisti in medio lapidum igneorum, abisti sine macula <tu> in diebus tuis ex qua die creatus es <tu>, donec inuenirentur iniquitates tuae in te a multitudine negotiationis tuae. implesti promptuaria tua iniquitate, et peccasti et uulneratus es a monte Dei, <et> abduxit te cherubim de medio lapidum igneorum. exaltatum est cor tuum in decore tuo, corrupta est doctrina tua cum decore tuo. propter multitudinem peccatorum <tuorum in terram proieci te, in conspectu regum dedi te dehonestari. propter multitudinem peccatorum tuorum> et iniquitatem negotiationis tuae contaminaui sancta tua; educam ignem de medio tui, hic te deuorabit. et dabo te in cinerem in terra tua in conspectu omnium uidentium te, et omnes qui te nouerunt inter nationes contristabuntur super te: perditio factus es, et non eris in aeternum.*

Eze xxviii 2 *Quoniam exaltatum est* inquit *cor tuum, et dixisti: Deus sum ego, habitationem Dei habitaui in corde maris.* et in
cf Mt xxiv 5 hominem conuenit *Ego sum Christus* et in diabolum, qui in
corde maris, id est populi, habitat, sicut Deus in corde
sanctorum suorum sedet. populus in corde maris, id est in
uoluptate uel altitudine saeculi, habitat, sicut in alio loco
Eze xxvii 25, 26 dicit Deus eidem ciuitati: *Satiata et onerata es nimis in*
corde maris. in aqua multa deduxerunt te remiges tui; spiritus Austri contriuit te in corde maris uirtutis tuae.

3 paradẏsi V habens] V; habes *p* 81^{31}, *sed cf Arnob* 4 et topazium et] topadiū V *tantum* 6 ligorium V achatim V 6, 7 ametistum crisolitum et berillum et onichinum V 8 apotecas V in te...es tu] *om* V; *suppleui ex pp* 81^{28}, 83^{8} 10 tu] *om* V 11 tu] *om* V 12 prumptuaria V* 13 peccasti] peccatis V; *uid p* 83^{23} monte] morte V et abduxit] *om* et V 14 igneorum] inferorum V 16, 18 tuorum...tuorum] *om* V; *suppleui ex p* $84^{6,13}$ 18 contaminaui] *conieci ex p* 84^{14}; contaminata sunt V 20 in cinere V 23 inquid V* 24 habitatione V 29 onerata] *coniecit Sabat.*; honorata V, *cf p* 63^{23}

V *Tu autem homo es, et non Deus.* et diabolus in homine Eze xxviii 2 homo dictus est, sicut Dominus dixit in Euangelio: *Inimicus* Mt xiii 28 *homo hoc fecit,* et interpretatus est dicens: *Qui ea seminat* Ib 39 *diabolus est.* homo diaboli Deus esse non potest. propterea in utrumque conuenit: *Tu homo es et non Deus.*

Dedisti cor tuum tamquam cor Dei. numquid sapientior Eze xxviii 2, 3 *es tu Danihele?* in Danihele totum corpus est Ecclesiae, quia non potest esse homo peccati sapientior in negotiis uitae, sicut ille *sapientior* est in suo *quam filii lucis.* potest etiam cf Lc xvi 8 in speciem conuenire, quoniam Danihel specialiter confudit regem Babylonis in figura, qui prophetico Spiritu regem superbum ad confessionem unius Dei Ecclesiae maiestate prostrauit, qui confessione suarum uirtutum et caelesti sapientia Babylonis superstitiones euertit.

Sapientes te non arguerunt sapientia sua? non solum Eze xxviii 3 enim Danihel sapiens, sed etiam tres pueri, qui regem et omne regnum eius cum ipsis diis suis unum Dominum asserendo eiusdem Dei praesente uirtute confuderunt. idem nunc usque generaliter eiusdem tam externas quam intestinas Babylonis tenebras lumine ueritatis disrumpunt.

Numquid in scientia tua aut sapientia tua fecisti tibi Eze xxviii 4, 5 *uirtutem, et aurum et argentum thesauris tuis? numquid in multa scientia et mercatu tuo multiplicasti tibi uirtutem tuam, et exaltatum est cor tuum in uirtute tua?* putant enim superbi et beneficiorum omnipotentis Dei ingrati sua uirtute aliquid posse et sapientia ditari, nescientes scriptum esse: *Non* Eccl ix 11 *leuibus cursus, non fortibus proelium, neque sapienti panis.* et iterum: *Numquid magnificabitur securis sine concisore?* Esai x 15 et non quidem prudentibus diuitiae, et non scientibus gratia. haec enim non sunt in nostra potestate, sed a Deo conferuntur. *Quid enim habes quod non accepisti? si autem* 1 Co iv 7 *accepisti, quid gloriaris tamquam non acceperis?* et iterum: *Non glorietur sapiens in sapientia sua.* Hier ix 23

Propterea haec dicit Dominus, Quoniam dedisti cor tuum Eze xxviii 6, 7 *sicut cor Dei, propterea ecce ego induco super te alienos, pestes*

7 danihelo V *utroque loco* ecclesia V* 11 figuram V 12 ecclesiae] ecclesiastica V; *cf Appx* II 13 prostrabit V 17 "suis" diis V 22 uirtute V 23 et mercatu] in mercatu V

ex gentibus, et exinanient gladios suos super te et super decorem V
scientiae tuae. etsi potest in speciem conuenire, quod reges
saeculi per suam superbiam dominos se appellari patiuntur,
tamen hoc quoque conuenit in genus. frequenter enim in-
ducit Deus in Ecclesiam alienigenas, et multos in mortem
uulnerant. sed etiam occulta persecutione multos inducit
cf Nu xxv 1ff ex gentibus, in quibus temptet populum suum, et occidat
nequam partem simul cum eis sicut Maziam.

Eze xxviii 7 *Et uulnerabunt decorem tuum in perditionem.* aliquos 66
Ib 8 enim non in perditionem sed cum spe sanitatis uulnerant. *Et*
deponent te, id est humiliabunt, *et morieris morte uulneratorum*
in corde maris. non diceret uulnerato *Morieris morte*
uulneratorum, nisi quia non aperte uulneratur et moritur;
sed ipse est, in quibus uulneratur.

Eze xxviii 9; cf Ps xxi 23 *Numquid narrabis in conspectu interficientium te: Deus*
sum ego? id est numquid diuini generis titulis terrebis
eos quibus traditus fueris occidendus tam spiritaliter quam
Ib 9, 10 carnaliter? *Tu uero homo <es> et non Deus; in multi-*
tudine incircumcisorum peribis in manibus alienorum, quia
ego locutus sum, dicit Dominus. nunc aperuit quo genere
se ille dicat Deum, dum minatur et in multitudine incircum-
cisorum periturum manibus alienorum, quod non conuenit
nisi in eum qui sibi circumcisus uidetur. rex enim Tyri
mortem solam potuit timere, non ne ab incircumcisis aut
cum eis moreretur.

Ib 11—13 *Et factus est sermo Domini ad me dicens: Fili hominis,*
accipe lamentum super principem Tyri, et dic illi: haec dicit
Dominus, Tu es signaculum similitudinis, et corona decoris
in paradiso Dei fuisti. numquid diabolo factus est paradisus,
ut ipse quod paradisum perdiderit increpetur? homo fuit
in deliciis paradisi, ipse est *signaculum similitudinis,* qui ad
cf Ge v 1 *similitudinem Dei* factus est. signaculum autem ad decorem
dixit, sicut per Aggeum dimicantibus huius aduersum se
Agg ii 22—24 fratribus promittit Deus Ecclesiae dicens: *Ego commouebo*
caelum et terram, mare et aridam. et conuertam currus et

5 in morte V 7 occidat. Nequam V (*sic*) 8 partem simul cum eis] *conieci*; persimiles V 15 narrabis] *uid Introd p* li; *pr* narrans V 18 es] *om* V; *cf p* 77^{30} 30 paradÿso V, *et sic infra* 33 dimicanti V*

V *sessores, et descendent equi et sessores eorum unusquisque in gladio ad fratrem suum. in illo die, dicit Dominus omnipotens, accipiam te Zorobabel filium Salathiel seruum meum, et ponam te signaculum, quoniam te elegi, dicit Dominus omnipotens.* Zorobabel omne corpus est, etenim exinde nusquam legimus commotis supra se <uniuersis> uenisse Zorobabel. hic est autem ex tribus, qui sub Dario meruit aedificare [cf 3 Esdr iv 13 *seq*] Hierusalem. ipse quoque in figura fundauit domum Dei et perfecit, sicut idem Dominus dixit: *Manus Zorobabel funda-* [Zech iv 9] *uerunt domum hanc, et manus eius perficient eam.* quod est autem *signaculum* hoc et *corona speciei*, sic Deus promittit Ecclesiae dicens: *Videbunt gentes iustitiam tuam, et reges* [Esai lxii 2–4] *claritatem tuam, et uocabunt nomen tuum nouum, quod Dominus nominabit illud. <et> eris corona speciei in manu Domini, et diadema regni in manu Dei tui. tu etiam non uocaberis Derelicta, et terra tua non uocabitur Deserta; tibi enim nomen uocabitur Voluntas mea, et terra tua Orbis terrarum.* homo est itaque *signaculum similitudinis* et *corona speciei*, cuius pars in [cf Ez xxviii 12, 13] ipso decore diuinae similitudinis et *deliciis paradisi*, id est Ecclesiae, perseuerat. altera uero pars, *ne in aeternum uiuat*, [cf Ge iii 22, 24] inter ipsam et arborem *flammeus ensis* euoluitur. *Adam* nam- [cf Ro v 14 (Col ii 17)] que, sicut apostolus dicit, *umbra est futuri*; sic et in fratres diuisus est in Cain et Abel.

Omnem lapidem optimum habens in te alligatum,—sardium [Eze xxviii 13] *et topazium et smaragdum et carbunculum et saffirum et iaspin <et> argentum et aurum et ligyrium et achaten et amethystum et chrysolithum et beryllum et onychinum,—et auro replesti thesauros tuos et apothecas tuas in te.* haec et in diabolum conueniunt et in hominem. isti enim duodecim lapides et aurum et argentum omnesque thesauri diabolo adhaerent delegati. denique *habes in te alligatum*, et iterum *apothecas tuas in te*, sicut corpus Domini a sanctis ornatur, promittente Deo et dicente: *Extolle oculos tuos in circuitu et uide omnes* [Esai xlix 18, 19]

3 salatihel V 6 uniuersis] *addidi, cf* 63^{22}, 66^{5}; *om* V 7 tribus] *scripsi*: tribu V 14 nominauit V et] *addidi*; *om* V 17 uoluntas] uoluptas V 19 paradysi V 22 in] *scripsi*; hi V 25 topadiū V iaspin et] iaspen V 26, 27 lygiriū et achathen et ametistū et crisolitū et berillū et onicinū V 28 apotecas V 31 apotechas V

filios tuos, collecti sunt et uenerunt ad te. uiuo ego, dicit Dominus, quia omnibus illis indueris, et superinpones illos tibi sicut ornamentum nouae nuptae; quia deserta tua et diruta et quae ceciderunt nunc angustiabuntur ab inhabitantibus. et in [cf Ap xxi 19, 20] Apocalypsi eadem ciuitas duodecim lapidibus fundata construitur. *Omnem* inquit *lapidem optimum,* et enumerauit duodecim, ut ostenderet in duodenario numero perfectionem. [cf Ge i 25] omnia enim quae fecit Deus bona sunt: horum diabolus usum non naturam mutauit. et omnes homines excellentis sensus et potentis ingenii aurum sunt et argentum et lapides pretiosi secundum naturam, sed eius erunt in cuius obsequio <uoluntate non> [cf Ro vi 16] natura suis fruuntur, *quoniam cui* se adsignauerit quis *in obedientiam, seruus est eius cui obaudit, siue peccati siue iustitiae.* ita fit ut et diabolus habeat aurum et argentum et lapides pretiosos; omnia quidem non sua secundum originem, sed sua secundum uoluntatem. nam et in [Iob xli 21] Iob scriptum est de diabolo: *Omne aurum maris sub eo est.* [cf 2 Tim ii 20] et apostolus *uasa aurea et argentea* dicit esse *quaedam in contumeliam.* non enim sicut quidam putant omnia *lignea* et *fictilia* reprobauit, cum ex eis sint aliqua in honorem, ipso [Ro ix 21] dicente *figulum luti aliud quidem* fingere *in honorem aliud uero in contumeliam,* et ex ligno, aliud ad praeparationem escae aliud in sacrilegium. ex auro et argento, id est ex magnis <et> perspicuis, dixit inmundos. nam et in Apoca- [Ap xvii 4] lypsi meretrix, id est corpus aduersum, *purpura cocco et auro* et argento *lapidibusque pretiosis* ornatur, *habens poculum aureum in manu plenum execrationum et inmunditiarum totius terrae.* ista sunt ergo diaboli ornamenta, lapides pre- [cf Eze xxviii 14] tiosi quibus *lapides igneos* imitatur. et homo in se habet thesauros tam facinorum quam perspicuos. ipse enim suorum portator est, quem facultates suae uelut compedes ligauerunt. praeter illa quae ab utroque sexu corporis diaboli ornanda [cf Mt vi 21] eduntur, etiam his quae defossa habent insitum est cor; *ubi enim erit thesaurus, illic erit et cor* hominis. uetus enim

3 nuptiae V* 5 apocalypsin V 9 excellentisensu V 11, 12 uoluntate non] *addidi* 13 in oboedientia V 18 uasa aurea &c] *cf Aug Retract* ii 18 18, 19 in contumelia V 20, 21 in honore V *utroque loco* 22 in contumelia V 23 escae] aesce V 24 et 1°] *om* V 24, 25 in apocalypsin V

V homo et terra eius unum corpus est, quoniam ipse quoque terra est. unde apostolus non solum ea, quae corpore admitti possunt, sed et auaritiam membrum esse possidentis ita definiuit dicens: *Mortificate itaque membra uestra quae in terra* [Col iii 5, 6] *sunt,—fornicationem, inmunditiam, passionem, concupiscentiam malam, et auaritiam, quae est idolorum seruitus,—propter quae uenit ira Dei.*

Ex qua die creatus es tu cum cherubim inposui te in monte [Eze xxviii 14] *sancto Dei,* id est in Christo uel in Ecclesia: *in medio lapidum igneorum fuisti,* id est hominum sanctorum, qui adunati montem Dei faciunt. angeli enim alterius substantiae lapides dici non possunt, quia corpus non habent. *Abisti sine* [Ib 15, 16] *macula tu in diebus tuis ex qua die creatus es tu, donec inuenirentur iniquitates tuae in te a multitudine negotiationis tuae.* lapides Ecclesiam dicit Petrus: *Et uos* fratres *tamquam lapi-* [1 Pet ii 5] *des uiui coaedificamini domus spiritalis,* quam domum igneam esse et hanc in malos fratres ardere sic dicit Deus: *Erit domus* [Abd 18] *Iacob ignis, domus autem Ioseph flamma, domus uero Esau stipula; et exardescent in illos et comedent eos, et non erit ignifer in domo Esau, quoniam Dominus locutus est.* cum enim peccat homo, deicitur de monte Dei, et *non erit ignifer* amisso Spiritu, et succenditur *in cinerem.* [cf Eze xxviii 18]

Peccasti et uulneratus es a monte Dei, et abduxit te cheru- [Ib 16] *bim de medio lapidum igneorum.* cherubim ministerium Dei est, quod exclusit uniuersos malos de Ecclesia, sed spiritaliter. qui enim *uestitum nuptialem* non habet, hic in saeculo exclu- [cf Mt xxii 11 ff] ditur de medio *recumbentium.* denique *in tenebras,* id est in obdurationem, *mittitur,* donec in ignem aeternum descendat. futuro enim saeculo nemo miscebitur choro sanctorum qui postea excludatur.

Exaltatum est cor tuum in decore tuo, corrupta est scientia [Eze xxviii 17] *tua in decore tuo.* corrupta est enim scientia eius qui sciens prudensque errat, et studio affectatae sapientiae asserit dissimulata ueritate mendacium, sicut Spiritus dicit: *Cum* [Ro i 21, 22]

1 et terra] *inter & et* terra *spatium trium litterarum in* V 3 auaritia V 8, 24 (2°) cherubin V 15 ecclesia V 16 domus spiritales V igneum V* 17 in malos] *om* in V 28 discendat V 29 choro] coro V

cognouissent Deum, non ut Deum magnificauerunt aut gratias V
egerunt, sed nugati sunt in cogitationibus suis, dicentes se esse sapientes. corrupta est scientia eius qui alios docet, se ipsum non docet. corruptus est decor <eius> qui generi suo operum similitudine non respondet.

Eze xxviii 17 *Propter multitudinem peccatorum tuorum in terram proieci te, in conspectu regum dedi te dehonestari.* et diabolus proiectus est in terram, id est in hominem, et homo de sublimitate Ecclesiae in conculcationem, sicut Hieremias dicit:
Thren ii 1 *Deiecit de caelo in terram gloriam Israhel. In conspectu* 67
regum: Christianorum dixit, quorum pedibus conculcatur diabolus et homo eius.

Eze xxviii 18 *Propter multitudinem peccatorum tuorum et iniquitatem negotiationis tuae contaminaui sancta tua.* uidetur ueluti principalem titulum exprobrasse corpori diaboli negotiationes—magis dicit et thesauros—spiritalis nequitiae. sicut enim spiritalis iustitiae negotiatio est thesaurus, ut Dominus
Mt xiii 45 dicit: *Simile est regnum caelorum homini negotiatori*, et
Mt vi 20 Mt xxv 14 iterum: *Thesaurizate uobis thesauros in caelo*, iterum *Dedit*
cf Eze xxxviii 13 *seruis suis substantiam suam* ut negotiarentur, iterum *Nego-*
Esai xxiii 18 *tiationes Carthaginenses* resistent tibi, iterum *Negotiatio eius*
1 Tim vi 6 *et merces sancta Domino*, et apostolus *Est* inquit *negotiatio magna pietas*; ita spiritalis nequitia negotiatio est, thesaurus
Mt xii 35 peccatorum, sicut Dominus dicit: *Homo malus de thesauro*
Ro ii 5 *cordis emittit mala*, et apostolus: *Thesaurizas tibi iram in die irae.*

Eze xxviii 18 *Propter iniquitatem* inquit *negotiationis tuae contaminetur sancta tua.* qui enim non recte sanctitate Dei utitur, suam
Esai i 13, 14 efficit, sicut Deus dicit de sabbatis suis: *Sabbata uestra odit anima mea.*

Eze xxviii 18 *Educam ignem de medio tui, hic te deuorabit.* ignis Ec-
cf 2 Thc ii 7 clesia est, quae cum discesserit e medio *mysterii facinoris*

1 deum] dnm V *utroque loco* 3 eius] eorum V 4 eius] *addidi*; *om* V 5 similitudinem V* *mox corr* 6 in terra V 10 deiecit] V* *vid*; deieci V *corr* 14 negationis V 15 exprobasse V 15, 16 negotiationes] *conieci*; negotiationis V 16, 17, 23 spiritales V 21 chartaginienses V*; chartaginenses V *corr* resistent] V; ἐροῦσιν LXX 27 inquid V* 28 s̄citatem V suam] sua V 32 mysteriis

V tunc pluet ignem Dominus a Domino de Ecclesia, sicut scriptum est: *Sol exortus est super terram, et Loth intrauit in* Ge xix 23, 24 *Segor. et pluit Dominus super Sodomam et Gomorram sulphur et ignem a Domino de caelo.* hic est ignis quem supra dixit: *Domus Iacob ignis, domus autem Esau stipula; et exardes-* Abd 18 *cent in eos et comedent illos, et non erit ignifer in domo Esau.* in Genesi iterum scriptum est: *Cum contereret Deus omnes* Ge xix 29 *ciuitates in circuitu, commemoratus est Deus Abrahae, et emisit Loth e medio subuersionis, cum subuerteret Deus ciuitates in quibus habitat in eis Loth.* numquid Loth non merebatur propria iustitia liberari, ut diceret Scriptura: *Commemoratus est Deus Abrahae, et emisit Loth e medio subuersionis*? aut in ciuitatibus habitabat, et non in ciuitate, ut diceret: *Ciuitates in quibus Loth habitabat*? sed prophetia est futurae discessionis. memor enim Deus promissionis ad Abraham eiecit Loth de omnibus ciuitatibus Sodomorum, quibus ueniet ignis ex igni Ecclesiae, quae de medio eorum educetur.

Et dabo te in cinerem in terra tua, id est in hominibus, Eze xxviii 18 uel ipsos homines in terra sua, qui in terra Dei esse noluerunt. *In conspectu omnium uidentium te,* id est intellegentium. numquid diabolus uideri potest nisi in homine?

Et omnes qui te nouerunt inter nationes contristabuntur Ib 19 *super te.* cum enim Dominus percutit aut detegit malos, contristantur qui eorum auxilio fulciri solent, corporis sui parte debilitata.

Perditio facta es, et non eris in aeternum. * * *

19 in cinere V* 21 omnium] hominum V 23 te nouerunt] tenuerunt V 27 in aeternu V* *vid*

Subscriptio. EXPLICIT DE DIABOLO ET CORPORE EIVS | LIBER SEPTIMVS V

MEMORIA TECHNICA

for the Rules of Tyconius, from a 13th cent MS at Laon (Departmental Catalogue of 1849, vol i, 88). See *Introd* p xxi.

Regula prima caput nostrum cum corpore iungit.
corpore de uero loquitur mixtoque secunda.
tertia describit quid lex quid gratia possit.
quarta genus speciem totum partemque rependit.
tempora disiungit maiora minoraque quinta.
sexta refert iterum que primo facta fuerunt.
septima serpentis sibi membra caputque resoluit.

Variants of the Roman MSS *Pal* 841 (14th cent) and *Vat* 4296 (15th cent).

2 corpore...secunda] nomine iustorum notat altera facta malorum *Vat*
3 describit] distinguit *Pal*
4 rependit] reuoluit *Pal*; resoluit *Vat*
5 disiungit] distinguit *Pal*; commutat *Vat*
7 sibi] tibi *Vat*   resoluit] reflectit *Pal*

APPENDICES.

THE MONZA EPITOME.

(*Codex Modoetianus, saec.* ix—x, *n°.* $\frac{c-2}{62}$.)

Note. The spelling and punctuation is that of the MS, but the contractions have been expanded throughout. Words in brackets are written above the line in the MS. The numbers at the side refer to the pages of this book. The sections not taken from the Book of Rules but from S. Augustine are printed in italics. See *Introd.* pp xxvii, xxxvi—xxxix.

(f. 206 v.) *Explicit tract. in epistola Pauli ad Hebreos.* ∴ VII. TICONII
1 REGVLAE: Necessarium dixi ante omnia quae mihi uidentur libellum regularem scribere et secretorum legis ueluti claues et luminaria fabricare; Sunt enim quaedam regulae mysticae quae uniuerse legis recessus obtinent. et ueritatis thesauros aliquibus inuisibiles faciunt; Quarum si ratio regularum sine inuidia ut communicamus accepta fuerit. clausa quaeque patefient. et obscura dilucidabuntur. ut quis prophetiae inmensam siluam perambulans his regulis quodammodo lucis tramitibus deductus ab errore liberetur; Sunt autem regulae istae: de domino et corpore eius. de domini corpore bipertito. de promissis et lege. de specie et genere. de
2 temporibus. de recapitulatione. de diabolo et eius corpore. Ecce esaias dicit. peccata nostra feret et pro nobis dolet et ipse uulneratus est propter facinora nostra et deus tradidit eum pro peccatis nostris et cetera quae domino conueniunt. Sequitur autem de eodem et deus uult purgare illum a plaga et uult deus a dolore auferre animam eius. ostendere illi lucem et formare illum p(ru)dentia; numquid ei quem tradidit pro peccatis nostris uult ostendere lucem et eum formare prudentia cum ipse sit lux et sapientia dei et non corpori eius? quare manifestum est sola ratione uideri posse quando a capite ad corpus transitum facit; Danihel quoque lapidem de monte praecisum dominum dicit. et implesse uniuersam terram corpus eius. non enim sunt audiendi qui potestate illum dicunt creuisse quia dominus ante mundi constitutionem hanc habuit potestatem et cum homo in illo dei filius fieret, non paulatim ut lapis sed uno tempore accepit
3 potestatem in caelo et in terra ∴ (f. 207 r.) Quod si potestate non corpore

implesset terram, lapidi non compararetur quia potestas. res est inpal-
pabilis. lapis uero res est palpabilis ; Nec sola ratione manifestatur corpus
non caput crescere sed etiam apostolica auctoritate. confirmatur. Cre-
scimus inquid in eum qui est caput christus ex quo omne corpus con-
structum et conexum per omne tactum subministrationis in mensuram
uniuscuiusque partis incrementum corporis facit in ædificationem sui. et
iterum non tenens caput ex quo omne corpus per tactum et coniunctiones
constructum et subministratum crescit in incrementum dei. Non ergo
caput quod ex origine idem est. sed corpus crescit ex capite : Ad propositum
redeamus ; Scriptum est de domino et eius corpore quid cui conueniat
ratione discernendum ; Angelis suis mandauit de te et cetera usque
ostendam illi salutare meum. numquid de cuius obsequio mandauit angelis
suis deus eidem ostendit salutare suum et non corpori eius ? Item. sicut
sponso inposuit mihi mitram et sicut sponsam ornauit me ornamento ;
Vnum corpus dixit utriusque sensus sponsi et sponsae. Sed quid in
domino quid in ecclesia conueniat ratione cognoscitur. Idem dicit in
apocalypsi. ego sum sponsus et sponsa. et iterum. exierunt obuiam sponso
et sponsae. Iterum quid capitis quid corporis ratione discernendum sit,
4 per esaiam declaratur. Sic dicit dominus christo meo domino cuius ego
tenui dexteram ut exaudiant eum gentes. Sequitur et dicit quod non nisi
corpori conueniat ; et dabo tibi thesauros absconditos inuisibiles aperiam
tibi ut scias quoniam ego sum dominus qui uoco nomen tuum deus israhel
propter iacob puerum meum et israhel electum meum ; propter testamenta
enim quae disposuit patribus.(ad)cognoscendum se deus aperit corpori
christi thesauros inuisibiles quod occul*us non uidit &c usque nec in cor
hominis ascendit id est obdurati hominis qui non est in corpore christi ;
Ecclesiæ autem reuelauit deus per spiritum suum ; Sunt enim in quibus
haec ratio minus claret eo quod siue in dominum siue in corpus eius
minus conuenit dictum. quam ob rem sola et maiora dei gratia uideri
possunt ; A modo inquid uidebitis filium hominis sedentem ad dexteram
uirtutis et uenientem in nubibus cæli ; Non uisuros uenientem in nubibus
cæli nisi in nouissimo tantum die plangent se omnes tribus terrae ; et
tunc uidebunt filium hominis uenientem in nubibus caeli ; Vtrumque
autem fieri necesse est. Sed primo corporis est aduentus id est æcclesiae
iugiter uenientis in eadem claritate ; Si enim diceret modo uidebitis
uenientem, solius corporis intelligendus esset aduentus ; Si autem uidebitis
capitis aduentus, Nunc uero a modo inquit uidebitis uenientem quoniam
corpore suo iugiter uenit natiuitatem et similium passionum claritatem.
Si enim renati christi membra efficiuntur et membra corpus efficiunt,
christus est qui uenit. quoniam natiuitas aduentus est ut illud inluminat
5 &c. usque in hunc mundum. Item generatio uadit et generatio uenit.
Item. sicut audistis antichristus uenit. Item de eodem corpore : si enim
iste qui uenit alium iesum predicat. unde dominus cum de signo aduentus
sui interrogaretur : de illo aduentu suo cepit disputare qui ab i(ni)mico
corpore signis et prodigiis imitari potest. cauete inquid ne quis uos

seducat. multi enim uenient in nomine meo id est in nomine corporis mei. Nouissimo autem aduentu domini id est consummationis et manifestationis totius aduentus eius nemo ut aliqui putant mentietur; Nec illud erit ab*sur*dum quod ex uno totum corpus uolumus intelligi ut filium hominis ecclesiam. quoniam ecclesia id est filii dei redacti in unum corpus. dicti unus homo dicti etiam deus. sicut per apostolum: super omne quod dicitur deus aut quod colitur. quoniam ecclesia dicitur, summus adoratur ut in templo dei sedeat ostendens se quod ipse sit deus id est ecclesia. quale si diceret in templo dei sedeat ostendens se quod ipse sit templum. aut in deum sedeat (f. 207 v.) ostendens se quod ipse sit deus. et dominus totum populum sponsam dicit et sororem et apostolus uirginem castam et aduersum corpus hominem peccati. et dauid totam ecclesiam christum dicit: faciens misericordias christo suo dauid. et semini eius in aeternum.
6 et apostolus corpus christi christum uocat; Sicut enim corpus unum est. membra autem habet multa. omnia autem membra ex uno corpore cum sint multa unum corpus est sic et christus. id est christi corpus quod ecclesia. Item. subpleo quae desunt pressurarum christi id est ecclesiae. nihil enim defuit christi passionibus quoniam sufficit discipulo ut sit sicut magister eius. Sic ergo aduentum christi pro locis sentiemus. legimus in exodo omnes filios dei unum filium. Israhel filius meus primogenitus. Item ibi omnes promitiuos unum primitiuum. Ecce ego occido filium tuum primitiuum. Et david uineam domini unum filium. uineam de egypto &c usque filium hominis quem confirmasti tibi. et apostolus filium dicit qui filium dei mixtus est paulus seruus christi iesu segregatus in euangelio dei &c usque iesu christi domini nostri. si diceret de filio suo ex resurrectione mortuorum unum ostenderet. nunc autem de filio inquit suo ex resurrectione mortuorum iesu christi domini nostri. Sed quis
7 factus sit filius dei ex resurrectione christi apertius ostendit dicens. de filio suo qui factus est &c usque secundum carnem qui predestinatus est filius dei. dominus enim noster non est predestinatus filius dei qui ex quo natus est hoc est. sed ille cui secundum lucam dicit in baptismo. filius meus es tu ego hodie genui te: Qui ex semine dauid mixtus est principali spiritui et factus est ipse filius dei ex resurrectione domini nostri iesu christi id est dum resurgit in christo semen dauid. non ille de quo ait ipse dauid. Dicit dominus domino meo; Itaque facti sunt duo una caro. uerbum caro factum est et caro deus. qui non ex sanguine sed ex deo nati sunt; Apostolus dicit. erunt duo in carne una quod interpretatur in christo et ecclesia. Vnum namque semen promisit deus abrahae: ut quanticumque in christo miscerentur: unus esset in christo. unde apostolus. omnes uos unum estis in christo iesu; si autem uos unum estis in christo iesu: ergo abrahae semen estis. et secundum promissionem heredes. Distat autem inter unum estis et unus estis. quotiescumque alter alteri voluntate myscetur * ut illud ego et pater unum sumus unum sunt. Quotiens autem et corporaliter myscentur et in unam carnem duo solidantur unus sunt; Corpus itaque in capite suo filius est dei. et deus

in corpore suo filius est hominis qui cotidie nascendo uenit et crescit in
templum sancti dei. Templum enim dei bipertitum est cuius pars altera
8 quamuis lapidibus magnis extruatur destruitur; neque in eo lapis super
lapidem relinquetur. Istius nobis iugis aduentus cauendus est donec de
medio eius discedat ecclesia: FINIT

Regula bipertiti corporis domini multo necessarior est et a nobis
diligentius perspicienda et per omnes scripturas ante oculos habenda est
sicut enim supradictum est. a capite ad corpus ratione sola uidetur. ita a
parte corporis ad partem. a dextera ad sinistram uel a sinistra ad dexteram
transitus reditusque ut in supradicto capite claret. Dum enim dicit uni
corpori. thesauros inuisibiles aperiam tibi ut scias quoniam ego sum
dominus et assumam te et adiecit. tu autem me non cognouisti et
nesciebas me. numquid licet unum corpus adloquatur in unam mentem
conuenit et thesaurorum dei apertio et dei ignorantia? non cognouisti
autem illi dicitur! qui licet ad hoc uocatus sit ut cognoscat et eiusdem
corporis sit uisibiliter et deo labiis appropinquet longe tamen corde
9 separatus est. Item. ducam cæcos in uiam quam ignorauerunt. et semitas
quas non nouerunt calcabunt et faciam illis tenebras in lucem. Haec
verba faciam et non derelinquam eos. Ipsi autem conuersi sunt retro:
numquid quos dixit non derelinquam idem conuersi sunt et non pars
eorum: Item dicit dominus ad iacob. Ab oriente adducam semen tuum
et ab occidente colligam te. dicam aquiloni da et austro noli prohibere et
paulo post. in gloriam enim meam (f. 208 r.) paraui illum et finxi et feci
illum. et produxi plebem caecam et oculi eorum sunt similiter caeci et
surdas aures habent. numquid quos in gloriam suam parauit idem sunt
caeci et surdi; Item dedi perire iacob et israhel i(n) maledictum. nunc
audi me puer meus iacob et israhel quem elegi; ostendit illum iacob et
israhel perire quem non elegit; Item scio quoniam reprobatus repro-
baberis. propter nomen meum ostendam tibi dignitatem meam. Numquid
10 reprobatio ostendit dignitatem suam? Item. breuiter bipertitum osten-
ditur christi corpus. fusca sum et decora. Absit enim ut ecclesia qui non
habet maculam aut rugam aliqua ex parte fusca sit nisi in parte sinistra
per quam nomen dei blasfematur in gentibus alias tota speciosa est sicut
dicit. tota speciosa es proxima mea et macula non est in te; quare fusca
sit et speciosa ostendit. ut tabernaculum cedar ut pellis salomonis. duo
tabernacula ostendit regium et seruile utrumque tamen semen abrahæ.
cedar enim filius est ismahel. cuius serui abrahæ cohabitationem sanctus
deplorat dicens. eu mihi quia incolatus meus prolongatus est. &c usque
inpugnabant me gratis; Non possumus autem dicere tabernaculum cedar
praeter ecclesiam esse unde cedar et salomonis inde fusca et decora, non
11 est fusca ecclesia in his qui foris sunt. hoc mysterio dominus in apocalypsi
septem angelos dicit id est ecclesiam septiformem nunc sanctos et pre-
ceptorum custodes nunc eosdem multorum criminum reos et pænitentia
dignos ostendit. Et in euangelio unum prepositorum corpus diuersi
meriti manifestat dicens; Beatus ille seruus quem cum uenerit dominus

inuenerit sic facientem. De eodem. si autem nequam fuerit diuidet eum
dominus et partem eius cum hypocritis ponet. non omnem sic diuidet aut
findet. denique non totum sed partem eius cum hypocritis ponet. In uno
enim corpus ostendit. Hoc itaque mysterio accipiendum est per omnes
scripturas sicubi deus dicit. ob merita. israhel periturum aut hereditatem
suam execrabilem. Apostolus enim copiose ita disputat maxime ad
romam in parte accipiendum quicquid de toto corpore dictum est ad
israhel inquid quid dicit. tota die expandi manus meas ad populum non
credentem. et ut ostenderet de parte dictum. dico inquid numquid
reppulit deus hereditatem suam? absit. nam et ego israhelita sum &c
usque presciuit: Et post quam ostendit quem ad modum. haec locutio
intelligenda esset' eodem genere locutionis ostendit unum corpus et
(26) bonum et malum esse dicens. § non de omnibus uobis dico; Magna breuitas
ostendentis unum corpus et separantis. si enim diceret non de uobis dico
(11) aut non de omnibus dico non ostenderet unum corpus. ¶ Secundum euangelium inquit inimici propter uos. secundum electionem autem dilecti
propter patres. Numquid idem dilecti. qui inimici? aut potest in caifan
utrumque conuenire? Ita dominus in omnibus scripturis unum corpus
seminis abrahae omnibus gentibus crescere et florere atque perire testatur;

DE CORPORE DOMINI BIPERTITO EXPLICIT. INCIPIT DE PROMISSIS ET LEGE:

12 Auctoritas est diuina nemine aliquando ex operibus legis iustificari
potuisse. eadem firmissimum est numquam defuisse qui legem facerent et
iustificarentur. Scriptum est quaecumque lex loquitur his qui in lege
sunt loquitur ut omne os obstruatur et subditus fiat omnis mundus deo
quia non iustificabitur ex lege omnis caro in conspectu eius. Item. si
enim data esset lex quae posset iustificare et reliqua usque credentibus ∴
Sed dicit quis. a christo et infra non iustificat lex. suo tamen tempore
iustificauit. Huic occurrit petrus. quid temptatis iugum imponere super
ceruices nostras &c usque illi. (f. 208 v.) Qui(s) uero tam peruersae
13 mentis est qui neget moysen uel reliquos sanctos legem fecisse? Sed
quomodo eos lex iustificauit qui ad hoc data est ut peccatum multiplicaretur. lex autem subintrauit ut habundaret delictum; Illud autem
scire debemus et tenere numquam omnino interceptum esse semen
abrahae ab isaac usque nunc. semen autem abrehae non carnale sed spiritale quod non ex lege sed ex promissione est ut illud quoniam qui ex fide
sunt hi sunt filii abrahae. si autem constat semen abrehae ante legem fuisse
et ex fide' constat et quia numquam fuit ex lege; Non enim potuit ex
lege esse et ex fide. lex enim et fides diuersa res est' quia lex non est fidei
sed operum. ut illud lex non est ex fide sed qui fecerit ea uiuet in eis;
14 uidemus legem ad promissionem non pertinere nec aliquando alteram in
alteram inpegisse. quia sicut lex numquam fidei obfuit' ita nec fides legem
destruxit. ut illud legem ergo destruimus per fidem? absit. sed legem
15 statuimus id est firmamus. Inuicem namque se firmant. Non enim
potuit quisquam iustus in lege positus uiuere nisi opera legis fecisset et
omnia. Sin maledictus esset neque aliquando liberari potuit nisi sola

gratia per fidem. est autem crimen magnum perfidiae non adtendisse
genus armorum quibus uiolentia peccatorum expugnaretur. e contra
magnificae fidei est inquisisse et uidisse bonum deum qui sciebat legem
16 non posse fieri alterum uitae aditum relinquisse. deus enim cum diceret
non concupisces! non nudauit quem ad modum id prouenire posset sed
seuere atque decise dixit non concupisces. quoniam id fide reperiendum
reliquid. Si enim mandaret a se prouentum postulari et legem destruxerat
et fidem. ut quid enim legem daret si se legem in omnibus factorum
polliceretur? aut quid fidei relinqueret si fidem auxilium pollicendo pro-
ueniret? nunc autem bono fidei legem ministram mortis ut amatores
uitae fide uitam uiderent et iusti fide uiuerent. qui opus legis non ex sua
18 uirtute sed ex dei dono fieri posse crederent: Dicit enim apostolus
propterea datam legem ut nos custodia sui concluderet in fidem quam
futurum erat reuelari in christum qui est finis legis qua uixerunt omnes
qui fide gratiam dei inquisierunt prius inquit quam ueniret fides sub lege
custodiebamur conclusi in eadem fidem. quam futurum erat reuelari; lex
itaque pedagogus noster fuit in christo. lex fidei erat demonstratrix; Sed
dicit quis si in utilitatem fidei data est lex cur non ab origine seminis
abrahae. si quidem iuge fuit. re uera iuge fuit iugis et fides ut genetrix
filiorum abrahae. Iugis et lex per dinoscentiam boni et mali. sed post
promissionem filiorum abrahae multiplicatis eis secundum carnem multi-
plicandum erat et semen abrahae quod non est nisi ex fide; Quae multi-
plicatio euenire non posset sine adiutorio legis multiplicate ut multitudo
in fidem necdum reuelatum ut iam dictum est uel necessitate deduceretur.
prouidentia itaque dei factum augendo gubernandoque semini abrahae ut
seueritate et metu legis multi conpellerentur in fidem et semen fulciretur
usque ad fidei reuelationem. lex subintrauit ut abundaret delictum et
reliqua usque gratia. non dixit ut daretur sed ut abundaret gratia; ab
inicio enim data est per christum fugientibus legis molestias atque domi-
19 niam. Idem namque spiritus eadem fides et gratia per christum semper
data est quorum plenitudinem * ueniens remoto legis uelamine omni genti
largitus est. si quis absque fide iustificatus est, non fuit filius abrahae;
21 quoniam filius abrahae non ex lege sed ex fide iustificatur: non
est bene et melius in lege! qui si iustificasset omnes iusti unius essent
22 meriti quia partem de omnibus exigit observationem; Cogimus autem
loqui ea qui sine igne doloris (f. 209 r.) fari non possumus. dicunt enim
quidam promis(is)se deum abrahae omnes gentes sed saluo libero arbitrio
23 si legem custodissent; Non enim si futuri essent et non quia futuri erant
promisit. quia non propter fidem abrahae placuit deo saluas fore gentes
quas non ante fidem abrahae sed ante mundi constitutionem possedit. sed
quisiuit fidelem cui donaret ex quo esset quod futurum statuerat;
Abraham ergo non id meruit ut essent sed ut per ipsum essent qui futuri
24 erant quos deus elegerat; Quid enim iusto lex qui propitio deo legem sine
25 lege faciunt qui ad imaginem dei uiuunt. uoluntate enim boni sunt. Non
est misericors qui timet esse crudelis. non furtum odit sed penam timet;

qui autem amat bonum imago dei est ut iam non sit ancillae filius. quia
28 timor non est in dilectione: De eo quod iacob et esau in uno sunt
corpore et ex uno semine propter duos populos futuros in uno corpore.
29 De eo quod numquam iacob id est ecclesia uenit ab benedictionem non
comitante dolo id est falsis fratribus sed non simul innocentia et dolus
benedicantur.

31 De specie et genere loquimur non secundum retoricam humanae
sapientiae quam qui magis omnibus potuit locutus non est ne crucem
christi fecisset inanem. si auxilio atque ornamento sermonis ut falsitas
indiguisset. Sed loquimur secundum mysteria caelestis sapientiae magisterio spiritus sancti: Qui cum ueritatis pretium fidem constitueret
mysteriis narrauit in specie genus abscondens. aut in ueterem hierusalem
totam qui nunc est per orbem. aut in unum membrum totum corpus ut
in salomone; Si hoc non tam occultum est quam cetera quae non solum
specie breuitate sed etiam mortiformi ratione occultantur; Quam ob rem
dei gratia in auxilio postulata elaborandum nobis est. Dum enim speciem
narrat ! ita in genus transit ! ut transitus non statim liquide appereat. sed
32 talia transiens ponit uerba qui in utrumque conueniant. donec paulatim
speciei modum excedat et transitus dilucidetur. cumque ab specie
coeperant non nisi in genus conuenerint. et eodem modo genus relinquid
in speciem rediens; Aliquando autem ab specie in genus non supradicto
modo sed euidenter transit et supradicto modo reuertitur; Aliquando
supradicto modo transit et euidenter reuertitur simili ordinis uarietate ut
ab speciae in genere. aut a genere in specie finit rationem. Aliquando
secedit ex hoc in illud non semel et omnis narratio nec speciem excedit
nec genus preterit in utrumque conueniens. haec uarietas translationis et
ordinis exigit fidem quae gratiam dei quaerat deus per ezechielem egressui
eorum qui ab hierusalem capti et dispersi fuerant gentium iungit aduentum. et in terram quam patres nostri possiderunt exprimit mundum;
Septem enim gentes abrahae promissae figura est omnium gentium;
factus est inquit sermo domini ad me dicens. fili hominis domus israhel
habitauit in terra et polluerunt illam in uia sua et in idolis suis. et post
33 aliqua incipit iungere genus: et sanctificabo nomen meum secundum
quod pollutum est inter gentes. et scient gentes quoniam ego sum
dominus dum sanctificor in uobis ante oculos eorum. Adtingit speciem
non tamen relinquens genus. et uocabo triticum et multiplicabo illud; In
figura uero terrae iudeae qui bellis uastata fuerat promittit inuocari
34 mundum qui a deo recesserat cum dicitur: Reaedificabuntur deserta et
terra quae exterminata fuerat coletur. Apostolus quoque in regressu
iacob promissum esse introitum gentium sic interpretatur. donec plenitudo
gentium intraret &c usque fiet. sicut scriptum est. ueniet a sion qui
liberet et auferat impietates ab iacob. Et eodem genere locutionis
redit in speciem dicens: Secundum euangelium inimici quid est propter
uos; Item. in ezechelo (f. 209 v.) Incipit ab specie qui conueniat in genus
et finit in solo genere. ostendens terra patrum mundi esse possessionem.

haec dicit dominus. ego accipiam omnem domum israhel de medio gentium.
et post aperte transit in genus : et seruus meus dauid princeps in medio
36 eorum. Item illic. ueluti in nouissima resurrectione prima significata est.
fili hominis ossa haec domus israhel est Ipsi dicunt arida facta sunt ossa
nostra et paulo post. ecce ego aperiam. monumenta uestra et scietis quia
ego dominus. numquid cum perspicue surrexerimus cognoscemus dominum
et non nunc cum per baptismum resurgimus. aut mortui possunt dicere.
Arida nostra sunt ossa? duas enim resurrectiones dominus ostendit
37 secundum iohannem. Item in uno homine totum corpus ostenditur
dicente deo ad dauid de salomone. suscitabo semen tuum post te et parabo
regnum eius. et excedit speciem dicendo. Et dirigam thronum eius in
38 aeternum. quae promissio ecclesiae congruit magis quam christo. Mani-
festum est salomonem sapientem et idolatrem figuram fuisse ecclesiae
39 bipertite cotidie disrumpit(ur) regnum salomonis in malis et cotidie
solidatur in bonis. In achan totum corpus malum intelligitur. Illud
etiam multo necessarium est scire omnes omnino ciuitates israhel uel
gentium uel prouintias quas scriptura adloquitur. aut (in) quibus aliquid
gestum refert figuram esse ecclesiae. aliquas quidem partis male aliquas
50 bonae. aliquas utriusque. Babilon inimica hierusalem totus est mundus.
51 Subtiliter inserit genus cum dicit. ecce excito uobis medos qui aurum non
53 quirint. quis enim hostis aurum non quaerit nisi ecclesia? ubicumque
autem idu(m)eam. theman. bosor. seir. nominat. malos significat. serras uero
55 ferreas homines durissimos qui secant parturientes ecclesias. temporum quan-
titas frequenter in scripturis mystica est tropo sinecdoc(h)e aut legitimis
numeris qui multis modis positi sunt et pro loco intellegendi. sinecdoc(h)e
uero aut parte totum est aut a toto pars. hoc tropo dictum est et adfligent eos
annis. CCCC qui post mortem ioseph coepit seruire populus ex CCCCXXX annis
deducemus LXXX annos regni ioseph. Regnauit autem a XXX annis usque
56 in .CX. et erunt reliqui seruitutis anni CCCL quos dixit CCCC. si autem omni
tempore peregrinationis suae israhel seruiuit plus est quam deus dixit. Si
autem ex morte ioseph secundum scripturae fidem minus. quo manifestum
est eum a toto parte esse nam post CCC annos pars aliorum annorum. C
propterea dixit CCCC annos. Sic in omni summa temporis ut puta post
VIIII dies prima hora xmi. dici dies est et post VIIII menses primus dies
mensis. mensis est ut illud. X mensuum tempore coagalatus sum in
sanguine. Sicut autem in prima parte cuius temporis totum tempus est
ita et nouissima. ut nouissima hora totus dies sit aut reliquiae mille
annorum mille anni sint. sex dies sunt mundi aetas id est $\overline{\text{VI}}$ annorum in
reliquiis sexti die id est mille annorum natus est dominus passus resurrexit.
Itidem reliquiae mille annorum dictae sunt mille anni primae resurrec-
tionis. Sicut enim reliquiae VI feriae id est III hore totus dies est unus
ex tribus sepulturae domini! Ita reliquiae VI diei maioris quo resurrexit
ecclesia totus dies est id est mille anni. hoc tropo soluitur quod dominus
59 tertia die surrexit. Ex legitimis autem numeris. denarius. XII denarius
idem autem est numerus cum multiplicantur ut LXX. DCC. Sed aut

perfectionem significant aut a parte totum aut simplicem summam perfectionem. ut VII spiritus ecclesiae. aut ut dicit septies in die laudem dixit. aut septies tantum recipies in hoc saeculo. similiter denarius ut centies
60 recipies in hoc saeculo. Et danihel decies milies dena milia. et dauid. currus dei decies milies tantum. Item per duodenarium CXLIIII milia (f. 210 r.) et XII milia tribus omnes gentes sicut iudicabitis XII tribus israhel ap(ar)te totum est. quoniam certum tempus legitimis numeris definitur ut in apocalypsi; habebitis pressuram X diebus cum significet usque in finem. ponitur hora pro tempore ut illud nouissima hora est dies ut illud ecce dies salutis annus ut illud. predicare annum domini. aliquando hora dies et annos et mensis est. sicut in apocalypsi. parati in horam et diem et mensem et annum quod est III anni et dimidius. Ibidem menses pro annis. datum est ledere homines mensibus. V. aliquando dies denario numero .C. dies sunt. sicut in apocalypsi dies CC.LX. Nam
61 milli dies ducentes centeni et sexagies centeni CCXXII. dies sunt. qui fiunt anni CCCL. mensibus tricenorum dierum. Ibidem unus mensis denario numero .C. menses sunt. ut ciuitatem sanctam calcabunt mensibus XL duobus. centeni IIII & CC menses sunt. qui sunt anni CCCL. Sicut per VI dies fecit mundum corporalem. ita per VI milium annos edificat spiritalem id est ecclesiam sanctificaturus VII quem benedixit fecitque aeternum.
62 Ideoque precipitur ut pondus peccati non inferatur per portas hierusalem.
64 In genere autem uno in tempore est uterque euentus sic XIIII anni sub ioseph ubertatis et steritalitatis. Isto enim tempore minatur dominus diuitibus famem pauperibus uero saturitatem promittit. uno in tempore
65 egyptus percutitur israhel saluatur. De eo quod XL. dies diluuii. CCCC anni in egypto XL in deserto et XL dies ieiunii et XL quibus apparet post resurrectionem manducans et XL diebus aqua in statuto suo totidem defecit; Nam in genere quo tempore inualescit carnaliter eo deficit spiritaliter. quia elatio defectio est sic mundus repugnans ponitur sub pedibus ecclesiae id est filii hominis; Qui sunt itaque XL dies idem CL dies; ezechihel namque XL diebus exsoluit peccata iudae et israhel CL quod est unum atque idem tempus. et VIImo mense sedit arca. Item tempus est et deficiebat aqua usque in Xmum mensem. Item tempus est exiuit de arca. XIImo mense. hic est annus libertatis domini acceptabilis: quo completo manifestabitur ecclesia mundi pertransisse diluuium. Vnaquaeque pars huius anni id est annus est. quale si diceret exiuit de arca. XL(mo) die. Aut mense VII.mo. aut X.mo sunt autem partes istae recapitulationis. sicut ab adam usque enoch id est ecclesiæ. translationem VII
66 generationes quod est omne tempus. rursum ab adam usque ad noe quod mundi reparatione. X generationes quod est tempus. et a noe usque abraham X generationes. nam et .C. anni quibus arca fabricatur omne tempus est quo ecclesia edificatur; Inter regulas quibus spiritus lege signauit quo luminis uia custodiretur non nihil custodit recapitulationis sigillus ea subtilitate ut continuatio magis narrationis quam recapitulatio uideatur. Sic enim aliquoties recapitulat: tun. illa hora. illo die. eo

tempore. ut illud. die qua exiit loth &c[1]; *Et in genesi plantauit deus paradisum in quo posuit et produxit adhuc de terra lignum. Ita dignum uidetur ut postea factum sit quam posuit deus hominem &c. Item in eodem libro cum commemorantur generationes filiorum noe hi filii cham in tribubus suis secundum linguas suas; Hoc autem quod adiunctum est et erat omnes terra labium unum. ita dictum uidetur ut eo tempore quo dispersi fuerunt super terram una fuerit lingua omnibus quod omnino superioribus repugnat ac per hoc recapitulando dictum est fit ista recapitulatio obscurius ut illud die quo exiit loth a sodomis et paulo post secundum haec erunt dies filii hominis quo reuelabitur in illa hora qui erit in tecto &c. numquid cum dominus fuerit reuelatus tunc ista seruanda sunt ne respiciat retro et non potius isto tempore? recapitulatio est; tempus ergo ipsum* (f. 210 v.) *q(uo) euangelium predicatur quousque dominus reueletur hora est in qua oportet ista seruari quia et ipsa reuelatio ad eandem horam pertinet qui die iudicii*
67 *terminabitur ut illud filioli nouissima hora est.* Aliquoties autem non sunt recapitulationes sed futurae similitudinis ut illud cum uideritis quod dictum est per danihelum prophetam. tunc qui in iudea sunt fugiant in mentes et inducit finem; Quod dixit in africa geritur. neque in eo tempore finis sed in eo tamen titulo futurum est propterea dixit tunc. id est cum similiter factum fuerit per orbem. id est reualatio antichristi; Et dauid ipso genere locutionis cum auerteret dominus captiui &c usque tunc repletum est gaudio os nostrum et usque laetante* per similitudinem tempus suum et nostrum [u]num fecit. Nec illud pretereundum puto
68 quod spiritus sine mysteriis ali[u]d [sonare] aliud intelligi uoluit. Omnis spiritus qui negat iesum in carne uenisse. &c usque in isto mundo est numquid omnes qui non negat spiritum * *[2] ista negatio non in uoce sed in opere est;[3] *Timothei*·

Omnes homines saluos fieri tamquam diceretur nullum hominem fieri saluum nisi quem fieri ipse uoluerit. Non quod nullus sit hominum nisi quem saluum fieri uelit sed quod nullus fiat nisi quem uelit et ideo sit rogandus ut uelit quia nece[sse] est fieri si uoluerit. De orando quippe deo agebat apostolus cum hoc diceret; Sic enim intelligimus quod dictum est qui inluminat omnem. et reliqua. id est qui inluminantur siue de omnibus gentibus ut illud decimatis omne olus;

Et illud obsecramus ut oretis pro scriptore ut deum omnipotentem habeatis protectorem

et ego Liuthprandus scripsi hoc librum ∴

[1] What follows in italics is from Aug *de Doct Christ* iii 36 (=*Eug* 873—875).

[2] 'habet' is supplied by a later hand.

[3] The passage in italics which follows is from Aug *Enchirid* 103.

ORTHOGRAPHY.

THE aim of an editor should be to reproduce the text of his author, even in matters of spelling, but in the case of a 4th cent. African writer like Tyconius it is very difficult to say what that spelling was likely to have been. I had therefore no other course than to be generally guided by the two MSS R and V. But it is improbable that 9th cent. MSS should have entirely retained the spelling of a 4th cent. author; the first question therefore is to try to isolate any peculiar element in the MSS themselves.

One of the most satisfactory methods of doing this is to compare the spellings of our MSS with the MSS of the Vulgate whose provenience is known. There is every probability that a learned scholar like S. Jerome would prefer correctness; irregular spellings therefore in an Irish or Spanish MS probably represent the local usage.

In this section Bp. Wordsworth's notation has been used for the Vulgate MSS of Mt Mc and Lc, but with italic instead of roman capitals.

1. *Spellings in cod.* R.

Cod. R was given by Hincmar to the Cathedral Library at Reims. It can hardly be earlier than the middle of the 9th century, but the MS bears no external marks of its origin. The most noticeable peculiar spellings are those generally classed as Irish.

SS for **S** *osse* R 28^{10}
issac R^{a} $13^{10, 20}$, 29^{25}, etc [=*DL* Mc xii 26, *D* having usually *issaac*]
precissum R 2^{15} [for *caesum* Mc xv 15, *DP* (*R*) have *cessum*]
cf. *dissimilitudine* R 67^{25} for *de similitudine*.

S for **SS** *promisis* R 1^{13} [=*Ept R* (not *D*) Lc xxiv 49]
presurarum R 6^{6} [=*D* (*EEptR H Y*) Lc xxi 23]
similarly *quatuor* R $53^{2, 4}$ [=$D^3/_3$ $Ept^7/_7$ $L^6/_7$ $R^3/_4$]
querela R* 13^{4} [=*J* (*K*) *V Mt W* as well as (*D*) *EptQ*].

IE for **I** in compounds of *iacere*.
subiecere R^{a} 26^{24} [=*D* Lc x 17]
deieceretur R 71^{12}
similarly *iesaiam* Rcorr 70^{14} [=*R* Mt viii 17, (*L*) Mt xiii 14, *Q* Mc i 2].

O for U *commone(m)* R 26^{14}, 30^{17} [=*DEptLQ* Mc vii 2, 5]
absordum R 5^{11} [*sordus D* passim, *Ept* Mc vii 32]
nobocodonosor R* 43^{26}
salamon $R^{4}/_{4}$ 38 and $^{2}/_{7}$ 39 (also R^{a} 39^{9}) [=*D L* passim]
sophyr (Σουφείρ) R 51^{15}.

Traces of the hand of the archetype of R may be seen in the confusions of

SS for **RS** *uessum* for *uersum* R 65^{6},
RS for **RR** *cursus* for *currus* R 60^{4}.

Other spellings rather suggest the 9th cent. French schools, such as *quoties*, *loquutus*, *sequutus*, etc (*loquutionis* R 34^{13}). *Obstupuerunt* (R 45^{11}) may be either Irish or French, and the same is true of *domu* (R 70^{24}), which occurs in $V^{23}/_{27}$ as well as in $D^{25}/_{27}$ $Q^{16}/_{27}$ $R^{15}/_{23}$ $Mt^{6}/_{27}$, the first-named MS being the best representative of Alcuin's recension. Hardly any other of Bp. Wordsworth's MSS have *domu* but these. In Old Latin MSS *domu* is never found in the Irish MS *r*, but it occurs in *d* Ac xvi 34, and in *k* Mt viii 6 *iacet domu mea* stands for βέβληται ἐν τῇ οἰκίᾳ (*cf* the Vulgate MSS *DL* but no other authority).

R has also a decided tendency to **AMM-** for **ADM-**. Thus we find constantly *quemammodum*[1], *ammonere*; also *ammodo* R 4^{16} for *a modo*, but *admisit* R 16^{1}.

There is also a tendency to **-ti-** for **-ci-** and **-si-** in R. Thus besides *conditio* (22^{8}, $24^{7,\,9,\,14}$, etc), we find *commertia* 46^{22} and *ostentio* 28^{21}.

Other noteworthy spellings are *actenus* 73^{15} (comp. *ericii* 42^{15}, and Lc xii 20 *d*), *alligoria* 67^{30} and *herimo* 65^{2}, *antichristi* (plene) 68^{28}, *archa* 64^{24}, *clusisset* 15^{29}, *clussise* 16^{4} (but *claudent* 47^{23}), *demitte(re)* 6^{13}, *insylę* 45^{22}, *iuncxit* 67^{27}, *praeliabitur* 49^{8} (also supported by *K Y* and Z^{2}), *sterelitatis* 64^{14}.

Many ancient forms have no doubt been corrected out of R. Thus *profecta* R* 42^{10} (*profeta* R^{a}) is good evidence for the spelling with *f* in R's ancestry, though *propheta* is the form in R elsewhere. Similarly *fili* for *filii* (nom. pl.) occurs nowhere in R, though it is frequent in V. But the vocative *fili* has also become *filii* in R 32^{18}, possibly by the same process. *Assumpsit* (sic) R 10^{2} points to the spelling *assumsit* adopted by Bp. Wordsworth.

R shews here and there a tendency to drop syllables, as *absolano* 40^{23} for *a subsolano*, and *illanineue* or *illamneue* R 42^{13} (there is often no difference

[1] Prof. Sanday suggests in *Studia Biblica* II 324 that *quemammodum* is a good test word. The evidence in Mt Mc Lc may therefore prove of interest.

Mt xxiii 37		*Y F*		*K V*		*X Z^{2}*	
Mc iv 26		*Y*	*I*	*K*		*Z^{2}*	
Lc viii 47		*A Y F G*	*H*		*Mt C T*	*X Z^{2}*	
xiii 34		*Y*				*X Z*	
xxi 14		*Y*	*I*			*Z*	
xxii 4	*M*	*Y*	*H*			*Z^{2}*	
xxiii 55			*H*			*X Z*	

Z^{2} is the contemporary corrector of B. M. Harl 1775 (6th or 7th cent).

Y the Lindisfarne Gospels.

M is the Ambrosian Gospels (6th cent), apparently the best MS of the Vulgate.

between *m* and *ni* in the hand of the MS) for *illam nineue.* This may explain the curious reading *cain.* R 11^{26} for *caifan*[1].

On the whole, from the affinities of R with Irish and Alcuinian spellings we may conjecture that it was written in northern France, and copied from a MS in an Irish hand.

2. *Spellings in cod.* V.

The orthography of V does not afford so many indications of local use. In spite however of the blunders of the scribe there is some reason to believe that most of the peculiarities of orthography in V are derived from its predecessor, not introduced into the text of Tyconius for the first time in our MS. Thus the constantly recurring *inquit* is spelt *inquid* by V*, but in 40^{26}, where *inquit* is wrongly inserted by V, the spelling is not *inquid* but *inquit.* In other words, the spelling *inquid* in V's ancestry is older than the insertion of *inquit* in 40^{26}.

Moreover many of the variations from the ordinary orthography are not those common in 9th and 10th cent. MSS, but those which we find in the MSS of the Old Latin. Thus

inquid V* (e.g. 32^{17}).
quodquod V* $49^{1, 13}$, but *quotquot* V 14^{19}.
cf also *numquit* V* 54^{14}.
hoc (=*huc*) V* 61^{14}.
Zaccharias V 13^{2} (not 22^{6}) is well supported both in the O. L. and vg.
dispargere V* 45^{5}, 52^{21} (not 47^{3}).

'Betacism' is not uncommon, e.g. *uiuere* V* 53^{12} for *bibere; uerbiante* V 31^{16} for *breuiante.*

Cod. V is given to false aspiration. Thus

amoneo (for *amo meo*) V* 44^{8} [*amum* Mt xvii 27 *M***J CT H O*^{c} *Q R*]
arena V $26^{20, 21}$ (not 39^{1}) [*arenam* Mt vii 26 *J T V** *Ept L W*]
olochausta V 62^{25}
ortus V 34^{4}, $74^{13, 15}$ [*ortum* Lc xiii 19 *a b R W*, see *Rönsch* 463]

but

humeris V 52^{18} [Mt xxiii 4, Lc xv 5 *codd. mult* incl *CT*Θ*O*$^{2}/_{2}$]
honera V 62^{17}, $63^{2, 23}$ (but *onera* 62^{13}) [=*CT O D Ept LR*].

PT for **BT** occurs in

optinere V $52^{5, 8}$ [*optentu* (Mt xxiii 14 *f,*) Mc xii 40 *b O W*]
suptile V 31^{19} [*suptus* Lc viii 16 *M*].

[1] A more serious fault in R, which hardly concerns Orthography, is the occasional substitution of an entirely different word. Instances are *gentes* R 42^{14} for *greges, ciuitas* R 42^{19} for *pascua, siluas* R 46^{5} for *insulas,* and *mitigare* R 50^{17} for *lenire.*

TI for **CI** or **SI** is not found in V, except in the well-known misspelling *conditio* for *condicio* (so $V^6/_7$, but *condicione* V 24[14]).

MM for **DM** is not found in V, but the following instances seem to suggest that this spelling may have occurred in its ancestry.

admonet V 68[9], *ammonet* R
amisit V 47[10], *admisit* R
admiserunt V 58[10], *amiserunt* R.

Compare *aiecta* V* 24[14], *aiecto* V 54[15] for *adiecta*, *adiecto*.

Spellings of a less ancient type are
dextra V 8[9] etc
intelligere V* 4[25] etc, but not e.g. 5[12]
epistola V 68[8] [$=\Theta^2/_2$ in '*epistola*' *ad Damasum*]
iocunditas V 35[29], 47[19, 24]
spiritales, e.g. V 84 *ter* for *spiritalis*.

Possibly *illum* V 33[5] (for *illud*) may be only a blunder, yet see *Rönsch* 276; *inimicum* V 41[4, 12] (for *iniquum*) may be a relic of the spelling *inicum* [Lc xvi 10, 11 *d T*]; *charismatum* is spelt *chrismatum* V* 69[9], but *carismatum* V 69[14].

3. *Spellings adopted in this Edition.*

The rule of following the MSS in matters of spelling has been very generally followed in this edition, even in such cases as *idolatria*, *Matheus* and *conditio*. The spelling *idololatria* is assured in Tertullian, but hardly in any later Latin writer[1]. *Matheus* on the other hand is rarely met with earlier than the 9th cent. *Conditio* is the spelling of R and of $V^6/_7$, and V has no general tendency to confuse 'ti' and 'ci'. Moreover Tyconius himself uses the word of the Cosmos in a sense half way between 'contract' and 'creation'. He says (p. 58) the three hours of darkness at the Crucifixion were 'praeter ordinem conditionis Dei. quicquid enim signi est non turbat elementorum rationalem cursum'. If the incorrect derivation of *condicio* from *condere* 'to create' were accepted by Tyconius, he would probably spell the word '*conditio*' as in this edition.

With regard to the termination -**i** for -**ii**, I have adopted *Aegypti* 43[7] and *reliquis* 58[16] on the authority of RV*, but to print *fili* for *filii*, which often occurs in V*, seemed to be introducing needless confusion. *Filii* occurs in R 32[18] for *fili*.

In questions of assimilation I have generally followed R.

The interchange of **F** and **PH** causes much difficulty. The best representative of the African text *k* has always F for ϕ, except in *Capharnaum* Mt iv 13, Mc ix 33. A good test word is *profeta*, which I have almost always spelt thus in the text of Tyconius. It is true that both R and V have generally

[1] See Koffmane, *Gesch. d. Kirchenlateins* 37. 'Idolatria' also occurs in Priscillian 21[3].

propheta, but each MS independently testifies to the original presence of *profeta* in their ancestry. Thus R* has *profecta* 42^{10}, a mistake which would only arise from the spelling *profeta*, and in 42^{26} V has *prophetant* for *profanant*, which points to an intermediate corrupt reading *profetant*. *Fanuhel* is the spelling of RV in 22^{6}, and therefore I have adopted *Farao* wherever V* supports it. On the other hand *scenophegiae* R 49^{15} (*scinofegiae* V*) has no good support, neither from the O. L. nor the good MSS of the Vulgate.

With regard to the spelling of the names *Iesus* and *Christus* I have followed the authority of Bp. Wordsworth, to whose exhaustive note on Mt i 1 I must refer the reader. Possibly however the form *Hiesus* is the best attested for African documents, and that is the spelling of R 39^{18} in the name of Joshua. Elsewhere both R and V use the ordinary contractions.

4. *The name 'Tyconius'.*

The name Tyconius appears to be quite unique. I have not been able to find an instance of it in the *Corpus Inscriptionum Latinorum*, though the names *Tychon* and *Tyche* occur in all sorts of spellings. Unfortunately the treatises of S. Augustine against the Donatists and his book *de Doctrina Christiana*, in which he mentions our author, have not yet appeared in the Vienna *Corpus Script. Eccl. Latt.*, so that the spellings in the ancient MSS of these works are not easily ascertainable. The passages of *de Doct Christ* III required for this purpose are however found in Eugippius, of which the leading MS (Knoell's V, *saec.* vii) appears to be very carefully written.

The following spellings occur. It will be seen at a glance that the oldest of each of our three main sources for the name of our author—MSS of the Book of Rules itself, MSS of S. Augustine, and MSS of Primasius—confirm the spelling with **-YCO-**. I have therefore uniformly printed Tyconius, not Tychonius or Ticonius.

1. MSS of the Book of Rules.

Tyconius	R
Thiconius	V and its copy P
Ticonius	M
Tichonius	O and Editions.

2. MSS of Augustine *de Doct Christ* III and of Eugippius.

Tyconius	*Eug* codd-opt (incl V *saec.* vii)
Tychonius	*Eug* codd. *Aug* cod pal 188 *saec.* ix
Ticonius	*Aug* cod B. M. addl 11873
Tichonius	later MSS and edd of *Aug.*

3. MSS of Primasius' commentary on the Apocalypse.

Thyconius	Bodl. Douce 140 (the oldest MS of Primasius)
Ticonius	other MSS.

INDEX OF BIBLICAL QUOTATIONS.

In this list the Psalms and the chapters of Jeremiah are uniformly given according to the Greek numeration.

15 *

MALACHIAS

ESAIAS

HIEREMIAS

THRENI

BARVCH

EZECHIEL

PETRI I

IOHANNIS I

AD ROMANOS

AD CORINTH. I

AD CORINTH. II

AD GALATOS

INDEX OF LATIN WORDS.

For the Latinity of the Biblical quotations in the Book of Rules see *Introd.* lxix—cv.